# DEF

## DISABILITY

*of related interest*

**Career Success of Disabled High-flyers**
*Sonali Shah*
ISBN 978 1 84310 208 3

**Disability and Impairment**
**Working with Children and Families**
*Peter Burke*
ISBN 978 1 84310 396 7

**Promoting Social Interaction for Individuals with Communicative**
**Impairments**
**Making Contact**
*Edited by M. Suzanne Zeedyk*
ISBN 978 1 84310 539 8

**Challenges to the Human Rights of People with Intellectual Disabilities**
*Edited by Frances Owen and Dorothy Griffiths*
*Foreword by Orville Endicott*
ISBN 978 1 84310 590 9

**Speaking Up**
**A Plain Text Guide to Advocacy 4-volume set**
*John Tufail and Kate Lyon*
ISBN 978 1 84310 474 2

**Autism, Discrimination and the Law**
**A Quick Guide for Parents, Educators and Employers**
*James Graham*
ISBN 978 1 84310 627 2

**Ageing, Disability and Spirituality**
**Addressing the Challenge of Disability in Later Life**
*Edited by Elizabeth Mackinlay*
ISBN 978 1 84310 584 8

**Community Care Practice and the Law**
**4th edition**
*Michael Mandelstam*
ISBN 978 1 85302 691 3

# DEFYING DISABILITY

The Lives and Legacies of Nine Disabled Leaders

MARY WILKINSON

Jessica Kingsley Publishers
London and Philadelphia

First published in 2009
by Jessica Kingsley Publishers
116 Pentonville Road
London N1 9JB, UK
and
400 Market Street, Suite 400
Philadelphia, PA 19106, USA

www.jkp.com

A CIP [...] gress

Defying [...] ilkinson.

ISBN 978-1-84310-415- [...] raphy. 2. Leadership—

362.4092'241–dc22

2008035881

ISBN 978 1 84310 415 5

Printed and bound in Great Britain by
Athenaeum Press, Gateshead, Tyne and Wear

# DEDICATION

For Rupert, who's been there from beginning to end.

# ACKNOWLEDGEMENTS

A great many people have helped me with this book, not least the subjects themselves, who were generous with their time and support. Some people have helped repeatedly, especially when my computer was stolen, while others have kindly checked chapters as well as contributing to them.

My very grateful thanks to Graham Bool, Stephen Bradshaw, Chris Hallam, Andrew Holman and Arthur Verney; also to my Editor at Jessica Kingsley Publishers, Stephen Jones, my Production Editor Lucia Ring-Watkins and my Marketing Manager Helen Longmate, and to my family, who have been patient and supportive. I want to especially thank Rupert (abridger in chief!), Matthew and Camilla, Imogen West and Richard Walters, who read chapters, watched a video, and in Richard's case gave much needed technical support.

I would also like to thank Geoff Adams-Spink, Ade Adepitan, Bill Albert, Kay Allen, Tim Anfilogoff, Geof Armstrong, Adrienne Baker, Clare Balding, Jenni Banks, Len Barton, Ruth Bashall, Roger Berry, Neil Betteridge, David Bonnett, Sue Bott, Chris Burns, Richard Caborn, Douglas Campbell, Jane Campbell, Mukti Jain Campion, Ellen Clifford, David Colley, Godfrey Davis, Martin Davison, Maria Eagle, Agnes Fletcher, Joe Fletcher, Tara Flood, Padraig Flynn, Barbara Follett, Ann Frye, Cheryl Gabriel, Kath Gillespie Sells, Caroline Gooding, Vicky Hanington, John Hannam, Elinor Harbridge, Dave Harvey, Joe Hennessy, Thena Heshel, Judy Heumann, Margaret Hodge, Richard Howitt, Raymond Johnson, Dan Jones, Neil Kinnock, Phil Lane, Sarah Langton-Lockton, Tracey Lazard, Clair Lewis, Richard Light, Michael Lynch, Anne McGuire, Julie McNamara, Ian Macrae, Joshua Malinga, Peter Mansell, Ewan Marshall, Simon Minty, David Moorcroft, Alf Morris, Dave Morris, Roger Mosey, Kevin Mulhern, Kate Nash, Caroline Parker, Eve Rank, Mary-Anne Rankin, Steve Regis, Isabella Rutter, Hilary Salmon, Susan Scott-Parker, David Sindall, Andrew Smith, Allan Sutherland, Adam Thomas, Jamie Trounce, Andrew Wakelin, Alison Walsh, Ed Warner, Nick Watson, Rosalie Wilkins, Jo Williams, and Robin Worman.

# CONTENTS

# INTRODUCTION

You look out of the window and see a disabled person going down the street. How you interpret that picture depends on what you know about disability or your own experiences of it. For many non-disabled people, the impairment still dominates the person. This book looks at the whole person in relation to society. It takes nine leaders and tells their story. What are they like? How have they responded to disability? What made them leaders? How, coming from different directions, have they made an impact on the disability community and the wider world?

Disability has had plenty of medical, academic and social science coverage. But apart from a few autobiographies, little has been written about individual disabled people. This is the first book to take a group of leaders and see how they operate, what they have achieved, and how the modern history of disability in the UK has been played out in their lives. It offers new insights for professionals into the role disabled leaders have played, the discrimination they have had to deal with, and how far society still has to go to achieve social justice. And for anyone interested in disability, these people provide an inspiring but realistic record of struggle and achievement.

The nine leaders I have chosen have not hidden their impairment, like Franklin D. Roosevelt, or brushed it aside as they climbed the political ladder, like David Blunkett; they have acknowledged that impairment is part of them – though Mat Fraser fought against it for a long time. They represent differences of class, ranging from the working-class deprivation of Jack Ashley and Bert Massie to the baronet, Tom Shakespeare; differences of education, from mainstream to various types of 'special' school; different opportunities; different impairments. The ratio of women to men is two to seven, which does not reflect the original plan; two women declined to take part. Also, no one is included from an ethnic minority, which I regret. Were the book being planned now, the choice would be greater, though such a small selection means, inevitably, that outstanding people have been omitted on every front. Similarly, I have not been able to represent every kind of impairment – someone with mental health issues or a degenerative condition, for example.

My only departure from one person per occupation was 'activist/campaigner', where it seemed right to include Rachel Hurst and Andrew Lee, so as to cover the different journeys taken by people with a physical disability and those with learning difficulties.

For readers outside the disability community, I should explain that the terms 'disabled', 'impairment' and 'learning difficulties' reflect the preferences of many disabled people and I have tried to use them. However, there are differences of opinion even within the community; for example, people with learning difficulties do not like the world 'impairment'.

The 'social model' keeps cropping up. It is the idea that people are disabled by physical and social barriers, such as the lack of a ramp or a discriminating attitude, not by their own impairments. In contrast, the 'medical model' concentrates attention on an individual's impairment, their defects, and how to cure or rehabilitate them. The idea of society disabling people was conceived by disability activists in the mid-1970s and named in the early 1980s. The social model has inspired a generation of activists to fight for their civil and human rights, yet recent government research found that when nearly 2000 disabled people were asked what impeded them from leading a full life, only 6 per cent mentioned the social model.

Some disabled people consider it not 'politically correct' to talk about a person's impairment. In this book 'impairment' is seen as part of the whole person, often providing a spur for action, so it will not be ignored.

This is not an academic book, so there are no references. The research has included in-depth interviews, sometimes as many as three or four with each subject, plus at least half-a-dozen interviews per person with friends, work colleagues, government ministers, Members of Parliament and civil servants. The interviews have been supplemented with information from autobiographies and other books, Hansard, academic journals, websites, newspaper articles, radio and TV.

# BERT MASSIE:
# PUBLIC SERVANT

*Photograph taken by PA Photos*

Debenhams, the second largest department store chain, with 126 shops and profits of £216.8 million in 2004–05, thought it could get away with flouting the 1995 Disability Discrimination Act (DDA). It had had nine years in which to make 'reasonable adjustments' to its stores, so disabled customers could be accommodated, before that section of the Act came into force. By then, Greg Jackson, a wheelchair user, had lost his patience. He could not reach the menswear department on the mezzanine floor of the Derby store because it was up a flight of steps. After repeatedly asking for changes to be made, he decided to sue in the county court. 'I'm in the embarrassing situation of having to ask for clothes to be brought down to me by a shop assistant, which means it's impossible to browse properly and places pressure on me to buy,' he said. 'It also emphasises and draws attention to my impairment and so I feel like I'm being singled out because of my disability.'

Jackson was supported by the Disability Rights Commission (DRC), which, since April 2000, had been protecting the rights of 10 million disabled people under the Act, in a similar way to the commissions for race and equal opportunities. The DRC did its homework. It funded an independent report which found that 20 other Debenhams stores had access barriers similar to the Derby one and, unlike its competitors, Debenhams had no centrally managed plan to meet its legal duties. 'Instead, they appear satisfied in doling out a second-class service to disabled customers,' said the commission's chair, Bert Massie. He also pointed out that disabled shoppers have a disposable income estimated at £80 billion a year. 'Bad access is bad for business,' he said.

Behind the threat of legal action, Massie tried negotiation. Bypassing the legal teams, he invited the chairman of Debenhams, John Lovering, to a meeting and persuaded him that it was in Debenhams' interests to conform to the DDA; Lovering could avoid one county court fine after another and secure favourable publicity if Debenhams signed a formal agreement with the DRC. In July 2006 Debenhams committed itself to providing access for disabled people in all its stores – the first major retailer to do so. High-profile cases like this showed the DRC had teeth. But in the long run, says Massie, it is only when courts set fines higher than the cost of adjustment that retailers will obey the law.

Over its short, seven-year life, the DRC successfully pressed the government to strengthen and extend disability discrimination law and won key court cases that clarified the law. It was behind Lord Ashley's pioneering bill to give disabled people stronger rights to independent living. Its formal investigations produced pointed reports that could, for example, make

National Health Service (NHS) managers wince. And it drew on the views of disabled people and others to produce a long-term disability agenda, relevant not only to itself but also to its successor, the Equality and Human Rights Commission.

Essentially, though, the DRC was pragmatic, aligning the rights of disabled people with the duties of employers and service providers through information, advice and negotiation, using legal action only as a last resort. This suited the style and personality of its chair.

Massie is a Scouser, resourceful, fast talking and funny, who, as a boy affected by polio, worked his way up from the back streets of Liverpool to become an expert on disability issues and director of an influential charity in London. He was knighted in 2007. Politicians, directors and civil servants feel comfortable with him. So, increasingly, do disability leaders. But he has been a hate figure for the radical end of the disability movement, who tend to discount his 'behind the scenes' impact on policy and legislation and distrust a man who is not on their wavelength. Back in the red-hot days of the 1995 civil rights campaign, the activist Rachel Hurst called him an Uncle Tom in the *Independent on Sunday* and said she wouldn't mind shooting him. Characteristically, he did not sue. Now, as a transitional commissioner, he is helping to keep the new commission up to the mark on disability matters. He has given up his adapted flat near the Broadwater Farm Estate in north London, his weekday home for over 30 years, and headed back to Liverpool for good. His wife, his roots and his heart are there.

Massie was born in 1949, the second of eight children and the eldest son. His father, Herbert, was a carter, who later became a ship welder and a keen trade unionist. His mother, Joan, had worked in the Barker & Dobson sweet factory in Liverpool.

Massie caught poliomyelitis at three months. There had been an epidemic in 1947 and polio remained prevalent in the UK until the Salk vaccine caught on in 1959, after the death of the England international footballer Jeff Hall. Massie was sent to Alder Hey children's hospital, where he stayed for almost five years, a guest of the new NHS. He remembers the long Nightingale wards, the high beds, the open verandah onto which the mattresses were pulled so the children could get fresh air. Sometimes snow would fall on them. 'They'd give you a balaclava to wear. We looked the likes of an IRA cell.' His mother walked across the city to visit him once a week.

'In many ways I was better off than other people, because in hospital I got fed, which wasn't happening outside quite often. And rationing was still going on. At least the hospitals had plenty of grub. And you were warm; the place was heated.'

The hospital aimed to rehabilitate its patients. 'I remember being forced into callipers and being made to walk. It was a bloody silly thing to do, to be honest, because I kept falling over. But that was the ideal at the time: if you were perpendicular you were normal.'

Massie doesn't recall being unhappy; he knew no other life. Aged five, he went on to a boarding school for about 50 disabled children at Greenbank in Liverpool. It was called the Children's School of Rest and Recovery. 'As you might imagine, we got no rest and no one recovered!' It was a brutal regime, punctuated by surprising gentleness. Children who broke the rules were beaten, kicked or punched in the face, and one child was slammed against a hot radiator. But if you were ill, says Massie, they took good care of you, and when the sun shone, you had to wear a sun hat. If a child showed an interest in a subject, the staff would bring in one of their own books. Even so, educational expectations were low, not helped by the time lost for operations and therapies. Massie estimates he lost two days of education a week because his twice-weekly hydrotherapy treatment was in a hospital nine miles away on the other side of Liverpool and the ambulance picked up and dropped other people along the way. He had five operations before he was 18; none of them helped. One friend, Mike, who had cerebral palsy, had 'artistically shaped' joints. His wealthy parents decided they should be straightened. Mike went to hospital and was never seen again. 'I remember thinking that Mike died because he didn't suit his mum's couch.'

One of the compensations for being at Greenbank was Christmas: the parties and presents.

> Everyone would buy toys for crippled children. I used to take them home and my mother would keep a few and wrap the rest and give them round the streets. I would see my fire engines come out of the houses on Christmas Day. Fine. What can you do with six fire engines?

As a new boy Massie had been physically weak, so he was immediately picked upon. 'But I sussed that out right away. I made a friend of someone with very strong arms, who bonked this bully on the nose, and I had no problem after that.' Later, when he was at secondary school and walked from the 622 school bus to his home in Tweed Street, he could run foul of a non-local gang, who kicked away his crutches and laughed when he fell over. He would tell a friendly gang, who retaliated on his behalf. If two local gangs were fighting it out, he was told to stand in a doorway and later they would get him home unharmed. Massie learned how to use whatever help was at hand.

At Greenbank, he and other boys learned to work the school system too. Parents visited every fortnight, which meant that for four days beforehand the staff would not thump the children because the bruises would show. So they concentrated their pranks in those days. From pranks, Massie moved on to escape. The escape committee had bus timetables and stolen food and would start diversionary fights so teachers failed to see somebody hobbling past the window in search of freedom. Once Massie escaped and was eventually stopped by a police car.

> They said, 'Are you Herbert Massie?' and I said no. They had pictures of me and said, 'You look like him.' So they said, 'Go on, get in the car.' And they took me round buying me sweets and all sorts and at the end of the afternoon they said, 'We've got to take you back now.'

He remembers the Liverpool City police with great affection.

When he was 12, Massie went on to Sandfield Park Special School and was able to live at home for the first time. Home was a three-up, three-down terrace house, with one open fire, one cold-water tap and a lavatory in the backyard. His mother, he says, had always spoiled him 'rotten', but his father was a lot tougher. 'He was a fairly brutal working-class guy and if he ever had to argue the toss he would use his fists, or his belt, or whatever. But that was pretty normal for the day.' His father wanted him to walk.

> He made me some parallel bars down the backyard with ropes and made me walk up and down them. Even when it was raining he wouldn't let me come in unless I had walked down these bloody ropes. He was always the one who made sure I did things for myself.

Sandfield took education seriously and had some very good teachers. With so much going on, he tried never to take a day off. He chaired the chess club, became a prefect and made some lifelong friends, but he was not one of the few to take O (Ordinary) levels.

From there, aged 16, he went to an employment rehabilitation centre in Aintree, where the first test they gave him was to saw a petrol can in half with a hacksaw. He wasn't having that. 'With respect, I'm never going to get a job sawing up petrol cans. I don't think this is a common trade.' They were testing his dexterity, they said. He told them he could hardly move his left arm, and his right arm was weak; he needed a job where he could use his head. They decided he was fit for training in clerical studies, but he failed the Portland Training College entrance exam, so, while waiting for another course there, he sought a job to tide him over for six months. By this time he was driving his 'Noddy car', the three-wheeled Invacar for disabled drivers.

His driving test had been to apply the brake as it went along a ward at the local hospital.

Massie became a lift attendant, the kind who knew everybody, supplementing his weekly pay of £5 (about £50 nowadays) with initiatives of his own – selling cut-price stamps to stamp collectors and personal stationery. He would tout for stationery custom at churches or garden fetes, offering a small commission, get paper and fonts for free and use the printing machine in his employer's basement, courtesy of the caretaker. From these two sidelines he made about £10 a week. Similarly, when he went on to a commercial course at Portland College, he and others supplemented their £1.25 a week benefit payment (about £12.50 today) by conning the social security officials into giving them cash for items like gloves when they were not needed. 'I think the staff knew what was going on. But they didn't want people to be pathetic; they found a way to help.'

His first real job was as a cost clerk at Coats & Son in Liverpool. He was the man on the end of the old-style aerial tube that passed money between floors, supplying the change. After a disagreement with the proprietor's son, who favoured fleecing a foreign customer, he was fired. From there he went to William Rainford, where he calculated the cost of transporting aggregates (clinkers) from power stations to building sites, and then to West Cheshire Newspapers as credit controller. To get that job he persuaded the disability rights officer to fill in job application forms for him because his handwriting was poor.

At West Cheshire Newspapers, Massie achieved a turn-around in the company's finances, and his own, when he persuaded his accountant boss to support him against the advertising sales team so he could tighten the credit restrictions on big advertising agencies. Since the parent company, the Liverpool Daily Post and Echo Ltd, controlled all the big Merseyside newspapers, the agencies could be brought to heel if the newspaper group acted as a group. Massie persuaded the other credit controllers. He asked the irate sales director, 'What's the point of selling advertising if nobody pays for it?' As a result, the average credit time fell from two years to three months.

Outside work, Massie was caught up in Swinging Sixties Liverpool and the explosion of new pop groups, one of which was the Beatles. At 16, he fell out with his father over late-night parties, and with his mother and the doctors over the useless hospital operations. He funded his own leisure activities. He was, an ex-social worker recalled, 'a right tear-away'. He went to soccer matches and gigs with non-disabled friends. At the Clubship Landfall, he had to be carried down the gangway and parked on a cool radiator. He treated this pragmatically: 'It got you in.' He was assistant manager of a minor pop group, and he took girls around in his one-seat Noddy car, which earned him a reprimand and a wink from the police. He got rejections from girls on account of his disability and he certainly missed opportunities to meet them, such as on the dance floor, but it doesn't seem to have upset him. 'You make other opportunities and you have disastrous relationships, just like everyone else. But I can't remember a time in my life when there hasn't been a woman around.' He was busy; life was to be lived; he wasn't going to break his heart about discrimination or a girl.

Among the clubs he went to was PHAB, where young 'physically handicapped and able bodied' people socialised. It was run by the indefatigable Eileen Bleasdale, who also chaired the Liverpool Association for the Disabled (LAD). Massie found it rather tame, with Monday evening speakers and no alcohol because the premises belonged to Liverpool Council. 'What the kids were looking for were relationships; it was no good talking about bloody Tibetan mountains.' When he became PHAB's leader in 1968 he set out to recruit more non-disabled members, instituted a post-meeting trip to the pub, brought in pop groups and a speaker on family planning, and later organised weekends away. The trips were funded by a small subscription and proceeds from an ambitious pop concert held in the 2000-seat Philharmonic Hall, which Massie hired for the night. Two well-known folk groups, the Spinners and the Crofters, were among the musicians who performed. 'We filled half the space and made a packet, which kept us going for three years.'

Through PHAB Massie met Maureen Shaw, who later became his partner and finally, in 2007, his wife. She never got involved in Massie's career, preferring to remain in Liverpool, where she works for a housing association. But she was one of the roots that drew him home from London every weekend to revive his energy and put his work in perspective.

Eileen Bleasdale appointed Massie to his first paid disability job, as senior administrative officer of LAD. It was 1970 and he was 21. Bleasdale came from a wealthy Liverpool family and was, says Massie, the best kind of 'do gooder'. She encouraged him to spread his wings. He had already started to do that himself. Lured by the campaign to replace the despised Invacar with an adapted Mini, he had joined the Disabled Drivers' Association and now represented the North West on its management committee.

At LAD, Massie was bookkeeper, but he also edited the newsletter and cut his teeth as a disability spokesperson on local radio and Granada TV. He went on a day trip to London to support Alf Morris' Chronically Sick and Disabled Persons' Bill and encountered Ted Heath, the likely next Prime Minister, outside Parliament. Not one to miss a chance, Massie asked Heath if he would introduce a comprehensive disablement income for disabled people (for which the pioneering Disablement Income Group (DIG) was lobbying and disabled people are still waiting). Heath just walked away. The young nobody could be ignored.

While Massie was at LAD he began to make up for lost schooling. Bleasdale arranged for him to have free private tuition from Ursuline nuns, which secured him five O levels. In 1972 he moved into full-time education, first at Hereward College in Coventry, the nearest accessible college, where he took three A (Advanced) levels, and then back to Liverpool Polytechnic (now Liverpool John Moores University) for a degree in sociology. He stayed in the area for domestic reasons. His parents' marriage had broken up and his mother was living in a homeless refuge with no money. As the oldest son, he took responsibility for helping her.

As home no longer existed, Massie asked for a room in a hall of residence owned by Liverpool Council. By this time he was using a wheelchair. The room turned out to be inaccessible because there was no ramp at the entrance, so he phoned Bleasdale's brother-in-law, who was number two in the housing department. The ramp was built in three days.

Massie acknowledges that middle-class people played an important part in his formative years. They often had the power to help him and he made the most of it. As a teenager, he went on holidays with the British Polio Fellowship, something his family had no chance to do. He went to garden parties on the smart side of town. He secured grants when he needed them. 'I think that's how I got the degree and all the rest of it. None of my siblings have any qualifications at all. Had I not been disabled, I would have had the same lifestyles they had.' But there was more to it than that. Cheerful, quick, bright, he could win over all sorts of people.

Massie went on to earn a graduate qualification in social work at Manchester Polytechnic (now Manchester Metropolitan University). It was a practical route to a job. He worked through his vacations at college and university. At one point he was research assistant to Mary Greaves, ex-director of DIG, working on her book, *Work and Disability*. When he landed a job at the London-based charity RADAR (Royal Association for Disability and Rehabilitation) in 1978, he found himself a modest, accessible flat through a housing association, and there he stayed, even as his jobs became better paid. 'I was never actually sure I would have a job in the following year at any point,' he says. 'I was always reluctant to have to land myself with a debt.' A concern for financial security never left him.

RADAR was a new charity created in 1977 from the merger of two others. Rooted in the establishment, it had the Queen Mother as patron, and the Duke of Buccleuch as chairman. Unlike most other charities, it was a campaigning organisation with affiliated local groups, not a service provider. Funding came from a Department of Health grant for charities, supplemented by legacies, advertising, fundraising and a nominal subscription. RADAR produced authoritative briefs for ministers and MPs and, as a result, had considerable political clout for a small charity. Well-known disabled people such as Vic Finkelstein, Peter Large and Peter Wade were associated with it. For a young disabled person it was the place to be. And the time was ripe too. The Labour government of Harold Wilson had made history in 1974 by appointing the first Minister for the Disabled, Alf Morris. He introduced four new disability allowances, looked favourably on the call for a comprehensive disablement income and instigated the merger that became RADAR. Committees set up by Morris slammed inaccessible buildings and the widespread discrimination of disabled people. They included the Warnock Committee (1978), which favoured mainstream education for children with special educational needs. The Conservative government's Education Act 1981 adopted this in principle.

Massie came to London already well informed about issues like access and employment. He and a friend had met Vic Finkelstein one night at Hereward College and discussed 'disabled people grabbing their identity back'. Finkelstein's view that disability organisations should be controlled by disabled people did not surprise Massie; that was how the British Polio Fellowship, the Disabled Drivers' Association and the Disablement Income Group worked. He had written his university dissertation on the application of the Chronically Sick and Disabled Persons Act 1970. He was an experienced campaigner in a local disability organisation and a confident and prolific media commentator.

As executive assistant to RADAR's director, George Wilson, he had a boss who allowed him the freedom to develop his skills. Wilson was a large, ebullient man, who enjoyed cocktail parties and meeting ministers. He knew the people who mattered. He had been a teacher in Uganda and helped to distribute the polio vaccine before being thrown out by the tyrant Idi Amin. Like a headmaster, he kept his finger on the pulse of RADAR; carbon copies of letters went the round of senior staff for information and would be returned with factual or grammatical corrections by Wilson. He also had to be persuaded that any new idea was his. But he let Massie represent the charity at meetings involving government ministers and highly paid civil servants. Massie did the same later. He would send someone off to see a civil servant and tell them not to come back if they hadn't won the argument.

Despite his low-level title, Massie was in charge of the 'professional' staff, including officers covering access, housing, holiday information and benefits. Soon he had a finger in other charitable pies as well, involving disabled professionals, teenagers with thalidomide, 'handicapped' children and information technology (IT) training.

In 1981, the International Year of Disabled Persons, Massie was secretary of an employment committee that ran conferences and produced an employers' guide to disabilities. Not much tangible change came out of the year, due to the Thatcher government cuts in public spending, but it raised awareness of disabled people. Massie joined various bodies, including Sir Richard Attenborough's pioneering inquiry into arts and disabled people, and the Access Committee for England, which secured the first minimum standards for disability access in the building regulations. His public appointments took off; he helped advise the government on special education, employment and transport. He persuaded the Department of Transport to make its disability advisory group a permanent body and was a member for 15 years.

Transport was his passion. Travelling to and from Liverpool every week in his wheelchair, he had first-hand knowledge of guards' vans and by 1986 he had written about rail travel and was advising British Rail on making new trains accessible. As disability transport developed, his interests fanned out into anything from local authority airports to wheelchair design.

Massie's best known campaign in the 1980s was for a wheelchair-accessible taxi that would help plug the gap in accessible public transport. Ann Frye, the young civil servant at the Department of Transport who worked with him to make it happen, found him radical at first and a bit scary. He had long hair, a big moustache and a strong Scouse accent. When he was nervous, he would talk so fast he was almost incomprehensible. He made her laugh, though; jokes were his way of breaking the ice. Frye credits Massie as 'the driving force' behind the project. The first accessible black taxi took to the road in 1985. With all 19,000 London taxis now accessible, the UK is world leader, but the taxis still cannot take large electric wheelchairs. The spread of accessible taxis may be speeded up now that local authorities, which license taxis, have been brought within the DDA 2005.

At the launch of the first prototype taxi, Massie's speech credited the courage and perseverance of Lynda Chalker, then the transport minister. It was not just flattery; he appreciated the political and economic pressures on ministers and how easily they could be disparaged for doing too little, too slowly. This understanding contributed to Chalker's high opinion of Massie, as it has done with other ministers. In Ann Frye's view, Massie's style of 'Even if we can only move an inch today and a foot tomorrow, let's get started,' was more effective than street demonstrations. 'If you are demanding the world today and government knows it can't deliver the world, they are going to do nothing.'

His skill as a negotiator put him on numerous committees, which added to his knowledge of disability issues and how to get what he wanted. Frye says:

> He has this very laid-back style but, if you know him, you know he has a whole game plan worked out and he's working his way through all the jokes and the niceties towards a pincer movement that's going to get them in the end.

Hostility and belligerence were not his normal weapons, but he could get angry. During the negotiations to include access in building regulations, builders won an exemption from the Government for land they had bought, and then, ahead of a government deadline, went out and bought more land. 'This is the skulduggery, really – the efforts which wealthy people go to to preserve their wealth and make more of it, and the complete disregard for building a better society for the country.'

In 1984 Massie, still only an executive assistant, received an OBE (Officer of the Order of the British Empire). The following year he became assistant director of RADAR, responsible for policy, information and parliamentary work. Internally, things were not going well. RADAR was running into what became a periodic financial crisis. Staff cuts had to be made, including young, non-disabled women who 'Georgy Porgy', as he was nicknamed, had been in the habit of recruiting. Then, in November 1986, Wilson was the subject of a *Sunday Times* article. It claimed the Charity Commission was investigating allegations of mismanagement and high living, including a drinks expense account, lavish entertaining at a conference, an abnormally high staff turnover and failure to fulfil RADAR's statutory functions of promoting legislation for disabled people. Many of the allegations were unjustified; others were scotched by phone calls to ministers and civil servants. But they ensured a reorganisation, which left more control in the hands of two directors, one of whom was Massie. Even so, the school culture persisted; staff balked, for example, at the imposition of rigid timekeeping and the rule about signing your name in a book if you wanted a first-class stamp.

Massie was freed up to develop grassroots organisation and use grassroots information more effectively for campaigning. He insisted that he or

Wilson should attend the regional forums, where local groups wrote the agenda. RADAR at last endorsed anti-discrimination legislation.

One of the young women recruited by RADAR had been Jane Campbell, fresh from university and keen to work for a disability charity. She was, however, severely impaired and a wheelchair user. Hired in 1982, she was set to type letters, which she could not do. 'I cried for seven months and an administrator used to tell me off for spending too long in the toilets.' She says Massie, then Wilson's executive assistant, told her that perhaps full-time employment was not suitable for someone like her. He clearly remembers saying she was in the wrong job, and trying, unsuccessfully, to get her into RADAR's research and intelligence unit. They also differ about when they made up their differences, but they both worked amicably on the Disability Rights Commission.

Campbell could not forget another experience at RADAR, overhearing an information officer disparaging 'these whingeing disabled people'. It all fuelled an anger that she took with her to a new organisation, the British Council of Organisations of Disabled People (BCODP), where she later became chair. Launched in 1981, BCODP saw itself as the hub of new disability theory and civil rights action, an umbrella organisation 'of' (run by) disabled people, the one that should rightfully be working with government.

The inevitable rivalry of a new organisation, which coveted the influence and funding of RADAR (on one occasion BCODP approached RADAR for money), was embittered by the view of Campbell and others. And when Massie did not give up his job to join an 'of' organisation, nor appear at BCODP demos, nor seemed to be working for full civil rights, but instead was suspected of schmoozing with ministers and compromising on issues that should never be compromised, it all added up, in the eyes of many BCODP members, to betrayal. 'They felt Bert was giving legitimacy to an organisation that was very bad news for disabled people,' says Campbell. Massie's chirpy Scouser style also seemed out of tune with serious radical debate, and the occasional laddish joke did not go down well with some of the female staff at RADAR, let alone radical feminists. He was distrusted, disliked, even hated. In some quarters he still is.

Time and energy were wasted during the 1980s and 1990s on the political rivalry between RADAR and BCODP. It also complicated campaigning because a lot of work had to go into keeping everyone on side. Campbell thinks it was inevitable; like the feminist movement, the disability movement had its internal rivalries. It certainly served BCODP's interests to be seen as the only legitimate disability group. RADAR, a small organisation – it never had more than 60 staff and £1 million a year to spend on campaigning and outreach – was lumped in with the big charities, a source of pride or shame, depending on which way you chose to look at it. Yet RADAR and BCODP memberships overlapped. There was cross-fertilisation all the time, Massie claims, and indeed it showed in the way RADAR began to pay more attention to its member groups and more disabled people appeared among its trustees and staff. Stephen Bradshaw, a BCODP founder member, known for his diplomatic skills, worked quietly with Massie to make change happen – though he never accepted invitations to join RADAR committees.

Massie acknowledged later that BCODP and the 'social model' had built the confidence and consciousness of disabled people in a way that RADAR and other groups had never done. But at the time he found the divide between organisations run by disabled people and charities run for them artificial and irksome. 'The organisations "of" and "for" disabled people is a load of baloney, it's political', he burst out in an interview with the newspaper *Disability Now* in 1990. He also questioned BCODP's idea of democracy. 'I am a member of three organisations that are members of BCODP, which says it represents 100,000 people. Nobody has ever asked me what I think of its policies.'

In spite of being blackballed, RADAR continued to attract clever, young disabled people who went on to become well-known figures in the disability field. It offered them a pan-disability perspective, links to government, detailed legislative knowledge, and a close relationship with key parliamentarians through the Parliamentary All Party Disablement (now Disability) Group to whom it supplied administrative backup. The group was composed of peers and MPs, chaired by the deaf MP, Jack (later Lord) Ashley, who introduced the first anti-discrimination legislation bill in 1982. Over the next 12 years Labour MPs produced 13 more, drafted with the help of RADAR, which all foundered on Tory government opposition to disability legislation and fears about cost.

In 1990, Wilson retired from RADAR and Massie was appointed director. It was a busy time for disability campaigners. Frustration with Tory government inertia was spilling over on many fronts – civil rights legislation, benefits, earlier legislation still not implemented. 'There is hardly any development in the disability world that doesn't pass through RADAR,' claimed the new director. 'I'm on loads of committees, trying to get the government to see things our way. You've got to be around the committee table, not on a street corner waving placards.'

This dig at direct action was unfair, but Massie probably felt his own efforts were being dismissed. Over the next five years he seemed to be everywhere, from persuading the Government to crack down on abuse of the 'orange badge' disabled parking scheme, to serving as the only disabled member of the Commission on Social Justice, set up by Labour leader John Smith; its report influenced the manifesto of the next Labour government. Massie's paper, *Disabled People and Social Justice*, calling for civil rights legislation and a disability commission, was supported by the other commissioners, though the draft, which included pro-life arguments, proved too hot for some and he was persuaded to tone it down.

At RADAR, Massie staved off another financial crisis with the help of a National Lottery grant and £60,000 from ITV's Telethon, the fundraising show that was picketed by disability campaigners for its negative, patronising attitude to disabled people. Massie says he took the money and gave a speech to camera about civil rights. By 1994, RADAR could afford to move from its West End offices, 'an ugly old 1960s monstrosity of a building', as one staff member put it, to brand new offices in Islington, where it had a modern computer network.

As a manager, Massie elicited different reactions, depending perhaps on your position in the hierarchy. 'Bert was the antithesis of corporate jargon', says Neil Betteridge, who started as information officer and ended up head of projects and campaigns. 'If you fouled up, he would come and tell you in words probably even less attractive.' Betteridge accepted this, as Massie also appreciated you 'when things worked well'. On the other hand, Vicky Scott, RADAR's parliamentary officer, thought Massie did not appreciate his staff enough and 'he helped to create an atmosphere of us and them between staff and management'. She also thought he contributed to the conflict between the 'ofs' and the 'fors'. Yes, he got a lot of flack from BCODP and others ('people were really, really horrible to each other'), but, as an umbrella organisation for disabled people, 'you have to be a bit more dynamic and a bit more able to take the punches and a bit less hermit crabby about it'.

Meanwhile the campaign for anti-discrimination legislation built up until, in 1994, it received an unexpected fillip. A civil rights bill originally introduced by Alf Morris was reintroduced by the Labour MP Dr Roger Berry. It won the backing of 231 MPs (none against) at its Second Reading, as well as support from the *Sun* newspaper, 250,000 postcards and a lobby of 2000 disabled people. It looked likely to succeed until 82 last-minute amendments tabled at Report Stage by five Tory MPs ensured the bill would run out of parliamentary time. The amendments, it turned out, had been authorised by the Minister for Disabled People, Nicholas Scott. At first he denied any involvement, but then he had to apologise to MPs. He did not resign, but was later sacked.

Vicky Scott was the minister's daughter. She had been working intensively on the bill and also with the coalition of disability groups, Rights

Now!, chaired by Stephen Bradshaw, which held its meetings at RADAR. When a late-night interview for BBC Radio 4's *Today* programme exposed her disagreement with her father, she little expected her comments to become the leading news story. Next morning journalists and TV crews crowded outside RADAR. The British public woke up to the fact that disabled people had no recourse in law against discrimination, unlike women or people from ethnic minorities. Wrong footed, the government was forced to bring in an anti-discrimination bill of its own.

For Nicholas Scott it was a personal tragedy. As the longest serving Minister for Disabled People, he had fought successfully to prevent cuts in disability benefits and increase the Independent Living Fund, but he could not get the Government to support civil rights. In the end, he put loyalty to the Government before principled resignation. He could have made a formal complaint about his daughter working for a campaigning organisation partially funded by the Government, but he refused, telling Sir John Hannam, secretary of the Parliamentary All Party Disability Group (APDG), that he admired her and supported the campaign.

Massie stood by Vicky Scott in those fraught days. 'Bert was lovely', she says, 'very supportive'. But he blotted his copybook later, when a senior civil servant, blaming Scott for her father's job loss, refused to work with her on the anti-discrimination bill, and Massie exchanged her for RADAR's legal officer, Caroline Gooding. Scott threatened to resign; Massie apologised.

A new private member's bill calling for full, enforceable civil rights went a lot further than the Government's anti-discrimination bill. The Government claimed the civil rights bill would cost £17 billion initially, plus £1 billion a year, but a report by RADAR on behalf of Rights Now! and the APDG counterclaimed that the Government had double accounted and failed to allow for welfare savings and tax revenues from disabled people in work. RADAR also commissioned a Gallop poll that showed, said Massie, strong public support for comprehensive legislation.

The pressure of the two bills on parliamentary time enabled Massie to be more demanding on ministers who wanted his support in getting their bill through. He had already had a one-to-one meeting – no civil servants – with William Hague, the new Minister for Disabled People, who had solicited RADAR's support for the proposed bill. Massie rejected it as being too weak, but was willing to support something stronger after it was made clear to him that the private member's bill had no future – Hague was facing heavyweight opposition in cabinet to any discrimination legislation. The resulting bill showed some improvements: it expanded the definition of disability and covered access to goods and services as well as jobs, but said little about access to transport.

Massie employed one of his pincer movements. He suggested the Government take the power to make transport regulations for accessible taxis, buses and trains. He then secured House of Lords pressure through the APDG to include the transport amendments. 'I remember talking to Bert on the phone late in the evening when we were drafting things,' says Frye. 'Do you think this form of words will work? Do you think we can get that past the Lords?' It was Massie and a few others working behind the scenes who brought it off, she says, not the street demonstrators. But Caroline Gooding believes the Government was softened up by the public protests.

Both lines of attack were probably needed, but Massie's backdoor diplomacy infuriated disability activists still holding out for full civil rights. Alan Holdsworth of the Disabled People's Direct Action Network (DAN) sold a T-shirt with 'Rights not Radar' on it. In April 1995 Rachel Hurst let fly to the *Independent on Sunday* her comment about Massie being an Uncle Tom, adding for good measure, 'He actually doesn't care a toss about the rights of disabled people.' Massie was upset, but his reply a week later dealt only with the rights point. He referred to his Commission on Social Justice paper and explained in a reasonable tone that RADAR would have preferred the civil rights bill, but since the Government would not accept civil rights, it was a matter of working with their bill or waiting for a Labour government, which could not be guaranteed to prioritise disability legislation.

In the final stages of the Government's bill in October, it became clear to everyone that they would not get a disability rights commission to enforce the law through the courts, only a toothless, advisory, National Disability Council. Furious, BCODP and other 'of' organisations on Rights Now! blamed the 'fors' for compromising, and split off. Massie's line was: 'If you are starving, you do not turn down beans on a plate just because it is not a banquet.' In October *Disability Now* reported that he was talking with Alistair Burt, the latest Minister for Disabled People. He later denied he was being too secretive.

The Disability Discrimination Act became law in November 1995. As deputy chair of the National Disability Council and a member of another advisory council on employment, Massie helped draw up codes of practice to make the Act work. Relationships he had built up with ministers earlier, sometimes when they were still backbenchers, came in useful and helped him outmanoeuvre unhelpful civil servants. When, for example, the Conservative Cabinet Office cut most of a key employment code of practice, approved by employers, disability organisations and the Trades Union Congress, Massie persuaded the cabinet minister, Roger Freeman, that the slimmed down version wouldn't work; it was so vague that every dispute would have to be settled at an employment tribunal and, anyway, no one had agreed it. Massie showed the first draft to Freeman, who had not seen it. Freeman saw the point and agreed. Similarly, when Nick Raynsford became housing minister in the Labour government, he extended the accessible building regulations to new houses, something Massie had persuaded him of years before.

Labour came into office in May 1997 on a manifesto pledge to support 'comprehensive and enforceable civil rights'. Massie already knew Andrew Smith, the minister responsible for equal opportunities, who forged the plan to implement the DDA, set up an independent commission, and a task force that would consider plugging gaps in the DDA. Massie and Rachel Hurst both served on the task force – without flare-ups. Massie said later that it takes too much energy to hate people or bear grudges; it's easier to move on.

He broke the ice quickly with Margaret Hodge, the latest disability minister, who chaired the task force. She cancelled their first one-to-one meeting, so he took along a RADAR diary and a RADAR calendar tile with contact details to the next one. 'Now, Margaret, as clearly your diary is all over the place, here's a new diary for you, and a calendar tile so you know where you are going.' Hodge found him funny and easy to get on with. Also, crucially, he was in tune with her aim of producing a practical agenda for the next phase of disability rights that she could sell within government and then implement. Hodge says, 'He nagged Number 10' to help her get parliamentary time to turn the proposals into legislation.

Massie gets an intellectual buzz from working with politicians, but he has no illusions about who calls the shots. 'Politicians have power. All the others have is influence.' On government committees, he knows you have little time and all around there are countervailing influences, hence the importance of building a relationship with the minister.

Hodge went on to appoint Massie chair of the new Disability Rights Commission (DRC). For some people it seemed an obvious choice: he was impaired and had expert knowledge; he also understood government and could 'play that bit of the game almost from the inside', says a senior civil servant. On the other hand, he lacked credibility with some disability groups. Hodge denies that the Government shilly-shallied over the decision. Massie, who was now getting more pain from his weakening arm muscles, used the 'reasonable adjustment' clause in the DDA to extend the three-day-a-week job to four, and also held out for his sickness benefit and pension to be continued. Whatever the reason, the commission started work three months late, in April 2000.

While Massie was securing his own financial future, RADAR's was slipping away. A fall in donations and trading income produced an operating loss of £410,000 in 2000 and a dangerous dip in reserves. Peter Mansell, previously at the Spinal Injuries Association, was brought in to deal with the crisis, which involved making staff redundant. 'We have had three years of growing deficits,' he said at the time. 'That trend has not been addressed.' Later he accepted Massie's argument that this was a recurring situation and if he had stayed he would have brought RADAR round. Nor did Mansell support the allegation that Massie jumped from a sinking ship.

The strength of RADAR's influence was brought home to Mansell a few days after he took over: Margaret Hodge phoned to ask what he thought about something.

> She didn't do that because she knew me from Adam. She did it because she saw the RADAR that Bert had generated as being powerful enough to seek its advice. Now that's pretty good going for an organisation with a couple of million quid and a few people in London.

The DRC started with a grant from the Department for Education and Employment (DfEE) of £11 million a year, roughly midway between the Equal Opportunities Commission (EOC) and the Commission for Racial Equality (CRE), and an agenda that was much more radical – no less than 'looking at how to change the whole structure of society', said Massie. To do this meant bringing different interests on board. The first 14 commissioners he helped to appoint were drawn from business, trade unions, public bodies and disability charities. Including Massie, two-thirds were disabled. In Bob Niven, former director of equal opportunities policy at the DfEE, he found a congenial chief executive who knew his way around Whitehall and whose hand on the tiller was said to be so safe that even the National Audit Office gave him top marks. Free from day-to-day management, Massie could concentrate on what he was best at – strategic leadership, problem solving and communication.

Charities grumbled as some of their brightest and best decamped to the exciting new organisation. The disabled proportion of staff grew to 31 per cent. Even so, it was a slow start, hampered by civil servant mistakes in the rush to set up and by most companies – those with fewer than 15 employees – having legal protection from the DDA until 2004. Inevitably, the commission was accused of being toothless. Massie replied that they had, at least, won the argument to get the exemption on companies removed.

The DRC set up offices in Manchester, London, Edinburgh and Cardiff. It advised government departments on complying with the DDA and pressed for more disability legislation. It supplied information, undertook formal investigations and ran national awareness campaigns. The helpline advised on the DDA, taking half a million calls in its first five years – although some people complained the lines were often engaged, advice was not always helpful and the DRC should have worked more closely with local organisations. There was a free, independent, conciliation service. When that failed, the DRC took employers or service providers to court and secured compensation – not often enough, some said; 55 cases were taken in 2005, the last year before funding was diverted to local organisations, such as law centres, ahead of the DRC's closure.

The commission also won high-profile appeals that clarified or widened interpretation of discrimination law; one of its last cases produced a landmark decision from the European Court of Justice in 2008 that protects carers of disabled people from discrimination in the workplace. Another landmark ruling in the House of Lords brought them the *Lawyer* magazine's Employment Team of the Year award in 2005. Though Massie failed to get the power to bring cases under the Human Rights Act 1998, the DRC intervened, with some success, in cases where a disabled person's dignity or independence were at risk.

Poised between the Government and the disability world, the DRC had to steer a tricky path. On the Government's side, it was seen as modern and well run. 'Of all three commissions, the DRC is by far the best,' said a senior civil servant. Each side needed the other to carry through an agenda for change. But of course there were private rows, and ministers had to be prodded to act faster or go further. Gaps in the DDA, such as education and wider coverage of transport, were plugged, and the definition of disability was widened. From December 2006, all public authorities have had a duty to promote equal opportunities for disabled people and, most importantly, involve them in drawing up action plans. Massie believes this proactive duty has enormous potential to change institutional attitudes and behaviour, though he fears that as the Equality and Human Rights Commission tries to include other groups, such as ethnic minorities, the message will get diluted.

On the disability side, too, the DRC was generally seen as having a higher profile and being more effective than the other commissions. 'I think the DRC has the best record of getting things done,' said the campaigning MP, Roger Berry, before the commission closed. 'It does Bert enormous credit.' When CRE chair Trevor Phillips joked about 'Bert's rat-like cunning', some people detected jealousy.

In 2005, Peter Mansell was a director at the National Patient Safety Agency. He appreciated the commission's down-to-earth attempts to improve people's lives. In one week he was asked to contribute to a DRC investigation into health care inequalities faced by people with learning difficulties or mental health problems and respond to a DRC revised code of practice. How many times, he asked, had he received something like that from the other two commissions during his three-and-a-half years in the job? 'I haven't. Isn't that strange?'

As a wheelchair user, he felt his daily life had been directly affected by the DRC. 'I can remember hearing on the radio that Bert was stuck at London City Airport because he couldn't get on the plane. The fact it was the chair of the DRC, that was good, and also that the DRC was supporting a case against Ryanair' – for charging for a wheelchair service.

During the life of the DRC, people saw a change in Massie. He became more confident, more certain of himself. 'Bert has come into his own,' said Baroness Jane Campbell, a commissioner from 2000 to 2007. 'Every year he's gone a little bit stronger and a little bit more edgy.'

By 2006, it did seem as if a pent-up anger against the poverty and inequality experienced by disabled people was spilling out in Massie's speeches. At Cambridge University, he talked of disabled people being 'incurably human', and gave examples of disabled people whose killings attracted light sentences because, he believed, disabled people have little real value, whatever their legal rights. This sounded more like Rachel Hurst's territory than Bert Massie's. A few months earlier, at Westminster Central Hall, he called for a fundamental shift in public policy towards disabled people. He criticised the 'lazy fatalism' of politicians and 'the cycle of low expectations' perpetuated by successive governments, which have resulted in more disabled adults living in 'frankly, obscene levels of poverty' than children or pensioners. He reminded his audience that disability can affect most people at some time: 'this is about our shared destiny'. And he positioned disability within the core concerns of mainstream politics: 'Unemployment, child poverty, skills, youth, safer communities and respect – successfully addressing the key challenges of public policy today rests on successfully addressing the circumstances of disabled people.' In another speech to the Advisory, Conciliation and Arbitration Service (ACAS), he pointed out that demographic changes – fewer young employees and more older people – will mean employers will have to employ more disabled people and people with long-term health conditions.

Speeches like these stimulated the national debate about the future of disability rights launched by the DRC a year earlier. Out of this came an agenda to take disabled people to the Government's promised land of equality in 2025. But it was also relevant to other groups. That was the DRC's legacy to the new Equality and Human Rights Commission (EHRC), which absorbed it and two other commissions in October 2007.

Massie's edginess may also have been because time was short. He postponed his retirement in 2004 because of fears that the new super-commission might sideline disability. The DRC persuaded the Government to appoint one disability commissioner – no other interest group secured that – and to have a disability committee, half of them disabled, with executive powers, a budget and staff, and a life of at least two years. Massie was to be a transitional commissioner. To get all this, 'we had more cups of tea with more people than you can imagine, right from Tony Blair downwards', he says.

The Minister for Disabled People at this time was Maria Eagle, another Scouser. Although she favoured a single commission, she understood how disability discrimination was different from the other groups and worked to secure the guarantees. Massie told her what disabled people would and would not accept, which helped her in negotiations. In return he could be relied upon to deliver support from the commission. 'Of all the commission chairmen, Bert told us what the bottom lines were and delivered exactly on them. And we were able to deliver further to the DRC.'

Some of Massie's fears about the EHRC have been justified. He finds it stuffy and hierarchical, more interested in formal investigations than taking legal cases, overly concerned about the 'cross strands' of its remit and fairly ignorant of disability. Massie had to stop them selecting an inaccessible office with no parking and he has had to point out that a door to a disabled loo is so heavy you can't open it. 'That lot know as much about disability as I do about the dark side of the moon,' he says in exasperation. He just hopes that when his term ends in 2009 he will have persuaded the EHRC that the disability committee is worth proper funding. He has yet to be persuaded that the Government's proposals for an equality bill, which aim to simplify and strengthen existing discrimination law, will really encompass the needs of disabled people and leave them better protected.

On another front, as Commissioner for the Compact between government and the Third Sector, he looks set to ginger things up, telling the Government how small organisations work, and getting user-led groups to campaign more boldly for services, including for disabled people.

Knighted: Sir Bert Massie, then chair of the
Disability Rights Commission, after his investiture in 2007. Photograph taken by DRC.

Nowadays, Massie enjoys the trappings of institutional achievement. He is sought after as a trustee, council member, governor. He is an honorary fellow and governor of John Moores University, his alma mater, and an honorary doctor of laws ('a doctor of outlaws would be more appropriate', he quips) of Bristol University. He is also a non-executive director of Appleshaw, which builds retirement homes and might, he thinks, offer a model to local authorities. He is still a Scouser, though. His off-the-cuff comments can woo the media and stay in the mind – even if the jokes in his speeches sometimes misfire. When an old work colleague hits trouble, he sends a personal email. And when *Disability Now* faced a crack-down on its editorial freedom by its publisher, Scope, he spoke out in support of the newspaper.

Massie has 'arrived', and he has helped disability rights arrive too. In its last year the DRC's grant of £21 million outstripped the other two commissions, though it was only scratching the surface of inequality, said Massie. Disabled people remained nearly twice as likely to be out of work, for example, and in spite of DRC efforts to include people with mental health conditions, severely disabled people and people with long-term health conditions still had no voice.

Yet many battles have been won, and Massie has been at the heart of them. Ministers acknowledge that disability is now on the inside track in government. Maria Eagle thinks it couldn't have been brought off better by anyone else. Andrew Smith, a former Work and Pensions Secretary, believes Massie played 'perhaps the leading role' in translating the shift in political thinking into practice, 'helping to give institutional, practical form to the rights which the movement was campaigning for, and being a very effective interface with government and the wider public'.

The strategy of gradualness and persuasion, so roundly derided in the 1990s, has come into its own, though it probably wouldn't have worked then without a backdrop of anger and demonstration. These days the anger is muted and the concessions Massie won for disability in the Equality Commission please everyone. Agnes Fletcher, who worked with Rachel Hurst, then at RADAR, and later as head of policy and communications at the DRC, suggests another legacy. Massie, she says, is very good at making it safe for people in powerful positions to do what is needed and wanted, and he does this through humour and a readiness to take flak from his own side. His example has:

> opened the doors for hundreds of other disabled people to get into positions of influence, for people to see the merit in that and not be scared of being denounced. He's shown people what is going on on the inside track.

As more disabled people move into high and exposed public posts, we should not forget that Massie helped lead the way.

# JACK ASHLEY:
# POLITICIAN

*Photograph taken by Pauline Ashley*

Jack Ashley (now Baron Ashley of Stoke and Widnes) was a fiery, extrovert, Labour MP aged 45 at the start of December 1967, a man at home in the cut and thrust of parliamentary debate and the banter of the Commons bar or tea room. Elected to the safe seat of Stoke-on-Trent South the previous year, he was Parliamentary Private Secretary to Michael Stewart, Secretary of State for Economic Affairs. He had fulfilled one dream, of becoming an MP, and now his hopes were pinned on becoming a minister, hopes supported by recent press speculation. But by Boxing Day Ashley was deaf. A minor operation to repair a perforated eardrum and improve his hearing had been allowed to go ahead even though he had a cold virus, and it failed; the hearing in his other ear had already deteriorated to nothing. He faced 'a growing, icy apprehension' about the future. How could a deaf MP hope to survive in the verbal hurly-burly of Parliament? How could he effectively represent his constituents?

The following April he put himself to the test. Armed with lip-reading skills from a crash course and hours of practice, feeling exhausted, apprehensive, 'but oddly hopeful', he went back to the Commons. He switched on his powerful hearing aid and turned it to full volume, but he could hear only vague, meaningless sounds. The Government speakers had their backs to him and the Opposition were too far away to lip-read. In the Commons bar, after the initial hand-shaking and back-slapping, he could not understand someone's question even though it was repeated at a volume which attracted the attention of nearly everyone else. 'It was the most embarrassing experience of my life,' he recalls in his autobiography, *Acts of Defiance* (1994).

Accompanied by a hard of hearing colleague, he went out on to the terrace overlooking the River Thames. The MP conveyed to Ashley that if Ashley could not follow him, a clear speaker, he would understand no one. Left alone in the early evening, Ashley gazed at the silent river. 'I thought I had known despair, but now I felt a chill and deeper sadness, as if a part of me was dead.' Even so, he went back into the Commons chamber to try again, but this time he could not pick up even a vague sound. He returned home prepared to resign.

Although Ashley posted the letter to his constituency chairman, and the news was made public, he did not resign. His constituency party voted for him to stay on; MPs supported him, and so did the Prime Minister, Harold Wilson. The constancy of his wife, Pauline, and his family was crucial. With a mixture of delight and trepidation, he decided to remain. Parliament had its first completely deaf MP.

Ashley feared he would not be able to make an effective contribution. If that meant being a minister or a shadow minister, then he did fail. Lord

(Neil) Kinnock, whose parliamentary career overlapped Ashley's, and who put the blind David Blunkett on the front bench, is sure Ashley was denied a post only because of his deafness. He puts it down to the novelty of Ashley and the technology he used, as well as attitudes towards disability in the 1970s when Jim Callaghan was Prime Minister. 'For Jim's generation, it would have been unthinkable,' he says.

Ashley soon found another role. Over the next 40 years he fought doggedly for social justice on many fronts – for children with thalidomide, battered wives, rape victims, vaccine-damaged children, bullied soldiers and many others, including, of course, deaf people. His main concern, though, was to end discrimination against all disabled people. He founded the influential Parliamentary All Party Disablement (now Disability) Group (APDG) of MPs and peers in 1969 and chaired it until January 2009. No legislation associated with disability has escaped the scrutiny or comment of the APDG. No disability minister could avoid its civilised grillings. It brought forward private members' bills and played a crucial role in the campaign for a comprehensive Disability Discrimination Act. It has been a conduit between parliamentarians and disabled people. 'We gave disabled people access to the corridors of power,' said Ashley.

As a backbench MP and then life peer, he has pulled every parliamentary lever for his causes – asking questions, introducing bills, initiating parliamentary debates, leading deputations to ministers, tabling motions. From his own experience, he knows what will get the media going. At the age of 86, he is still at the hub of disability politics, having piloted a bill twice through the House of Lords that would sweep away barriers to disabled people living independently. The widespread respect in which he is held was summed up by Gordon Brown in 2003, when, as Chancellor of the Exchequer, he presented Ashley with the first ePolitix.com Charity Champions Lifetime Award. 'He is a great man, someone who has been a shining beacon of honour and decency in our society, who has proved that one life can transform many lives.'

In his autobiography, Ashley wondered if, as a deaf man, he was perverse to choose Parliament over a quiet job and an easier life. He decided: 'I was fighting back, but there was nothing noble about that. It was an instinctive reaction, influenced by my upbringing and my nature.'

Ashley has been a fighter all his life. That was how he coped with a childhood of extreme poverty in the Merseyside town of Widnes, where the chemical industry and the Catholic church dominated the workers. Ashley's father, John, was a labourer who became night-watchman for ICI. He died of pneumonia in 1927, when Ashley was five, leaving his widow, Isobel, to bring up three children on her own. Ashley was the middle child, the only boy. The family shared a two-up, two-down decrepit terrace house. There was a scullery for cooking, a lavatory at the end of the back yard, a coal fire and gas lighting delivered via a meter. 'Mam', to whom Ashley was devoted, made ends meet by cleaning office floors. In spite of the long hours that wore her out, she kept her rooms and her children clean and created a close-knit family. In appreciation, the children sometimes clubbed together to spend a penny on a slice of coconut iced cake for her, which she shared with them.

While his mother was shy and respectful of authority, Ashley was spirited, competitive, and willing to take risks, whether it was whizzing down the street on his 'gooch' – a home-made scooter – or trying various ploys with his friends to get into the cinema for free. At the Catholic school he did not shine scholastically, but he loved singing in a special section of the choir. On Sundays he sang in the church choir, which operated from a high balcony at the back of the church. At evening Benediction a bald man would sit beneath the balcony. 'I used to compete with a mischievous friend to see who could form a bubble on his tongue then blow it down on the inviting head.'

Ashley left school at 14, like most of the other children. Neither he nor his sisters tried for the grammar school; they were Catholics, and the grammar school was not. With no father to recommend him for a job, he took matters into his own hands and applied for an office job at ICI, which was a cut above factory work in job security and wages. Hearing nothing, and needing to earn money for the family, he took a labouring job at an asbestos factory. On his first day, holding bacon sandwiches and an old tea can, he clattered down the dark street to the bus stop wearing leather clogs with metal reinforcements. He says he was alert and curious rather than scared. He liked the comradeship of the job ('a feeling that we were all in it together'), but not the pay – 12s 3d a week (about £24 today). ICI came through with an interview and when he turned up in a collar and tie he found he was to be a labourer helping to fill carboys – thick glass bottles two feet high – with formic acid. He took the job, but didn't always push himself, incurring reprimands from the foreman.

When he was 16 he again looked for a better-paid job, to the consternation of his mother and now his stepfather too, who was unemployed. After several casual jobs he landed one at Bolton's, a copper-smelting works down the road. He cursed a workmate as stupid because he was faster and more conscientious at unloading wagons of coal dust, but, generally, he got on well with his workmates, and with girls. Dancing in one of the local church halls led to him becoming a master of ceremonies – the first sign of an aptitude for public speaking.

War broke out in 1939 and, as soon as he was 18, Ashley applied to be an air gunner in the Royal Air Force (RAF). There followed a series of painful rejections. He was turned down by the RAF because his maths was poor and then discharged from the Royal Army Service Corps because his hearing deteriorated – luckily his perforated eardrum was patched up successfully when he got home. So it was back to Bolton's, where, after an emergency appendicitis operation, he asked the foreman for a temporary light job, and was refused until he could load the furnaces again. For someone who had had his brushes with the foreman, this response was probably inevitable. But it set Ashley on the road to rebellion. He went off to find out about trade unions, talked to the secretary of the Widnes branch of the Chemical Workers' Union and discovered Bolton's would be eligible. 'When I eventually returned to the factory I was fit, broke and bitter – and supplied with hundreds of application forms.'

What happened next takes some believing. Ashley persuaded 400 workers to abandon years of deference to a powerful company, vote to support a trade union and then strike twice, for union recognition and restitution of pay withheld and a sacked colleague. The workers may have been ripe for action, but they put their trust in a youth of 20, inexperienced in trade union ways, and voted him chairman of their shop stewards' committee. He showed he could select able lieutenants, act decisively under pressure, control his anger – most of the time – and plan and organise resistance. His success at Bolton's started Ashley on a trajectory that carried him to the union's national executive council a year later.

Meanwhile, appalled by the slum condition of the houses around his home in Wellington Street, Ashley embarked on a campaign for repairs and reduced rent, which won the support of his neighbours and led to him being elected a town councillor at the age of 22. He canvassed every house in the ward, and outwitted his opponents by turning their loudspeakers to his advantage: he addressed the crowds they left behind and used children to drown their speeches with chanting.

All this ended in 1946, when he chanced to read about scholarships for working men at Ruskin College, Oxford. He applied and, notwithstanding his frank admission that he had read very little, he was accepted. He knew his pay packet would be missed, but going away to college was a big opportunity. Even so, he returned home often and never lost his roots.

From a diploma in economics and political science at Ruskin, he went on to get an honours degree at Cambridge University, helped by another scholarship. While books still deterred him, he relished debate, and at Cambridge he rose swiftly through the ranks of the University Labour Club and then the Cambridge Union to become in 1951 the Union's first working-class president. He broke with the tradition of evening dress and wore a suit. As president he got to know famous guest speakers, including government ministers. Ashley and the previous union president were invited to tour 20 American universities to debate various motions, including that they regretted the American way of life. They did this in style, even though they were minimally prepared – the entertainment on the *Queen Elizabeth* had been too beguiling. Similarly, on the voyage back, Ashley did precious little revision for his final examinations.

From Cambridge he got more than a degree. After graduating, he became engaged to Pauline Crispin, a mathematics student from middle-class Surrey, 'a lovely young woman with dark brown hair and blue eyes', as he describes her. He wanted to be an MP, and Hugh Dalton, who was a cabinet minister and one of his Cambridge Union speakers, helped him to get the Labour candidacy for Finchley in the 1951 general election – a contest he predictably lost as Finchley was a safe Conservative seat (later Margaret Thatcher's).

For nearly 15 years Ashley was a BBC radio and television producer and then editor, a period broken only by a year's travelling fellowship in the USA. His background in industrial working-class politics gave him an inside track at the BBC on issues like labour relations and unemployment. He worked on *Panorama* and also on his own documentary programmes. In 1966, now married and the father of three daughters, he entered Parliament as MP for the safe Labour seat of Stoke-on-Trent South.

Although social security and disability were on his political horizon, he was most involved in supporting government efforts to stabilise the economy by controlling prices and incomes, a policy opposed by left-wing Labour MPs as well as the Tories. A prickly pride could land him in scrapes. When the Prime Minister, Harold Wilson, seemed to ignore Ashley at a Labour Party Conference party to concentrate on left-wing members, Ashley was miffed. He sent a sharp message to Wilson saying he was 'stupid to ignore his supporters and soft-soap his critics'. Since Wilson had chosen Ashley to second the Loyal Address to the Queen's Speech in the new parliamentary session, he later had to apologise to Wilson – who handsomely waved it aside.

By 1967, Ashley thought his political career was flourishing. And then, abruptly, he became deaf, unable to hear any sound from outside his head, yet beset by terrible roaring and shrieking noises within it – tinnitus. There were the practicalities of communication to deal with as well as the reaction of MPs. He felt out of touch with political events and he was unable to keep abreast of something immediate, like a speech, or to comment on it to someone else, because he was excluded from the informal network of corridor and tea room conversations. Even good friends avoided protracted contact with him. Ashley remembers sitting in the Commons library, hoping that David Owen and David Marquand would ask him to join them for dinner. They just walked past, smiling and nodding affably. 'I turned to look at the retreating figures of my two friends, feeling unbearably isolated, and went to eat alone in the cafeteria.'

Nevertheless, he determinedly broke the ice, speaking up at a meeting of the Parliamentary Labour Party. A few days later he spoke in the Commons, championing a bill that called for a commission to consider introducing a disablement income. He relied on a fellow MP to signal if he was speaking too loudly or too softly. His speech was warmly received and even the Prime Minister congratulated him, which made him feel more confident.

In everything except parliamentary debates, Pauline was at his side to help interpret conversations, take notes, relay telephone calls he could then reply to, or exchange with him almost imperceptible signals at meetings. She also did the research behind Ashley's speeches and parliamentary questions, and inspired many of his campaigns. 'Without Pauline it would have been impossible to carry on,' he said.

Invited to speak at a conference of the Royal National Institute for the Deaf (RNID), he asked himself if he should start campaigning for deaf people or whether it would look like special pleading. Characteristically, he went ahead and gave a barnstorming speech about the discrimination faced by deaf people and the need to change public attitudes. The speech got media attention and prompted a spate of letters that encouraged him to become a disability campaigner. It was a role that could replace his ambitions, now dashed, for ministerial office. He had already championed the cause of a disablement income and there were many other areas to improve, such as transport, housing and employment. Parliament had shown little concern for disability since the Second World War, except to help disabled ex-service personnel find employment. 'It became clear to me that some kind of parliamentary organisation was needed to stimulate political interest in disability and to establish cooperation between MPs and the voluntary organisations,' he wrote. The result was the Parliamentary All Party Disablement Group (APDG). Ashley was elected chair and the Tory MP John Astor secretary.

The APDG took off when Alf Morris, a fellow MP from Manchester, who, like Ashley, had followed the Ruskin-Oxbridge route, introduced his

own Chronically Sick and Disabled Persons' Bill. It was the first comprehensive disability bill, requiring local authorities to identify disabled people,
assess their needs and provide services and adaptations for them. APDG
members helped him with ideas for the bill and briefed other MPs to secure
all-party support. Ashley threw himself into the fray, supporting the bill at
every stage, arguing for the provisions and battling the let-out phrase 'as
far as is practicable', which civil servants kept trying to include. He also
met Harold Wilson and softened him to the idea that people with haemo-
philia needed special help. When the Government gave the bill its financial
blessing, Ashley could tell *The Times* with justification that it was 'a major
breakthrough for the disabled people of Britain'. The bill became law in
May 1970, just scraping through before the general election, though the
fight to implement it continued under a Tory government.

All this activity helped to jerk Ashley out of his isolation. It gave him
a sense of purpose and worth. People sought his views again. With this
'psychological tonic', as he called it, he felt he could continue to be an MP, a
belief confirmed by his constituents when he retained his seat in the Tories'
landslide victory.

Heavy handed: Jack Ashley and other MPs receive a 258,000 signature petition for a
national disablement income in November 1972. On Ashley's left is
Rosalie (now Baroness) Wilkins; on his right, Mary Greaves, director of the
Disablement Income Group. Photograph taken by NI Syndication/The Times

Ashley believed the pressure in Parliament for disabled people's rights was
becoming irresistible. In 1972 he presented a petition for a national disablement income signed by 258,000 people; it took four people to carry it in.

When Harold Wilson returned to power in 1974, he appointed Alf Morris the first ever Minister for the Disabled (later Minister for Disabled People). Faced with severe public spending cuts on one side and pressure from disability groups and the APDG on the other, Morris succeeded in introducing four new cash benefits for disabled people and their carers, 'as of right', not based on financial need. And he more than trebled spending on disability benefits over his five years in office.

The APDG was growing stronger. Every fortnight a core of MPs and peers, some of them disabled, would meet to discuss disability issues and hear the views of disability groups. Minutes of the meetings went to others, eventually reaching about 150 people. The Royal Association for Disability and Rehabilitation (RADAR) supplied admin support and expert briefings, which continue today. Ashley had reckoned that disability would lend itself to an all-party grouping. 'I thought there must be areas of agreement on disability because there was such vast scope for good work to be done.' By making the most of neutral territory and not forcing a consensus when there was a division along party lines, such as over anti-discrimination bills in the 1980s, he kept the group together.

John (later Sir John) Hannam, an influential Tory backbencher, was secretary from 1974. He says the two of them worked harmoniously together for nearly 20 years, 'always pushing the boundaries back'. In the early days they made the most of small government majorities in the Commons. On one occasion Ashley's amendment to exempt war-disabled pensioners from vehicle excise duty elicited so much support that the Government's majority was threatened and the Tory Chancellor, Anthony Barber, was hastily summoned back to Parliament to concede defeat. Hannam says: 'We would prepare the ground in the Commons and having got the amendments accepted, they thought they would reverse them in the Lords and we made damn sure they wouldn't. We had a very effective second chamber.' Over the years he consolidated Tory support until, by the 1990s, some MPs were ready to back even civil rights for disabled people. Colleagues would come and ask him how they should vote on amendments and motions.

Ashley saw the APDG as channelling sustainable ideas from the disability community, such as integrated education or an Independent Living Fund, through to Parliament. Sometimes, though, even with the group's support, he could make no headway. Improving job prospects for disabled people was one of them. Successive governments took no action against most of the companies flouting the 3 per cent quota of disabled employees, or they just issued exemption permits, he said, 'like confetti'. In 1982, a committee originally set up by Morris called for legislation to counter the widespread discrimination against disabled people that it had found. The Tory government took no action, so Ashley did. He introduced a bill to prohibit unjustifiable discrimination on grounds of disability and to set up a commission to tackle complaints. The bill predictably failed, but a precedent had been set. Over the next 11 years other Labour APDG members kept up the pressure with a run of bills, which were duly knocked down by a Tory government averse to regulation and fearful of cost.

During the 1970s and 1980s Ashley espoused many causes, many of them to do with disability compensation. The most famous was the campaign against Distillers Company, to reverse the woefully inadequate compensation it was prepared to pay 450 children, whose mothers had taken the supposedly 'safe' sedative, thalidomide, during pregnancy. It was Ashley's first major campaign since he had become deaf.

The scandal had been kept out of the news for ten years by an unexpected alliance of the Attorney-General and Distillers: with compensation claims ongoing, the matter was *sub judice*, so public discussion was forbidden, including in Parliament. Ashley read about the children's plight in the *Sunday Times* in September 1972. Harold Evans, the editor, bravely ran a front page story and an editorial, and then another story a week later, thereby losing his biggest advertiser, Distillers, worth £600,000 a year (over £4 million today), and incurring an injunction preventing any follow-up. Ashley wanted to find a way of raising the subject in Parliament. If he could, parliamentary 'privilege' would protect him and any reporters from prosecution. He also had to balance hitting the company hard with keeping his Tory APDG members on board, and getting wide parliamentary support. Thanks to Harold Evans, he knew the Attorney-General had accepted a distinction between moral and legal justice, so he spoke in the House of '*moral* justice' and argued that since this was not a question of law, his motion could not be *sub judice*. He also asked the Tory Speaker, Selwyn Lloyd, to allow the House to condemn the 'contemptible' offer of £3.25 million to 389 of the families. Later, Selwyn Lloyd gave Ashley the go-ahead for an amended motion, which called upon Distillers to face up to its moral responsibilities. The motion secured an impressive 266 signatures. Still, the Prime Minister, Edward Heath, refused to intervene, harassed though he was by incessant parliamentary questions from Ashley, Alf Morris, and others.

The APDG invited Distillers' chairman to discuss compensation, but he refused. Instead, Distillers threatened to break off negotiations with the parents. Unsure if the company was bluffing, Ashley risked attacking again and secured an adjournment debate – a 30-minute debate at the end of the day. Better still, Labour leader Harold Wilson allowed some of the Opposition's limited parliamentary time for a full-scale debate on thalidomide and invited Ashley to open the debate from the front bench. Alf Morris, by then shadow spokesman on social policy, who had asked Wilson for parliamentary time, wound up the debate.

Just before the debate, Distillers increased its offer to the parents from £3.25 million to £5 million – not nearly enough. In his speech, Ashley vividly described the impact of thalidomide on two children, and this was picked up by radio, TV and national newspapers. Of Distillers he said: 'There are a thousand excuses why these children should receive no money and every excuse has been scavenged by the company throughout the last decade.' The Government offered £3 million to help congenitally disabled children in general, but, more than this, the debate sparked new public pressure on Distillers. It increased its offer to £11.9 million, thinking that the method of payment would be tax deductible, but the Chancellor of the Exchequer scotched that. Ashley then turned to the Trades Union Congress, which contacted the main union of Distillers' employees. A parent, David Mason, urged a boycott of Distillers products on both sides of the Atlantic supported by the American consumer champion Ralph Nader; and Tony Lynes, a Distillers shareholder and social policy analyst, got together with other shareholders to form a committee. When the *Sunday Times* published a list of large shareholders, the press started asking them where they stood. The Legal & General Assurance Society, one of the biggest shareholders, sided with the shareholders' committee, and others followed suit.

Distillers gave way in January 1973 and offered the £20 million the campaign had been demanding. Ashley headed the liaison committee that worked out a compensation scheme. His final battle was to persuade the Treasury not to tax the investment income the children would receive.

The thalidomide case put Ashley on the public map as a parliamentary campaigner for disabled people. It took a confluence of forces to beat the powerful Distillers Company – a courageous editor followed by the media in general, militant parents and shareholders, big institutional investors, and public opinion. But it was Ashley who got past legal and political obstacles to make the case a *cause célèbre* in Parliament. As Lord Kinnock noted, it was the first time that compensation was won in the public domain, not the law courts.

As one campaign died down, another started. Ashley took up the cause of children who had been severely damaged by vaccines in the government's immunisation scheme, particularly whooping cough vaccine. Six countries, including Japan and Germany, already offered compensation, but not Britain. Ashley reckoned that there might be ten times as many cases as the 170 a year reported to the government, and he found that brain damage in one-third of them could have been avoided if the vaccine had not been administered when there were contra-indications, such as fever – an echo of the way he himself went deaf.

Six months into the campaign, Labour won the general election and Barbara Castle, the new Secretary of State for Health and Social Services, asked him to be her Parliamentary Private Secretary (PPS). Ashley was in a quandary. The unpaid job of a PPS is to keep the minister in touch with backbench opinion, but he thought he could also influence health policy. On the other hand, he would be unable to campaign on health issues or have a high public profile in that field. He accepted the offer. He was back in a role he had had before he went deaf. For the next two years, he worked closely with Barbara Castle. She wrote in her diary: 'One by one I am trying to take his pet projects on board.' She approved, for example, an Institute of Hearing Research that Ashley and Morris wanted, but the Medical Research Council and her own civil servants opposed.

Later in 1974, Ashley featured in the TV show *This Is Your Life* and the following year he became a Companion of Honour, which ranks higher than a knighthood. From 1976 to 1978, he was an elected member of Labour's National Executive Committee, coinciding with Jim Callaghan's premiership – two right-wingers among the lefties.

Callaghan replaced Barbara Castle with David Ennals, who also asked Ashley to be his PPS. But this time Ashley said no; he wanted more time and freedom to do what he knew best, campaigning as a backbencher. When Callaghan was defeated in 1979, he ensured Ashley became a member of the Privy Council – an honour rare for a backbencher.

Ashley had many campaigns on the go in the mid-1970s, but he re-turned to the vaccine issue with gusto, producing masses of parliamentary questions with the help of Pauline. It fell to Alf Morris, as Minister for the Disabled, to answer them. Morris had to take the government line that he could not comment on the merits of particular compensation schemes ahead of the report from a Royal Commission set up by the Tories. Ashley called this a 'stonewalling response', and argued that a Royal Commission should not prohibit a government from taking action.

He then persuaded the Parliamentary Ombudsman to look at four cases to see if there had been official maladministration – whether warnings of danger, such as vaccinating a sick child, had not been passed on to local authorities. In the Commons he accused the Government of shirking its responsibility. Ennals retorted that Ashley was risking the health and lives of children by insisting he was right and the medical experts were wrong.

Ashley 'exploded'. Doctors themselves had been questioning the safety of the vaccine, he said; that was why he was calling for a new, independent inquiry. As Ennals prepared to leave, Ashley shouted: 'That was a shabby and squalid speech.'

Pauline Ashley's research found that the Government's figures for vaccine damage were unsound, and Ashley accused Ennals of making a false statement to the House. The press were now on Ennals' tail, so much so that Ashley wrote to the *Daily Mail* defending him against swingeing condemnation that went beyond the vaccine controversy and seemed unfair. The situation was saved by the Prime Minister, Jim Callaghan, who got the Royal Commission to indicate in advance that it would recommend financial help for very serious injury. Ennals accepted this in principle and the Ombudsman added his weight with criticism of the Health Department.

It looked like victory. But in the wake of the Royal Commission's report, Ennals announced a tax-free payment which did not meet the lifetime needs of the severely disabled children and included only those disabled since 1948. The Tories offered no more help when they came to office in 1979. Finally, a judge put the kibosh on future compensation payments for whooping cough alone by concluding that 'on the balance of probabilities' it could not be shown that whooping cough vaccine could cause permanent brain damage to young children. Against all this resistance, Ashley tried everything possible – from legislation to a judicial review – without success. He felt he had let the families down. Still, the principle of government payment for vaccine damage had been established and the public and doctors were alerted to the risk of vaccinating children with contra-indications.

The campaign also showed the tension that can exist between ministers and MPs, who are nominally on the same side. Ashley and Morris, in particular, came from similar backgrounds and had the same commitment to disabled people. They were both fiery: on one occasion Ashley lost his temper with Jim Callaghan in the Commons, misinterpreting what he had said; and on another, Morris, somewhat the worse for wear, took a swing at Kinnock and ended up on the floor of the division lobby.

As Minister for the Disabled, Morris produced concrete improvements and a focus for fresh thinking about disability, yet his power was curtailed by the Treasury and his bosses. Ashley, the maverick MP who had a severe impairment, led an influential backbench group, could beard governments and win headlines, but not wield power as a minister. Each man, perhaps, coveted something of the other. Both became privy councillors in the same year, 1979. Some see a rivalry between them, especially felt by Morris, but they have remained good friends.

In 1977, among all his campaigns, Ashley won one for himself. His Achilles heel had always been parliamentary debates, where he lacked Pauline's help and had to keep up as best he could by lip-reading. For someone completely deaf this was a great strain and could lead to embarrassing gaffes. Then, in 1974, he and Pauline heard of Palantype, a device which allows the operator, typing at the speed of normal speech, to use a phonetic shorthand that prints out as a pattern of dots which can then be transcribed. Perhaps a computer could read the dots and produce phonetic English on a monitor, Pauline thought. To develop this needed money as well as permission from the Commons, neither of which seemed forthcoming from the Services Committee. However, two technical experts were found to take on the task, and Ashley secured parliamentary support and funding.

The Services Committee agreed to see a test of the system. Concentrating hard on the small screen and phonetic language which 'looked like gobbledegook', Ashley managed a halting conversation. Then the committee chairman, Robert Cooke, surmising, correctly, that Ashley was also lip-reading, moved behind him. Ashley said he 'half-calculated and half-guessed' that he was being asked how he would react if Cooke became Foreign Secretary. 'I replied, "To suppose that you were Foreign Secretary would be to face disaster, because you are a Tory MP."' He got it right, everyone laughed, and Ashley felt elated. 'For the first time in eight years I had communicated directly with a person I could not see.'

Southampton University's version of Palantype was approved and Ashley began using it in February 1977. Over the years, the script became easier to understand. Palantype was taken up by deaf organisations and used at disability conferences.

The International Year of Disabled Persons in 1981 heralded a decade where the discrimination that disabled people faced on all fronts was coming to light through official reports, some commissioned in the Labour years, and through the efforts of disabled people themselves. The momentum for equal rights was building up against a Tory government, led by Margaret Thatcher, that was determined to curb public spending and encourage people to stand on their own feet. It was an inauspicious time for poor and vulnerable people. Unemployment in Stoke doubled, to 20,000, in the first 18 months of the Tory government; disabled people saw the value of their social security benefits fall while local authorities cut back on services.

Amid all this, the APDG grew in influence and activity. Apart from fostering private members' anti-discrimination bills, it tackled the Government over social security cuts and secured mobility allowance for deaf-blind people and those with learning difficulties. 'Adequate resources are the key,' wrote Ashley. 'Only then will disabled people escape poverty and patronage.'

In 1986 the APDG helped strengthen a bill introduced by Labour MP Tom Clarke, which, among other things, required local authorities to make an assessment for services if asked to by a disabled person or carer. Although the bill got through, it was a hollow victory, because the Government dragged its feet on implementing the more expensive sections, such as drawing up statements of need and providing services for school leavers. Ashley criticised the Government for its 'bogus' support of the bill, condemning it as a public relations exercise. Frustrated by the delay, over 1000 disabled people descended on Westminster in April 1987 for a mass lobby of Parliament. APDG supporters alerted other MPs, 200 of whom went along.

Ashley was pleased to see among the demonstrators hundreds of deaf people and their interpreters. He had long ago jettisoned his concern that parliamentary campaigning for the UK's 9 million deaf and hard of hearing people would look like special pleading. He knew the terrible social isolation of deafness and what it had cost him. Years later, when the pluses of disability were being discussed, he said: 'There's nothing good about being deaf.'

He persuaded the Tory Health Secretary, Sir Keith Joseph, to introduce behind-the-ear hearing aids on the NHS in 1973 by mocking the list of fudging replies Joseph had given and making MPs laugh. He set up the British Tinnitus Association supported by the Royal National Institute for the Deaf (now for Deaf People) and became the RNID president in 1987. He pushed successfully for the Broadcasting Act 1990 to include tougher targets for subtitling ITV programmes and has kept up the pressure ever since.

He also became president of the Hearing Research Trust (now Deafness Research UK), set up by Pauline Ashley in 1985 to attract funding for medical research into deafness. This included the cochlear implant, designed for severely deaf people who cannot benefit from hearing aids; by electrically stimulating the auditory nerve it allows the brain to understand sound. He helped secure the first government funding for six NHS cochlear implant centres.

Ashley's own cochlear implant in 1993, when he was 70, allowed him to hear his four-year-old grandson for the first time and improved his tinnitus too. 'I can best describe what I hear as being like a croaking Dalek with laryngitis,' he joked, and then, more seriously, 'The difference between a world of total silence and being able to hear, not perfectly but well, is absolutely fantastic.' He wanted others to have the device, but the high cost (about £27,000 for an adult nowadays, including assessment and rehabilitation over the first year) has deterred primary care trusts. If an appraisal by the National Institute for Health and Clinical Excellence (NICE) shows that cochlear implants are cost effective and it issues commissioning guidelines, the postcode lottery uncovered by the Ashleys could become a thing of the past. Ashley has taken up the cases of many people seeking an implant, and with Pauline he set up the National Cochlear Implant Users' Association.

Campaigning for medical answers to deafness and working with the RNID, the biggest deaf charity, which is not run by deaf people, have set Ashley at odds with deaf activists from the British Deaf Association, who celebrate their deaf culture, use British sign language and call themselves 'the Deaf community'. They see cochlear implants as dangerous and robbing people of their inherited degree of deafness. Ironically, Ashley received an honorary degree in 1977 from America's only university for deaf people, Gallaudet, where the students converse in sign language, though he himself cannot sign. He saw there the confidence that a common culture and language brought them, but he was not persuaded that when they entered 'a new and perhaps alien world' of non-deaf people their burden of disability would be lightened.

He deeply resents the 'propaganda' put out by the Deaf community against cochlear implants. When the BBC's *Children in Need* appeal cancelled its plan to include a video of deaf children with implants at the last moment, in November 2004 (after criticism from deaf leaders), Ashley told Mark Thompson, the BBC's Director-General, that he had been gagged. 'Let them be proud of their history,' he says, ' let them be proud of their culture, but actually to attack something that has proved of enormous benefit to thousands of people is to me outrageous and irresponsible.'

Ashley has also been out of step with many disabled people, including the Disability Rights Commission, about euthanasia and assisted dying. One of his strongest memories of Parliament was hearing the MP Roland Boyes passionately advocating euthanasia after his mother had died an agonising death. He is one of the very few well-known disabled people – Tom Shakespeare is another – who supported Lord Joffe's assisted dying bill.

Today, most people seem to overlook these lapses in disability correctness from such a veteran campaigner, but in the late 1990s the radical end of the movement, disappointed at not getting a civil rights act, was openly critical. 'It took an extremely long time for the APDG to understand that disability is a rights issue,' said Barbara Lisicki, spokesperson for the Disabled People's Direct Action Network (DAN) in 1998. 'Some say people like

Lord Ashley are champions. But he is not in touch with the disabled people's movement.'

To some extent that was true. No mention of the British Council of Organisations of Disabled People, which thought of itself as the movement – let alone of DAN – appears in Ashley's autobiography, even though BCODP began in 1981 and the book ends in 1992, the year he retired from the Commons. Nor does he talk about the 'social model' of disability. What is more, the All Party Group, chaired by him, worked closely with RADAR, for years BCODP's sworn enemy. Even so, BCODP representatives have been invited to speak at All Party Group meetings and they worked with the group as members of Rights Now!, the coalition of disability groups that campaigned for legislation.

When Ashley left the Commons, he could no longer represent Stoke South, but he took Stoke and Widnes as his title when he was made a life baron the same year. Sir John Hannam, who became chair of the APDG in the Commons, recognised the influence of the Lords and asked Ashley to share the post with him. So Ashley was as busy as ever. Behind the scenes the APDG influenced government policy. It prevented, for example, the new Access to Work scheme, designed to help disabled employees with equipment and support, from being half funded by employers; if firms had to fork out half the money needed to help disabled employees, they would have an incentive not to hire them in the first place. More importantly, the APDG worked with the disability lobby to secure civil rights legislation that would outlaw discrimination across the board, not bit by bit. The Americans with Disabilities Act 1990 proved helpful, supplying a definition of disability and requiring employers to make 'reasonable accommodation' to disabled employees.

The Conservative government, fearful of the cost of disability legislation and the burdensome regulations it would impose on businesses and employers, always argued for education and persuasion. Faced by a widely supported private member's civil rights bill, introduced by Alf Morris at the end of 1991, government forces ditched it through the backdoor parliamentary procedure of talking it out – using up its limited debating time. Ironically, the Tory MP who did the deed, Rob Hayward, had multiple sclerosis.

The Government used more chicanery to defeat another civil rights bill, despite active lobbying by the APDG, led in the Lords by Ashley, and Rights Now!. In the end, it was forced to bring in an anti-discrimination bill of its own, which addressed employment and access to goods and services. Limited as it was, it marked a new stage in the development of disability rights. 'There was a U-turn in legislation,' says Labour MP, Dr Roger Berry. 'It was the APDG inside Parliament and Rights Now! outside that brought that about. I'm not aware of any select committee being as effective as that.'

Indeed, the APDG was now the biggest and most powerful all-party campaigning group, with the authority of a parliamentary select committee. (Select committees monitor government departments.) Ann Frye, head of the Department of Transport's Mobility and Inclusion Unit, remembers that speakers were quizzed closely: 'You were quite nervous about it.' Ministers did not turn down an invitation to speak and they would be given a rough ride if they had not mastered their brief. Vicky Scott, RADAR's parliamentary officer, recalls a meeting attended by the Prime Minister, John Major, where Ashley spoke with a 'wonderful directness' about disability as a rights issue. It was her responsibility to record the minutes of the meetings, without shorthand or a tape recorder; they had to be accurate because Ashley wanted them as a parliamentary record. 'If something was not up to scratch, he would really tell you about it.' He expected the same high standards and fast service from disability organisations that supplied him with briefings.

The APDG worked hard to strengthen the Government's weak discrimination bill, influencing William Hague, the Minister for Disabled People, who was sympathetic to the cause, and introducing hundreds of amendments. Most of them failed. The Government allowed some extension to the bill – on transport, for example – but it refused to exempt employers with fewer than 20 employees or to give enforcement powers to the National Disability Council (described in heated debates as having gums, but no teeth).

In the Lords, Ashley relished the battle. He called the bill 'a midget milestone on which we need to build', and attacked its serious omissions, loopholes and 'lack of enforcement procedures'. He unsuccessfully introduced three amendments of his own, including a deadline for subtitling all TV programmes and provision for programmes using sign language. When the Tory minister, Lord Mackay of Arbrecknish, talked about the difficulties and cost of extending subtitling to, say, TV news, Ashley accused him of being old fashioned for not knowing that all TV programmes can be subtitled in seconds. Mackay got his own back later. Ashley had been arguing for further and higher education to be brought within the bill, pointing out the patchwork provision for disabled people; only 300 deaf students were at universities, he said, and the Government should get started on funding them. Mackay quoted Ashley from the BBC's programme *See Hear*: 'I believe in demanding everything and letting ministers try to knock you down. Then you reach something satisfactory for the people concerned.' Mackay commented amiably: 'In future, when the noble Lord tries to appeal to my conscience and I knock him down, I shall not feel as guilty.'

When the bill passed the Lords and returned to the Commons, to be enacted later as the Disability Discrimination Act 1995, Ashley commented that at least 'We have managed to show that vigorous debating can still be civilised debating.' Characteristically, he acknowledged 'the marvellous work' of backroom researchers like Caroline Gooding of RADAR. But he had 'a stark message' for disabled people: 'We still require hard pounding and vigorous campaigning to get comprehensive anti-discrimination legislation in Britain.'

Fortunately, Labour's manifesto included comprehensive and enforceable civil rights. When the party came to power 18 months later, in May 1997, it opted to build on the framework of the DDA and plug the gaps, starting with the Disability Rights Commission, then education and, in 2005, another Disability Discrimination Act. Even so, nagging was needed to push the Government to fulfil its pledges. Ashley and Roger Berry, now the group's secretary, were better placed to squeeze more out of fellow ministers than members from other parties.

Sometimes Labour seemed to get things plain wrong. It produced a report showing how it was tackling poverty and social exclusion, yet tried to cut the number of people on Incapacity Benefit (IB) by raising the bar for new claimants. The resulting Welfare Reform and Pensions Bill of 1999 outraged disability organisations. The APDG went into action. In the Lords, Ashley's sense of injustice outweighed his natural loyalty to the party and he paid for this by being cold-shouldered at a meeting of Labour peers about the bill. Undaunted, he scored a memorable hat trick, defeating government amendments in the Lords to means-test occupational pensions, abolish Severe Disability Allowance for most groups and stop Incapacity Benefit if you had not made insurance contributions for two years. Strong cross-party support produced exceptional majorities against the amendments; one reached 156.

Tactfully, Ashley praised the Labour minister, Baroness (Patricia) Hollis, for her eloquence and offered compromise amendments, which she did not accept. But his moral arguments were adamant: 170,000 poor and disabled people would lose out if the two-year rule for insurance contributions went through. The Government was taking no account of the fact that it was much harder in some regions than in others to get employment and make insurance contributions.

The Government's plan to means-test pensions stuck in his gullet too. He was opposed to a principle which might be extended to other benefits and shocked that disabled people who had paid their insurance contributions would lose 50p out of every £1 of IB they received if their occupational pension was over £50 a week (£6123 a year). 'For a Labour government, historically committed to helping the poor, that is amazing.'

The bill ping-ponged between majority votes in the House of Commons and a stubborn House of Lords, until the Lords had to back down. But out of what was considered a disaster for disabled people some concessions had been won: the £50 pension bar was raised to £85 and the two-year limit for paying national insurance to get IB was extended to three years.

While thundering on the floor of the Lords, Ashley could be influencing ministers more gently behind the scenes – Margaret Hodge, for example. Labour's Minister for Disabled People in the key years 1998 to 2001, she was new to the disability field and felt slightly in awe of Ashley. The two of them would have regular cups of tea together as she developed the agenda for the Disability Rights Task Force, planned the Disability Rights Commission and considered welfare reform. Like others, she found him kind, someone to trust. 'I'd go and pick his brains – how do I deal with this? I'm thinking about doing that, what do you think?' She thought him 'very wise and honest and open', but not for turning once he had made up his mind about something.

Ashley's stubbornness was, perhaps, best suited to campaigning. Hodge's successor, Maria Eagle, recognised a 'superb parliamentarian', but says he could still be 'an awkward sod' who used every trick in the book to get what he wanted and scared some people with his forceful personality.

> He might chuck you a little compliment occasionally. But he never stopped for a minute. It can be a bit wearisome for a minister at times – go on, give me a break. But he never did give you a break.

He's an oppositionist, she concludes. He has never had to juggle priorities as a minister; if he did, he would want them all.

His forcefulness, though, could be practical. A few years ago the APDG was being so swamped by different organisations expressing their views that Roger Berry feared it was losing direction. Ashley, who does not normally take kindly to anyone encroaching on his domain, responded by limiting the group's agendas to impending legislation and campaigns that others might not do. Even so, the APDG is not what it was in the heady days of civil rights campaigning. Key battles have been won, new channels opened to government – most recently, the advisory group of disabled people, Equality 2025 – and the Labour government's big majority has shifted MPs' interests away from all-party groups towards select committees. But no one thinks the role of the APDG is over.

In 2003 Pauline Ashley died of a heart attack, quite unexpectedly. She was the mainstay of Ashley's life, his partner personally and professionally. 'There was this person called JackandPauline,' says Lord Kinnock. People could not see how he would recover from the blow, even though he had a close family and nine grandchildren to support him. He dealt with the bereavement as he had dealt with the onset of deafness, by fighting back and not wanting to be treated differently. The very next day colleagues received a letter from him breaking the news; he continued his routines of working at home in the morning with his personal assistant and travelling to the Lords most afternoons; he did not dwell openly on his loss. There was a good political reason, too, for remaining clearly vigorous. To be effective in Parliament, you need to 'appear utterly on form', says Agnes Fletcher, former parliamentary officer at RADAR and later head of policy and communications at the Disability Rights Commission (DRC).

Physically frail now, with Parkinson's disease, Ashley seems as mentally switched on as ever. His latest battle is to totally reform the social care system and give disabled people the right to choose the kind of life they lead and control the money they are entitled to from different support agencies. Helped by the DRC, he produced a private members' bill, the Disabled Persons (Independent Living) bill, and has steered it through the House of Lords twice, reintroducing it yet again in December 2008. While the Bill has got nowhere in the Commons, it has snapped at the heels of a government committed to giving disabled people choice and control. Ashley argued that 'The measures will get more disabled people back to work; there will be more income from taxes; there will be less spending. It will transform the whole situation.' From dismissing the Bill as unnecessary, the Government has now promised its own legislation to give disabled people the all-important right to control their support services.

The bill has had cross-party support. Disability rights, as Ashley envisaged when he set up the APDG, can reach beyond party loyalty. Now they have come to occupy the centre ground in politics and there is no going back for either major party. 'Jack will be regarded as a seminal and leading figure in that shift,' says Andrew Smith, former Secretary of State for Work and Pensions. He also thinks that Ashley, as a role model, has contributed to a parallel, cultural shift in people's attitudes to disability. Lord Kinnock sees Ashley as the crucial voice in Parliament for disabled people, and also the 'walking miracle', who still communicated when he was completely deaf. People had to listen.

Festooned with awards and honorary degrees, a national treasure to some people, the man himself remains the same: tough, shrewd, resourceful, persistent, charming, at times belligerent and intimidating. He still wants to win. It intrigues him that one can mobilise public opinion against injustice and use it to wear down ministers. One of his joys, as he explained at the e.Politix.com awards, is to see how, as a result of campaigning, 'the Chancellor says "it's impossible"; next week, "it's impossible"; next week, "it's almost impossible"; next week, "it's very difficult"; and eventually, "we feel it is the right thing to do".' This is Ashley's brand of power.

He refuses to celebrate deafness, yet deafness has given disabled people a great political champion.

# RACHEL HURST:
# ACTIVIST/CAMPAIGNER

*Photograph taken by Scope*

The day disabled people took over the European Parliament building was a watershed for disability rights. It was also a high point in Rachel Hurst's life. She made it happen, but not without a fight.

On 3 December 1993, 440 disabled people from all over Europe filed into the huge, semicircular debating chamber of the European Parliament in Brussels, recently completed at a cost of £756 million. They had come to celebrate the first Day of Disabled People and to affirm their human rights under the European Convention – rights that included life, liberty and security, freedom of expression (including receiving and imparting information), privacy, marriage, education, free movement, and protection against discrimination. The Social Affairs Commissioner, Padraig Flynn, was there with Members of the European Parliament (MEPs). The president of the European Parliament, Egon Klepsch, opened the proceedings. Hurst sat on the podium under the flags and symbol of the European Union. She was both co-chair and choreographer.

'It was pure theatre,' she says with glee. But the spectacle packed a punch. During the day 72 disabled people took the floor to explain, in three-minute presentations, the abuse, segregation, neglect and isolation they had experienced. Eighteen interpreters for deaf people of different nationalities supplemented the usual aural translators. At midday, Flynn, MEPs and European officials marched into the chamber accompanied by Beethoven's prelude to *Ode to Joy*, the European anthem. They signed a commitment to human rights for disabled people and to the Standard Rules on the Equalization of Opportunities for Persons with Disabilities agreed by the United Nations (UN) earlier in the year. Then they walked out to Joan Baez's recording of *We Shall Overcome*. One or two of them tried to speak out of turn, but Hurst allowed them only a minute each; Euro rhetoric was not to be encouraged.

By the end of the day, the first European Parliament of Disabled People had agreed a lengthy resolution, drawn up by Hurst. It called on the then 12 states of the European Community to take practical steps to guarantee the human rights of disabled people, to accept and implement the UN's Standard Rules (which covered everything from education to sexual relationships) and to include a specific non-discrimination clause when the Maastricht Treaty came up for revision. (The Maastricht Treaty of 1992, which heralded the European Union, had established a principle of social equality that Hurst and her colleagues were quick to grasp.)

The resolution also asked the European Commission, among other things, to set up a new directorate to develop equal opportunities policies and present a progress report to the next Disabled People's Parliament. Ambitious stuff. The Standard Rules were approved in 1996, and the 1997

Amsterdam Treaty did contain a non-discrimination clause; it led to a directive that member states must legislate against job discrimination by 2006 and make workplaces reasonably accessible for disabled people.

Winding up the day, Hurst exhorted the disabled representatives to have 'strength in unity', and from all round the debating chamber came the response, 'strength in unity'.

Padraig Flynn was impressed by the Parliament. As Social Affairs Commissioner until 1999, he was well placed to change the attitudes of other commissioners towards disabled people and push through legislation. The aspirations of disabled people fitted his policy of social inclusion, 'a people's Europe', so they featured in his employment strategy and other initiatives such as public transport. But to achieve this disability perspective required, he says, 'an enormous shift of emphasis' in European Community thinking, and he needed the cooperation of different groups, including non-governmental organisations (NGOs), if his plans were to stick. He and Hurst shared the same aims and respected each other. 'Rachel was hugely persuasive; she wanted disability highlighted and that exactly fitted into my schedule of things.' Luck played a part too. She was the right person at the right time, Flynn says. 'My memory of the whole business was that she was at the leading edge of the reforms that were contemplated by me and others for people with disabilities.'

Other officials were visibly moved by what they heard in the Parliament, says Arthur Verney, who worked alongside Hurst. The effects of the Parliament rippled out like a stone in a pond.

> It brought about a greater respect for disabled people and a massive shift from the old medical model of seeing people as pathetic individuals. From then on, funding was made available to far more ventures run and managed by disabled people.

Disability NGOs also gained in confidence, he says. Disabled people recognised they were European citizens with human rights, which should be addressed in Brussels and by their national governments.

The night before the Parliament, about 200 disabled people had braved cold and rain to take part in a vigil in the botanical gardens. Holding candles, and led by Hurst, they sang or kept silent, remembering disabled people everywhere, especially those living in institutions against their will.

Hurst herself had a sore throat at the vigil and by the next morning it had turned into a fever of 102 degrees. Unable to take the usual painkillers, she just kept going. She had planned and worked hard for this historical day and she was going to see it through. It was one of the battles she fought for the Disabled People's Parliament.

The others began a year earlier, when the United Nations General Assembly in New York approved an annual Day of Disabled People as a follow-up to the Decade of Disabled People, just ending. Good news on the face of it, but in fact a disappointment because Hurst had been hoping for a UN convention after all the hard work of the Decade. What was more, she feared the day would be used to promote charity, not rights. She alerted Joshua Malinga, co-founder and chair of Disabled People's International (DPI), which saw itself as the true representative of disabled people. 'We were absolutely horrified,' she says, 'because we knew that everyone around the world would have just rattled tins – disabled people would have gone backwards.' So they rushed off to the president of the General Assembly and UN officials and persuaded them to make the focus of the day human rights. 'We made the best of a bad job as quickly as we could.'

Hurst tended to leave the talking to the men. 'I don't mind doing the work to get people to somewhere and then taking a slightly back seat. But I will always interrupt if I think the men are pussyfooting around.'

The idea of marking the day with a European parliament came from Arthur Verney, who shared Hurst's office as DPI Europe's development worker. Verney had spent many years in Brussels working for what is now the European Union of the Deaf. He and Hurst hit it off. 'We were a good team,' says Hurst. 'He'd have a lot of ideas and I had the knowledge of where to put them to.'

Between them, they secured funding of 1 million euros (about £683,000 then) from the European Commission, which covered a year's work of organising, marketing and promoting the Parliament in six languages. 'Everyone mucked in', says Hurst – three part-time staff, one full-timer, and a lot of volunteers.

Getting permission from the College of Questors, the Parliament's gate-keepers, to use the new building led to 'a real fight'. The first time Hurst asked, she was turned down.

> So I went to Brussels and padded around all the MEPs' offices. It needed a lot of courage, actually, because I didn't know anybody; I didn't work there; so I just went up to the corridors where all these MEPs were, and put my head round each door and said, 'Can I have a word with you?'

Although some of them were helpful, the College of Questors turned down Hurst's request a second time. So she turned to direct action:

I got in the heavy mob from northern France. I made contact with DPI in France and they sent half-a-dozen fierce young men in large wheelchairs, with posters. The Parliament went completely egg-shaped and refused to allow them into the building with their posters. So I said, 'Why not? This is a place of democracy and they are entitled to come in.'

Faced by concerted lobbying, the questors capitulated. 'We found out later that the reason they had said no in the first place was because they thought we were going to pee on the seats!'

The whole episode of the Disabled People's Parliament reveals why Hurst is the *grande dame* of the disability world and why she was given an OBE 'for services to disabled people' just over a year later, which was converted to a CBE (Commander of the Order of the British Empire) in 2008. She can operate successfully at many levels, recognising opportunities and taking them. She is a great rabble-rouser. She can find common ground among different viewpoints and run up resolutions that pack a strong message. And the demands she makes in Europe or at the UN are rooted in the experiences of ordinary disabled people.

Had I not had Mrs Bloggs on the phone who was still peeing in a bucket downstairs because bloody social services weren't doing anything, I would never have been able to cope and translate high-flown principles into reality. It isn't any good talking wonderful words that don't mean anything if they're not grounded in practical reality.

Out of the oppression she has seen and felt has come a vision of a world that acknowledges the human rights of disabled people, and for this she has fought tirelessly. She offends some people, patronises others, and doesn't suffer fools gladly. She likes being centre stage and running the show. But, surprisingly, her professional aggressiveness is undercut by personal shyness. 'I've had to work very hard at overcoming lack of confidence,' she admits. 'There are still times when I go into something extremely insecurely. But then everyone else is insecure – that is one of the things I've learned.'

Hurst looks and sounds like 'a lady'. She maintains the stiff upper lip of her class and training, but underneath she cares and has suffered. Her life has not been easy.

She was born into a family of actors and weavers in 1939, the youngest of three sisters. Being seven and a half years younger than the next sister, Elizabeth, it felt to her like being an only child.

Her parents, Eileen and Leo Baker, had been at the Old Vic theatre in London in the 1920s before setting up a successful weaving workshop in the Cotswold village of Chipping Camden, where the Guild of Handicrafts had flourished earlier in the century. They moved back to Streatham in 1938, only to be forced out by Second World War bombing. From then on their life was peripatetic, governed by job opportunities, usually teaching, which continued all through Hurst's childhood and teens. It meant that she went to five schools, and even shared a governess at one point. As a result, she found it difficult to make friends.

Her earliest memories, aged two, are of being boarded at a Rudolph Steiner junior school while her parents taught at the senior school several miles away. She remembers the hard edge of the potty on which she was left to sit, and running through a cabbage patch, almost her height, to greet her mother on one of the occasional visits. 'Why', she asked her mother later, 'did you send me to boarding school and not the other two?' 'Because I thought you could cope,' her mother replied. When they were finally reunited, Hurst did not want to let her mother out of her sight for many years afterwards.

Putting a brave face on things was what she grew up to do. Unbeknown to her family, or in the early years to herself, she had been born with a rare neuromuscular impairment, probably the result of her mother catching rubella in the fourth month of pregnancy. Having damaged nerve endings meant that if Hurst tried to do too much, she would be in severe pain by the end of the day. For three periods, before she reached 20, she was unable to walk. Neither her family nor the general practitioners (GPs) recognised what was wrong – they did not notice, for example, that she had scoliosis, with one leg longer than the other – they just put it down to growing pains. It did not help that her father used to stick pins into the girls if they failed to sit up, so important was deportment in an acting family. But this was a small discomfort compared to the pain in her back or limbs.

> I never told anybody about the pain because I thought everybody was like that. I thought it was terribly wimpish to make a fuss. Everybody was so busy, we were very poor, and anyway there was an assumption that art and the journey of the soul were the things that mattered.

A family trust provided money for the girls' education. The oldest, Susan, went to the Royal Academy of Music and became a violinist; Elizabeth went to Chelsea College of Art and became a painter. Hurst wanted to be an actor and dancer. The dancing was always marred by her not being able to stand straight, but by her mid-teens she was quite an experienced actress. Her mother founded a semi-professional theatre company, which took plays, mainly by Shakespeare, around theatres, pubs and town halls in London. Hurst's first part, aged seven, was at Catford town hall, playing the fairy Peaseblossom in *A Midsummer Night's Dream*.

When she was almost 16, and had passed seven O levels, the question of university came up. By this time the family trust was running low, Hurst thinks, and her father suggested she should go to the new Rose Bruford College of Speech and Drama in Sidcup, where he was chairman of the governors. Hurst was very pleased at the idea, having no inclination to aim for university. Her father told her she would have to get a grant. 'So I went off to the Middlesex County Council offices and did an audition – Juliet's "Gallop apace, you fiery-footed steeds" speech. When it came to theatre, I was absolutely confident.' She got the grant and started at the college in 1955, living in digs because her current home, at Potters Bar, was too far for commuting. The work was hard and Hurst loved it, especially theatre production – managing – and verse speaking.

But the days were clouded by her mother's growing illness. Eileen Baker had suffered from an overactive thyroid for many years and nothing could be done until iodine appeared towards the end of her life. She had bipolar disorder, and only Hurst, who loved her mother dearly, could handle the moods. Once again, she pushed herself too hard, to the point where she could not walk. With two of her three college years completed, she had to drop out, and this time it took two years for her to recover. She spent the time aged 18 to 20 looking after her mother, cooking meals and reading 'anything and everything'.

> Those two years hit home and I realised there was something different about me. I had always had this energy, but only for a limited time. If only I had realised that it didn't stretch to a full day. By the time I did my third year at the college, it was quite clear I was not going to have a future in the theatre.

Thwarted in her career, Hurst consoled herself with a job in the production department of *Queen* magazine in the days of the iconoclastic fashion designer Mary Quant and the flamboyant Jocelyn Stevens, who owned and edited the magazine.

She also married Charles Gane, a solicitor. 'We bought this little house in Blackheath and life was great.' Her daughter, Kate, was born in 1964 and Daniel a year later. Daniel was impaired but it was not until he was 15 months old that he was diagnosed with malformed kidneys. Coping with a baby who had a strangulated hernia, repeated hospital operations, a tight feeding routine and sleeplessness wore Hurst down. She laughs now at her resolution: 'My stiff upper lip – God was it stiff! I could smile and do anything.'

Not, she says, that she wouldn't complain to a doctor if she got the chance. The trouble was they didn't believe her.

> One of the reasons is that I don't behave like a 'disabled' person. When I feel tired and exhausted, I do everything in my power not to let myself look tired and exhausted, so I don't think they understand the seriousness of the situation.

Having said that, it was her GP who persuaded her husband to take the family somewhere warm in the spring of 1968. The 'holiday' in southern Spain nearly ended in tragedy. The second day there was a magnitude five earthquake followed by rain for the next two weeks. Kate caught chickenpox, Daniel caught mumps, and Hurst herself had a bad attack of mumps followed by encephalitis (brain fever). Her husband, who had returned to England, came back to collect the children; it was decided she would recuperate on her own. One night she awoke in the hotel to find herself completely paralysed. 'I could barely breathe, and in fact if I had not known how to breathe because of the acting…' Hotel staff and two guests helped to pull her through. Back home, she struggled on with more illness until at last she was diagnosed with Myasthenic Syndrome. She was approaching 40.

As with other people, knowing what was wrong brought relief, and she found out that the now recurrent paralytic crises could be relieved by an injection of calcium. She became a volunteer at Daniel's school so she could help him with his reading. When the head teacher offered her a remedial teaching job, she agreed only on condition she could also teach dance and drama throughout the school. By 1970 she was back working, and at something she loved. 'I used to put on the school play. I would write the background and the children added to it and each child had a part to play. It was great fun.'

During this time she was divorced from Gane and married Christopher Hurst, an independent publisher who lived next door in Blackheath. He later helped promote disability studies by publishing some key books.

Trying to do everything, as usual, took its toll on Hurst. She was in and out of hospital. She took up physical exercises developed for the Canadian Air Force in an attempt to get fit. 'Within three months, I was in a wheelchair – for good. When you are somebody like me, you never listen!'

Becoming a wheelchair user was a turning point. She discovered how it felt to be a disabled person in 1976. She lost her teaching job, even though the school was wheelchair-accessible. But what stuck in her memory was her first trip in the wheelchair. As her husband pushed her to the shops, one woman she knew well crossed the road to avoid her and others could not face acknowledging her. Hurst cried at her predicament and the rejection. She had been a teacher in the local school and a good neighbour; she ran the local branch of the National Association for the Welfare of Children in Hospital and she had campaigned for surgical screening. Now she was just a label. 'I was different. And it was interesting that I also realised in the ensuing months what women's rights were all about too.'

Eventually, she found her way to the Greenwich Association of Disabled People (GAD), its positive name belying a meagre offering of 'tea and buns' every six months to disabled people who were bussed in from their homes or day centres. No one was remotely campaigning. By the time the next meeting came round, Hurst had been fired up by a film she had seen on the ITV disability programme, *Link*. Made by Rosalie (now Baroness) Wilkins, it was about the pioneering Centre for Independent Living in Berkeley, California, where severely disabled people had devised strategies for living independent lives. A couple of years later Hurst was one of the first disabled activists from the UK to visit Berkeley; she marvelled at how disabled people could get around on their own and no one stared at them.

Meanwhile, if she was to improve things for herself and others, she needed to join GAD. 'I realised I had to do something at the grassroots and the only way to do it was to join up.' So she put herself forward as a trustee and was accepted. Of the 12 trustees, only one other person was disabled.

Her first campaign was to reverse a plan for a 22-bed respite centre costing several million pounds, favoured by the chairwoman. She managed this by bringing in some new trustees and challenging the plan during a fundraiser she had organised, attended by staff from social services. She argued against spending so much money on just 22 people. The chairwoman retired in protest. 'She thought we couldn't do without her, but we gave her a glass bowl and said thank you very much, and I took over the chair and we stormed ahead!'

Hurst had got her way, but she knew she was a novice when it came to disability issues, so she read widely. The problems of GAD members kept her feet firmly on the ground.

The year 1981, when she took over as chair of GAD, was a historic one for disabled people. Not only was it the UN's International Year of Disabled Persons, from which flowed other UN initiatives, but the British Council of Organisations of Disabled People (BCODP) was formed. BCODP brought together organisations run by disabled people, who saw themselves as oppressed and wanted to bring about social change. GAD became a member the following year. Hurst remembers those early, ideological, annual meetings.

We had workshops where everybody sounded off, but there would be a lot of play too. You know, we would arrive on Friday evening and stay up to God knows what hour, and Johnny Crescendo (the Pete Seeger of disability) and stand-up comics Ian Stanton and, later, Tom Shakespeare would do their bit.

(Others found those early meetings frighteningly dogmatic.)

Hurst learned a lot from talking to other disabled representatives, such as John Evans from Hampshire and Ken Davies from Derbyshire, who were starting independent living centres in the UK. She came to understand the social model as a tool for change. But she never forgot the first feeling she had as a wheelchair user, of being no longer part of the human race, and it drove her to see disability as a matter of basic human rights. Yet international and European declarations of human rights did not specifically include disabled people.

BCODP also gave Hurst something she had always lacked – a sense of belonging.

I just found it terribly exciting. It was new friends with a shared vision, a shared interest, something I had only had when I was with a company putting on a play or at college, but otherwise never. It was and has always been very heady stuff.

One thing which irked her was that the BCODP constitution allowed only national organisations to have a vote, not local groups like her own, so, supported by others, she secured a change in 1983.

Meanwhile, plenty was going on at GAD. Hurst relied on just a handful of people, as local groups usually do. One of her first moves was to change the constitution so GAD became a genuinely 'of' organisation (representing disabled people and run by them). It became a limited company in 1983 so it could take over responsibility for the local Dial-a-Ride transport from the Greater London Council. Working with council departments, GAD also started putting independent living into practice by developing housing projects for wheelchair users and a personal assistants' scheme.

Although the Conservatives dominated national politics, there were many radical, left-wing local authorities at this time and Greenwich, according to Hurst, was 'a particular hotbed'. Martin Manby, the director of social services, was an ally and so were John Austin and Clive Efford, now MPs. The senior occupational therapist, Beth Atkinson, also understood that services should be geared to the needs of disabled people – government policy now, but very advanced in the 1980s. John Austin, leader of Greenwich council in the 1980s and then mayor, says they were one of the first councils to use the word 'empowerment' and set up equality committees. And when the council introduced a public question session before committee or council meetings, Hurst had her chance to air the disability viewpoint on housing, education or social services. While she was 'challenging', Austin says, 'she was very forthcoming in her praise when the council made some progress'. It gave her a good grounding in public lobbying.

One other thing was unusual about GAD at this time. Members were encouraged to look beyond local and national disability politics. This was because Hurst herself, already dedicated to human rights, kept an eye on what was happening at UN level. Out of the International Year had come the Decade of Disabled People (1983–92) with a World Programme of Action to make equal opportunities for disabled people, including housing, a reality – not that many nations, apart from the UK, took much notice.

In 1985 Hurst became chair of BCODP. It was all rather unexpected. Vic Finkelstein, who had been chair from the beginning, telephoned to ask if she would stand, and she was duly elected. 'I have a feeling that the men thought they could do a certain amount of manipulation,' she says.

That same year, DPI held its second world congress in the Bahamas and, as chair, Hurst was due to accompany some of the founders of BCODP. She says it was agreed they should each seek funding for the whole group, but she failed to find it. The others raised funding for themselves and off they went. They sent Hurst a postcard along the lines of 'wish you were here'. Determined to go, she succeeded in getting funding for herself from the borough of Greenwich and arrived just in time, to the considerable surprise of the men. She then teamed up with Judy Heumann, an American activist from the Center for Independent Living in Berkeley, to break the male hegemony in the conference. This involved persuading the small number of less radical women to support a resolution to change the DPI constitution and to stage a walkout – similar to the one that had produced DPI itself – if their demands were not met. They wanted all DPI delegations to councils and assemblies to be 50 per cent women and DPI to have at least two serving women officers. Hurst and Heumann realised the men were likely to be more receptive to the demands if they came from a woman of age and gravitas, so Dr Fatima Shah from Pakistan was persuaded to be spokesperson. The plan worked. According to Joshua Malinga, 'The withdrawal of disabled women from DPI could have spelt the end. DPI couldn't exist without disabled women, who are the majority of the disabled population.'

Hurst thought that rebellion was 'one of the most terrifying things I have ever done'. But Heumann, now director of disability services in Washington DC, saw only 'a take charge woman', steadfast in her vision, yet ready to relax when off duty and be teased about using the Queen's English. 'She's been a great role model for myself and many other disabled women around the world for many years.'

Back home, the pressing need for BCODP in 1985 was to build itself into a credible force capable of influencing government policy. But for that it needed money. Competition came from another umbrella group, the Royal Association for Disability and Rehabilitation (RADAR), which received government funding, as well as from big, well-heeled charities like the Spastics Society (later Scope) and the RNID, known as the 'for' organisations because they were run not by disabled people but on behalf of them.

Over the next two years Hurst worked with Stephen Bradshaw, director of the Spinal Injuries Association, and the academic Dr Mike Oliver to secure funding from the Department of Health, as well as Comic Relief and other charities. A part-time worker was appointed, and membership rose from 12 organisations to over 30. BCODP ran two conferences, on housing and independent living.

There were successes and failures. BCODP's earliest national demo in support of an anti-discrimination bill, introduced by the Labour MP Bob Wareing in 1983, was a flop; plenty of deaf people appeared in Parliament Square but only five wheelchair users. BCODP helped to draft Labour MP Tom Clarke's private member's bill calling for local authorities to assess disabled people's needs, improve services, and allow disabled people authorised representatives – in other words, advocates. Hurst persuaded Clarke to extend the bill beyond people with learning difficulties to all disabled people. It became law, though many of the clauses were never enforced because of cost.

Hurst was the only honorary officer of BCODP not to have a full-time job, so she was able to throw herself into all these activities. 'It was vital that our voice should be heard,' she says, so she went wherever she was invited, including to meetings headed by Lord Snowdon or the Duke of Buccleuch, where people did not take kindly to the idea that only BCODP truly represented the voice of disabled people.

Yet BCODP was beginning to realise that alliances could further the cause. It joined the Voluntary Organisations for Anti-Discrimination Legislation (VOADL) in 1985, a new group of the 'of' and 'for' organisations, which later became Rights Now!, chaired by Bradshaw. They tried, for example, to avert Tory government plans to overhaul the benefits system, which, it was claimed, would leave severely disabled people worse off by up to £50 a week. But the government's Social Security Act was passed in 1986.

Meanwhile, inside BCODP people were beginning to question Hurst's style of leadership as being too dictatorial, too autonomous. Ann Rae, from the radical Manchester Coalition of Disabled People, masterminded a campaign that ousted Hurst from the chair in 1987. It was a cruel blow for someone who had given herself so completely to the cause of disabled people.

Baroness Jane Campbell, now disability commissioner on the Equality and Human Rights Commission, was a young idealist in those days, captivated by Hurst.

> She was charismatic. She had that theatrical air. I loved all her speeches — they used to make me come out in goose bumps. She was a woman, so for me that was better than having a man leading. She knew everything; she could explain everything. And she was radical in her thinking and would go and say much further and not give a toss. I loved her for that.

Yet Campbell was torn about which way BCODP should be going.

> Rachel has always been a leader and she wanted that control and more flexibility to exert her own influence and ideas. Whereas there was this huge, democratic, centralist idea that the people must decide everything down to what stamps you put on the envelopes.

Few people realised what was happening, she says. They were caught up in the politics of leadership and 'it was all a bit Machiavellian'. She voted against Hurst.

> If we had been a bit more mature, maybe it would not have happened. But we weren't. We were in constant struggle. And when there's struggle, there's struggle within struggle. People have different views and they will fight it out because they have come from being very oppressed, and once you have been oppressed you can't always deal with that in the best way.

Hurst rejects the claim that she was undemocratic. She points to the meetings and the social times that gave members a sense of community. With the instincts of a hostess, she knew that getting people to relax socially over a drink could help iron out differences and subsequently get things done. Yet over the years she has underestimated how her moral certainty in public can put people down, and humiliation is not a good recipe for creating unity.

Hurst thinks she fell foul of the Manchester Coalition's radical approach to politics:

> which is that 'We [disabled people] won't ever talk to non-disabled people; it is us first, and until you see that, we are not in dialogue.' I have never been

prepared to compromise my principles, but I will dialogue until the cows come home in order to get somewhere.

Bradshaw saw the affair as a stab in the back for Hurst and admired the way she dealt with it. 'She wasn't a person who sought revenge. She didn't seem to bear malice against people at a personal level, only focusing on her objectives.'

The rejection by BCODP still left Hurst with GAD, which she continued to build up. In 1990 it became the Greenwich Centre for Independent Living and the same year she received the freedom of the borough of Greenwich. (Later, one of her two honorary doctorates came from the University of Greenwich.)

On the warpath: Rachel Hurst with other members of the Disability
Benefits Consortium at the 'Bridge the Gap' demonstration in
November 1989, where they demanded a review of disability benefits
by the Conservative government. Photograph taken by Chris Killick

On the national front, the cause came before personalities, so in July 1988 she was among 2000 disabled people from different organisations who demonstrated against the Social Security Act, which had come into force three months earlier. Disabled people feared the cuts would force them back into institutions. They marched on the Department of Health and Social Security office at Elephant and Castle, London, and delivered a letter to the Tory Minister for Disabled People, Nicholas Scott. Misjudging the situation, Scott declined to meet them, whereupon some of the demonstrators sat down, blocking traffic on the busy roundabout. This spontaneous act of civil disobedience is seen as a watershed in the history of UK disability rights. The march itself was conceived in a back room of Hurst's house in Blackheath. So was the slogan, 'Rights not Charity', which has become part of the disability movement.

Although still an officer of BCODP, she needed another battlefield and, luckily, one was already to hand. The walkout she helped to engineer on behalf of women at the Bahamas World Congress in 1985 had paid off in personal terms: it parachuted her into disability at the international level. By 1987 she was a member of DPI's world council and in the same year she was asked to chair a UN meeting in Yugoslavia, which was evaluating the UN's Decade of Disabled People at its half-way point (not much achieved, inevitably). She also became vice-chair of a small, unique, UK aid and development agency, Action on Disability and Development, where disabled people were working to relieve poverty and build disabled people's organisations worldwide. From now on, she had a hand in many disability pies at European and international level, influencing policy and legislation – often after arduous hours of discussion – building up organisations, getting out information, pushing all the time for the human rights of disabled people to be taken seriously. She loved the travel, the debates, and getting to know disabled people all over the world. She had found a bigger family than BCODP.

Her paid job at this time was as project director of the UN Global Project, dreamed up by the blind innovator, Sir John Wilson, to help the Decade of Disabled People by raising awareness of disability and finding money for projects. For the first time, the UN worked with disability NGOs, which Hurst thought was a breakthrough. The UK government lent them an office. But the Global Project was built on an assumption of commercial sponsorship, which proved to be wrong. The point was finally made in 1991 when Hurst optimistically booked the Royal Albert Hall in London, persuaded musicians like Yehudi Menuhin and Mstislav Rostropovich to play in a concert marking the end of the Decade, and failed to get commercial support. Companies still saw disability through a charity lens and offered only small donations. The concert had to be abandoned amid red faces.

The Global Project did reveal how little disabled people all over the world knew about each other or about their human rights. In an attempt to fill the gap, Hurst worked with Henry Enns, then chair of DPI, on a funding proposal for an international information network. This time some money was forthcoming. They were allowed to keep the London office, and in 1992 Disability Awareness in Action (DAA) opened, initially with just two staff, Hurst and her daughter Kate.

DAA has always operated on a shoestring, as rights-based organisations do. Hurst says: 'If I'd been trying to fund prosthetics for poor little cripples in Africa, I'd have had money coming out of my ears!' Yet over the next 14 years DAA became a focal point for national and local disability organisations around the world, sharing news and information and supporting their struggle for disability rights. It ran a bi-monthly newsletter, produced resource and information kits, and worked with UNESCO and the BBC World Service. Between 1992 and 1993, it produced eight volumes of testimony by disabled people about their lives. *Letters from our Lives* was presented to the UN High Commissioner for Human Rights, Mary Robinson, who passed it on to the UN Secretary-General. It helped nudge the General Assembly towards deciding that disabled people needed the protection of an international convention and also kick-started members of the ad-hoc committee.

Around the same time, DPI reaffirmed itself as a human rights organisation – something Hurst and others had pushed for – and resolved to investigate how to obtain evidence of the violations of disabled people's rights – another of her long-term concerns. This resulted in a database of violations, set up in 1999, the first of its kind. Helped by trained reporters, DPI and DAA have recorded over 2,400 cases affecting 2.4 million disabled people worldwide. Some people question the validity of the entries. Hurst bristles: 'I can assure you that I'm very tough and we don't put anything on the database that I think might be in the slightest bit dubious. It's a snapshot of what is going on; I don't claim anything else.'

The database is very close to her heart. She understands the ethical issues surrounding disability – not just traditional abuse, but how easily support for assisted dying or the hype surrounding genetic research can infringe the right to life of disabled people. She has used evidence from the database to argue her case at international conferences. In 2000 she challenged doctors and scientists at the Fifth World Congress of Bioethics to explain why the theoretical physicist Dr Stephen Hawking should live, but a 14-year-old boy with hydrocephalus should die when he 'is making as good a contribution to life as any other son or daughter – it just happens to be different'. In the same year, she drew up a DPI declaration in Solihull, calling for disabled people to have the right to live and be different, and to be included in bioethical debates.

Dr Bill Albert chaired that meeting. He has represented BCODP many times at international level and was a disabled member of the government's Human Genetics Commission for six years. 'Rachel is the one person I know who really understands what human rights is about,' he says. 'She's been so strong on that both domestically and internationally, and internationally she's a power.'

Hurst was also active in Europe. In the late 1980s, disability NGOs were increasing in number and securing more funding, but they were generally groups 'for' disabled people, which caused friction with an emerging DPI. Under European treaties, disabled people had no legal status, so no legal redress. Programmes designed to integrate them, called Helios, were based on rehabilitation and spiked with rhetoric, and disabled people had little say in their planning or in mainstream policy making.

In 1990 Hurst persuaded the world council of DPI to give $40,000 (about £34,000 today) to its Europe region. She recruited Arthur Verney to be the development worker, based in her London office. A year later she won agreement from DPI for a new committee, composed of disabled members of European Union national assemblies, and became its chair. The time was ripe because the European Parliament, supported by ambitious disabled people's NGOs, had refused to pass the budget for the second Helios programme.

The new committee was deliberately set up as a charity so it could apply for funding. Hurst says: 'I took it upon myself, with Arthur's help, to put together a funding proposal. We got initial funding from the European Commission and never looked back.' They lobbied, organised projects such as the Disabled People's Parliament and, as the membership rose, helped emerging disability groups with advice and support.

So much was happening; Hurst was riding high; and then came the fall. In September 1994 she went to the DPI world assembly in Australia, confident she would be elected chair of DPI and beat the other contestant, the Finnish politician Kalle Konkkolla. The night before the vote, she thought she had a 50:50 chance. But when the votes were counted next day she had only two, one of which was her own. It felt like a repeat of the BCODP rejection. She gave Konkkolla a congratulatory kiss, but she was very hurt, says Arthur Verney. He thinks she did not take sufficient account of a predominantly male organisation, some of them unused to seeing a competent woman in authority. Also, 'in her usual Rachel upfront way', he says, she had probably upset one or two people, whereas Konkkolla was an adroit politician.

Konkkolla often used Hurst as a source of advice during his four years in office, as many people did and still do. She was always answering calls, says Verney; he wondered how she ever got her work done.

When Joshua Malinga was elected chair next time round, he bypassed the election process by appointing Hurst as vice-chair and then as a special rapporteur for human rights, which gave her influence over DPI decisions at international level. Looking back, he sees her rejection as a long-term setback for DPI. 'At the time, we needed a person of Rachel's character and ability to develop DPI, and we didn't vote for her. The organisation has been bleeding from that and it will take some time to mend.'

Hurst's methods have often been intemperate. She believed in attending international meetings 'to make sure they do nothing without you' and also 'shouting and screaming', if necessary, to make change happen. 'I was able to help other disabled people who were involved at EU level to be bolshie.' Being polite does not pay off, she thinks, when you are completely at odds with what the establishment – usually government officials – is trying to do, because then 'the reality is you sit on the fence and you're not doing anything for the people you are fighting the battles for'.

She has had some memorable confrontations. One was at a women's unit meeting in Brussels where the talk was all of equal opportunities from a gender point of view and Hurst introduced disability. She was asked to stop speaking because what was important was the gender issue. She refused. 'Then one or two other women got strength from me and agreed,' and her point was made.

Again, her impatience spilled out as she tried to convert health professionals to the social model. It happened when she was chairing the World Health Organisation's environmental task force from 1998 to 2001, in the closing stages of a nine-year revision of the International Classification of Functioning, Disability and Health. 'I made such a nuisance of myself that they didn't want me there.' Notices of meetings seemed to go astray and once they invited a more placatory DPI representative, whereupon Hurst gatecrashed the meeting in Paris and told them they were behaving outrageously. 'If it's for the cause, I will confront who you like,' she says. She got some of her way in 2001 when a new classification was approved accepting that social environment as well as the body affects disability – a move away from seeing disabled people as just medical problems. But that was not enough for BCODP. 'She got a lot of stick,' says Dr Bill Albert.

Sometimes Hurst's efforts misfire. She has misjudged people and events – at BCODP or DPI, for example – and made, as she says herself, some 'lousy' decisions. In 1999 she accosted Labour's Secretary of State for Social Security, Alistair Darling, over possible cuts in disability benefit, and emerged from his office in tears. Later, she said she had 'put on a little show'. But she had chosen the wrong person; the mistake deepened the chill between Darling and the disability lobby.

Yet she can be the soul of diplomacy. In Europe, Verney says she had Padraig Flynn and MEPs eating out of her hand; Flynn himself found her 'quite charming'. She also inspired loyalty in her staff, in spite of relatively poor management. Many people, including Joshua Malinga, Bill Albert and Sarah Langton-Lockton, who became a pioneer in disability access to the environment, felt her warmth and support at times of despair or self-questioning. Vicky Hanington remembers Hurst's empathy. In 1994 she was parliamentary officer for the disability lobbying group RADAR, but she was also the daughter of the Tory Minister for Disabled People, Nicholas Scott. She split with her father amid a wave of publicity after Scott's civil servants helped some Tory MPs to sink a strongly supported civil rights bill. At a painful meeting, where she had to watch her father apologise to Parliament on TV, Hurst held her hand. She says, affectionately, 'I think she's an old pussy, actually. She was always incredibly nice to me.'

Towards the end of the 1990s, things began to fall apart. The European Parliament suspended funding temporarily to all disability NGOs, then Verney resigned because of ill health, and the Commission refused further money to DPI Europe. The paperwork involved in putting forward a proposal is a real burden for small organisations, says MEP Richard Howitt, president of the All-Party Disability Intergroup at the European Parliament. This is where he thinks DPI Europe came to grief. There were suspicions of waste and fraud, but Howitt believes the problem was lack of capacity. By 2003, Hurst was 'clearing up'. She resigned from DPI's world council after 16 years. Lack of funding hit DAA too, with the loss of the office and the newsletter. In 2005 the organisation and its database moved with Hurst – now divorced from Christopher Hurst – to her retirement house in Wiltshire.

In spite of the setbacks, there was a sense of achievement. All the activity of the 1990s had forced the huge European Union ship of state to change course and now it was gathering steam. By 2001, there was a EU disability strategy aiming for 'a society open and accessible to all', and the commissioners were expected to consider the rights of disabled people in all policy making and involve them in planning and monitoring. The European Disability Forum of disability NGOs – another Verney idea – had come into its own, and Hurst was chair of its human rights committee. The year 2003 became the European Year of Disabled People, another Disabled People's Parliament was held, and commissioners adopted the social model, committing themselves to removing environmental barriers. True, disability as a human rights issue is still resisted; state follow-through has been slow and a fully comprehensive disability directive is elusive. But Hurst has been the key figure in moving things forward, says Richard Howitt. 'Rachel has been the principal advocate for a human rights approach in European politics.' In

2003 she received a People of the Year award from the UK disability network RADAR and an honorary degree from the Robert Gordon University in Aberdeen.

While Hurst concentrated mainly on Europe and the international disability scene during the 1990s, she kept up her arts interest in various advisory capacities – for the BBC, the Arts Council and as vice-chair of Graeae, the leading disabled-led theatre company. She was also involved with the energetic campaign for civil rights legislation being organised by Rights Now!, the volatile group of 'for' and 'of' organisations, chaired by Stephen Bradshaw. She did some constructive negotiating with the 'of' organisations, to keep them on board, recalls the solicitor Caroline Gooding, later a special adviser to the Disability Rights Commission. But when the Conservative government passed only a limited Disability Discrimination Act in 1995, she shared the double frustration felt by leaders of BCODP, with the Act itself and that they had not been consulted. BCODP even wanted the Act repealed and a new bill drafted. Rights Now! was weary and divided, the 'for' organisations preferring to build on what had been achieved. Hurst took the chair in 1997 and tried to stimulate – 'harangue' some people said – a flagging enterprise. Eventually the 'for' organisations were forced out and, by 2004, the group was dead. At the time, members of Rights Now! saw Hurst taking the BCODP line, yet later she admitted that trying to repeal the Act was unrealistic and time wasting. She ended up pleasing no one.

Rights Now! also lost focus because there was now a new Labour government, which had comprehensive, enforceable civil rights squarely in its manifesto and had set up a Disability Rights Task Force to include key disabled people, such as Hurst, Bert Massie, Jane Campbell and Caroline Gooding. The task force called for a Disability Rights Commission (DRC) with teeth, which was generally welcomed. It made many other recommendations too, but Hurst – who certainly said her bit – thought key things were missing, such as extending the definition of disability and setting deadlines for fully accessible public transport. Margaret Hodge, Minister for Disabled People and chair of the task force, disliked confrontation, complains Hurst. For her part, Hodge found Hurst belligerent and oppositionist. 'She just wanted to sit there and shout about how horrible society and the government were, and it was everybody else's fault.' In truth, they were both strong women who liked to win, but Hodge wanted consensus and an agenda she could sell to government. From this unlikely start, based on mutual suspicion, they grew to understand and respect each other, helped perhaps by a series of task force 'girls' dinners'. They became 'great buddies', says Hurst, though they never did agree on abortion or the integrity of the social model.

Generally speaking, Hurst does not have much time for government ministers of any political creed, nor civil servants – which is probably reciprocated. But Maria Eagle, Minister for Disabled People from 2001 to 2005, was an exception: 'She was a force for good and she did her damnedest as a junior minister.' Supported by successive Work and Pensions Secretaries, Andrew Smith and Alan Johnson, Eagle pushed through a further Disability Discrimination Act and initiated a key report from the Prime Minister's Strategy Unit which actually set a date, 2025, when disabled people should be equal members of society. She also appointed the first independent disabled adviser to a UK delegation working on an international human rights law, the UN Convention on the Rights of Persons with Disabilities. Nominated by BCODP, Dr Richard Light is a respected civil rights activist – and Hurst's son-in-law.

Eagle met Hurst regularly; she even visited her office, which was considered unusual. She valued Hurst's experience: 'The genuine voice of the oppressed, which she represents, is incredibly important for the government to hear.' Eagle and her boss Andrew Smith understood where Hurst was coming from and did not take her public criticisms personally, though Eagle thought Hurst's relentless cup-half-empty stance 'could be a bit churlish'. The approach wouldn't work on a government that was not set on change, she thinks, which might help explain Hurst's successes and failures.

Smith voices what others have said of Hurst, that she is a 'philosophic outrider', one step beyond the usual disability lobbyists. 'She does have influence. Apart from anything else, she makes you measure your statements.' It was Hurst who introduced Smith to 'disablism' – systemic discrimination against disabled people based on their perceived inferiority – a word that she would like to see in the dictionary alongside racism and sexism.

A chance to help end disablism set Hurst off in a new direction, even as she was retiring. She agreed to work with Tony Manwaring, the new chief executive of Scope, on his Time To Get Equal campaign and accept a small retainer. Traditionally, Scope has been one of the big, rich, 'for' charities that the disability movement loved to hate (even though by the late 1990s over 50 per cent of its trustees had a disability). Hurst herself said not so long ago: 'The money is in the voluntary sector. Where would all the Scopes and RNIBs of this world be if they weren't able to raise money on the backs of disabled people?'

She joined up because she thought Manwaring understood disablism and 'it was a marvellous opportunity to harness the resources of an enormous organisation to the good of equality for disabled people'. Her decision surprised people in the disability movement. It could have driven a wedge through her friendship with Jane Campbell had they not agreed to avoid discussing the matter. Both say they rely on gut feelings, which in the case of Manwaring were at odds.

In 2006, Manwaring resigned suddenly, leaving a deficit of £10 million and a lot of ill will. Hurst rallied from the setback. She kept on good terms with Manwaring's successor and his team, who needed her knowledge and authority. The liaison has paid off for both. Scope now bankrolls events that disability organisations really care about and works with them, such as celebrating the UK's signing of the UN Convention and demonstrating on behalf of the Independent Living Bill. Hurst looks more in her element at a demo – fist clenched, smiling, chanting: 'What do we want?' 'Civil rights.' 'When do we want them?' 'Now.'

In 2008 Scope members voted for a new constitution and a disabled chair of trustees. Currently 22 per cent of the staff are disabled. Perhaps, as Hurst dreams, Scope can become a model for other big charities and development agencies around the world, to 'transform themselves and really be an ally to disabled people so that we can all go forward together'. It would be a worthy legacy.

Meanwhile, sitting in her adapted bungalow, offering tea and windfall apples, with Polly, a Miniature Schnauzer, beside her, she looks the picture of a contented granny. But then she stresses a point, drops her chin and stares intently at you over her glasses, challenging you to disagree. She is as fired up about the poverty, cruelty and lack of opportunity that disabled people face as she ever was, and disheartened too by the lack of progress.

> One of the reasons I am always so angry and always so clear, and I couldn't care less if individuals get hurt by my anger, is that I really do want the world to recognise the shit that most disabled people are living in. And I know that very few people will take any notice, which is why, like Martin Luther King, I think we need legislation and we need resolutions and we need everything to try and change behaviour rather than attitudes.

Might she have achieved more if she had been more diplomatic, more wedded to the politicians' 'inevitability of gradualness' (Padraig Flynn's phrase)? Would money have been in less short supply? Maybe. But most people agree that the disability movement and mainstream society have needed people with Hurst's undiluted vision to goad them on.

# TOM SHAKESPEARE:
# ACADEMIC

*Photograph taken by Caroline Bowditch*

When a book is worth five reviews in the same edition of an academic journal, it must be important. This is what happened to Dr Tom Shakespeare's *Disability Rights and Wrongs* in 2007. It was his parting shot on the subject of disability, a consolidation of his thinking and research over 17 years.

Once again, this maverick of the disability world challenged the received wisdom of the UK disability movement in an effort to kick-start a new understanding of disability. He thinks academic disability studies have come to a dead end and the disability movement is stagnating because both rely on the 'social model', which defines disability as social discrimination – the barriers and attitudes that disadvantage people with impairments. Shakespeare acknowledges that the social model has given disabled people a sense of liberation, identity and purpose, and secured important political victories, but he thinks it is narrow, outdated and 'wrong'. It allows disabled people to escape from the traditional view of disability – medical defect – to seeing disability in a social context, but in doing that it ignores the reality of impairment: 'people are disabled not just by society but by their own bodies'. It makes cures and medical help suspect, and eclipses the organisations and research devoted to specific impairments. It also fosters a 'them' and 'us' view of the world.

Shakespeare challenges other cherished beliefs too. For example, he does not see pre-natal screening as a serious threat to disabled people; he accepts early abortion for 'significant impairment', and assisted dying in the end stage of terminal illness. He defends modern charities and the emotional side of 'care', and he thinks the autonomy of 'independent living' may not be the promised land for all disabled people.

He wants academics in disability studies to value open debate and bin the social model orthodoxy in favour of a 'practical research agenda' that explores how different people experience impairment and social barriers. Similarly, he thinks the disability movement should aim beyond disability 'rights' to a broader social justice, making common cause with other groups, such as older people. For disabled people to flourish, he says in his final sentence, it is 'vital' that they should be positive about non-disabled people and see the mutual advantages of working together.

From being heretical, the idea of working with other groups is now in the vanguard of disability thinking, urged on by an all-embracing Equality and Human Rights Commission and the crisis in social care funding that also affects elderly people and unpaid carers. 'The challenges we now face demand that our slogan, "Nothing about us without us", must speak less of our separateness and difference and more of our interdependence and connection with others,' argued Baroness Jane Campbell, chair of the commission's disability committee, in *Society Guardian* in April 2008. She was for joining forces with other groups while at the same time promoting the ideas of the disability movement as a blueprint for the wider battle for equality and human rights – a neat solution that combined change and continuity.

Not so Shakespeare, who puts more stress on change. He knew from past experience that his views would elicit a harsh response and, indeed, the four British reviewers all marked him down; only an academic in disability studies from the University of Iceland welcomed the book warmly. Professor Mike Oliver, author of the term 'social model' and known as its policeman, was particularly scathing. He accused Shakespeare of 'confused and distorted thinking' leading to 'fundamentally flawed and dangerous positions'. As a severely impaired person, who uses a wheelchair, Oliver argued that impairment is central to his work and that Shakespeare just didn't understand; he had, for example, no concrete proposals about improving care. 'Only a relatively affluent person with a minor impairment who is never going to be at the sharp end of personal support services could write such well-intentioned but meaningless platitudes.' In sum, Oliver saw no new, exciting, constructive theories, but just an attempt 'to rewrite history and diminish our past achievements'.

It takes conviction and chutzpah to question the ideas behind a movement that has nurtured you and your academic career and to take on one of its intellectual lions. Last time Shakespeare did it, in 1999, Campbell, a protégé of Oliver, saw 'a bit of boy competition going on between Mike and Tom'.

If Shakespeare has not been able to shift the hegemony of the social model, he has made people think about it and acknowledge more openly the relevance of impairment. As a sociologist, he has also pushed disability research into new areas, such as cultural imagery, sexual politics, bioethics and postmodernism. Clever, restless, fast thinking, he has worked for change on many fronts. He set up arts and political groups in the North East of England. He spent eight years at the Policy, Ethics and Life Sciences Research Institute (PEALS), University of Newcastle, starting as its only employee and developing research and ethical debate around the new genetics. He and eight experts across the world have edited a major World Health Organisation report, to be published in 2009, that, unusually, concentrates on measures to include disabled people, not eliminate their impairments. Now he is more than ever into creative writing as a way of changing public opinion.

His greatest strength is communication. He is at home with academics, doctors, Arts Council members, disability organisations and lay audiences.

He appears on radio and TV programmes, discusses bioethics and religion on the *Guardian* website, and has a regular column on the BBC disability website, Ouch! There he stimulates discussion on topics people may not have thought about, like the privileges they are likely to lose in return for equality, and shares his daily experiences of disability – chronic back pain or the cost of pedal extensions for his car. In September 2008 he announced 'This week, I have mainly been trying to wet my bed. No, not some obscure sexual fetish. Merely the frustration of lack of bladder control.' He had become paraplegic, unexpectedly, perhaps permanently. He explained how he felt – 'not freaked out', but mourning his mobility and freedom – and what medical treatment he was having, 'I am embarking on two months of rehabilitation in Middlesbrough (not an address I'd ever envisaged admitting to).'

People's opinions of Shakespeare tend to be polarised: at one end, intense respect and appreciation; at the other, teeth-grinding annoyance and academic disdain.

Shakespeare's family is only tenuously related to the Bard. His father, Sir William Shakespeare, was a GP and the first member of his family to have achondroplasia. Tom, born in 1966, has it too: the genetic mutation – a biological 'spelling mistake', he calls it – which produces restricted growth.

He has also inherited the baronetcy conferred on his grandfather, the Liberal MP for Norwich, Geoffrey Shakespeare, a junior minister in national governments of the 1930s. This has been an unavoidable embarrassment for someone who describes himself as a democrat and a republican. 'It's the skeleton in my cupboard,' he told the audience of *No Small Inheritance*, a monologue he performed in Newcastle in 2004. 'You see before you Sir Tom Shakespeare, who had a title thrust upon him.'

Shakespeare grew up largely undeterred by his short stature (he is 4ft 5in). He can remember no illnesses except the odd earache which people with achondroplasia are prone to. He was treated no differently by his family, and his impairment did not stop him doing most physical things. But he did have to cope with the stares and comments of strangers, and all his life he has had to run the gauntlet every time he goes out. 'It's almost like being a celebrity without having done anything special,' he told Joan Bakewell on the BBC Radio Three *Belief* programme in 2007. 'It's not a serious burden. But it is a sort of existential… sometimes, y'know, I go to bed and cry.'

His father, one of the first GPs with a disability, had a busy practice in Aylesbury. 'He was not loud, flamboyant, conceited, demonstrative or ambitious,' Shakespeare said in *No Small Inheritance*, perhaps cartooning himself. 'He set out not to change the world in large things, but to make a difference in small ways.' An unassuming man, dressed in a sports jacket or a three-piece suit, he sat on various disability committees. He was vice-president of PHAB (which runs clubs for people with and without physical disabilities) and a founder of what is now the Restricted Growth Association. For Shakespeare, he was a role model. 'He showed that disability didn't mean you couldn't be normal.'

William Shakespeare was a member of Lord Snowdon's working party, which produced a report arguing for *Integrating the Disabled* in 1976. The Shakespeare family featured in a documentary made by Snowdon. In one shot you see the young Shakespeare unconcernedly stuffing his face at a picnic. His parents remembered how Snowdon arrived for filming dressed in black leather and driving an Aston Martin Lagonda.

Shakespeare talks of his mother, Susan, as 'a force of nature', with tremendous drive and a seemingly overpowering hospitality acquired from her childhood in Sri Lanka. She was a nurse before marrying William, and had a son, Matthew Luck Galpin, who has become a visual artist and master blacksmith. Later, she took on many public service roles, imbuing Tom with the idea that he should contribute to making the world a better place. He inherited her drive, he thinks, which translates into working fast, having many projects on the go, and feeling guilty when he wastes time. He has adopted his mother's mannerisms and behaviour too: he cooks her dishes and encourages second helpings. 'You may think you are your own person,' he says, 'but you haven't noticed that you are what your parents made you.'

True to his upper-class background, he went off to boarding school at the age of nine, and then to Radley College, the public school near Oxford, where his father had been before him. His younger brother James followed, and later became a Church of England priest. Shakespeare was teased and bullied, but he still managed to enjoy himself. He appreciated how his schools taught him independence and the confidence to speak up for himself and debate.

He could not play team games, but his lack of sporting options at a sporty school did not upset him or the school, though his father was disappointed that he did not follow family tradition and cox the school boat. Instead, he was into books and his friends were 'the bookish people'.

Equipped with A levels in English, History and History of Art, two of them at A grade, he went to Cambridge in 1984. He took a two-year course in an unexpected subject, Anglo-Saxon, Norse and Celtic. 'I was very into Tolkien and Norse and Old English legends. I do get a bit obsessed about things and this was my little obsession.'

One of his regrets now is that by being away at school for so long, he grew apart from his parents. 'I think I was rather snooty about my parents. I'm quite intellectually arrogant and they weren't intellectually exciting in the way that discussions at school or university were. I didn't value them enough.' Later he did come to value them, and wishes now that he had had more time to cement the bond with his father. William Shakespeare died in 1996 when his son was 30.

At Cambridge Shakespeare was free to try anything and think anything. He did it very thoroughly. More than most people. Nothing was fixed; spiritual beliefs, intellectual ideas, friendships, sexuality, drugs, food, were all up for exploration and assessment. He abandoned the liberal, Anglican, middle-class views of his family and threw himself into student politics, supporting left-wing causes like Campaign for Nuclear Disarmament (CND), anti-Apartheid, the women's movement, the gay and lesbian movement. He joined the Communist Party, but moved on a year later, disenchanted by its doctrinaire constraints, though he remained influenced by Marxism for many years.

In the final year of his undergraduate degree he switched to social and political science. By now he had gravitated to disability politics and was involved with the National Union of Students' disability campaign along with other disabled left-wing students. What attracted him was not just the activism, but the theory. 'In sociology you hear about Marxism and all the other isms. I was increasingly interested in applying all those insights to disability. And it hadn't been done before – or at least I wasn't aware it had been done.'

He got a first-class degree. Two years later he started an MPhil. His thesis about the politics of disability was written in 1989.

> I wrote it on my own, as it were. There was very little published in those days, though I had read Vic Finkelstein. I constructed a politics of disability for myself by analogy with Marxism and feminism and other things.

Expanding on this for his PhD in sociology in the early 1990s, he wrote what he calls a critical examination of the social model and other ways of thinking about disability from the social perspective. For Shakespeare, the social model was never a blinding-flash, a starting point, as it was for many impaired people; it was a viewpoint. As books began to appear by academics like Mike Oliver and Colin Barnes, he read them objectively. 'I approached them from the position that they weren't a revelation. They were something to critically engage with.' He had read widely in feminist literature, and when Jenny Morris produced *Pride against Prejudice* (1991) he thought it was 'brilliant', because her account of disability was close to his own – she too thought the social model did not take enough account of a person's impairment and individual experiences.

Opportunities for Shakespeare at Cambridge went beyond ideas and activism. Disabled men often lack sexual confidence, says Kath Gillespie Sells, who founded and chaired Regard, the disability lesbian and gay group, between 1989 and 1999. But Shakespeare was not like that, or at least he appeared not to be. He fathered two children by different mothers in 1988. There was a 50 per cent chance that he would pass on his achondroplasia; his son and daughter both have it. He then became a popular and flamboyant figure on the disability gay scene before getting married in 2002.

Shakespeare has no ready explanation of his bisexuality. He thinks it is partly a reaction to his disability, partly about not liking categories, maybe to do with genetics. 'I've always found it very hard to understand why somebody could be exclusively heterosexual or homosexual,' he said in 2005. 'I like people. I'm a married, monogamous man, but I've got many close, gay friends still. I don't think I'd say I was heterosexual. I've still got a gay sensibility.'

Out of his experiences and Regard meetings came several academic papers, as well as *The Sexual Politics of Disability* (1996), written with Kath Gillespie Sells and Dominic Davies. The first book to look at the sexual politics of disability from a disability rights perspective, it sought to make disability and sexuality 'a key political and sociological issue'.

The authors talked to 44 disabled people. The evidence they gleaned put paid to the myth that disability and sexuality were incompatible. They found many people were lonely, but they also secured surprisingly frank comments about sexual experiences that were used to highlight chapters such as 'identity and imagery', 'barriers to being sexual', 'bad sex' or 'double the trouble' (to be lesbian or gay and disabled).

While they acknowledged that the social model and the disabled people's movement were essential for giving people self-confidence and securing improvements in their lives, they said there were still 'minorities within minorities' and 'multiple oppressions' to contend with. 'If disability politics is centrally about civil rights and citizenship demands, its failure to campaign in the area of sexual citizenship is a major omission.'

The book's content and academic authority were welcomed, but its impact was mainly outside the UK. The disability movement in the UK did not take up the challenge. While Mike Oliver thought it would become 'a key text in disability studies', he marked it down for under-representing heterosexual men and paying only lip-service to the social model. It was, he thought, too centred on the individual at the expense of radical collective action for a better society. As such, he feared the book might be 'confined to the dustbins of academic history'.

Yet, more than ten years later, *Sexual Politics* is still relevant. Disabled people still face discrimination, loneliness, and lack of information and support, as a survey in the newspaper *Disability Now* showed in 2005.

In the two years between degrees Shakespeare worked as an administrator in the alternative Works Theatre Cooperative and as a printer at the Cambridge Free Press. In 1991, he went north, to become a lecturer in sociology at the University of Sunderland. It opened up new opportunities to him, not least in arts and political activism, as well as the chance to 'reinvent' himself.

He was already into disability cabaret and had been doing stand-up in the street, complete with juggling and fire-eating – all high-risk stuff. Live performance, he says, is in his nature. Others call it showing off. Given that his appearance attracts attention anyway, live performance is a way of turning something disagreeable to positive effect.

Geof Armstrong, former director of the National Disability Arts Forum, remembers Shakespeare on the cabaret circuit.

> He covered disability issues head on. He used the social model as a starting point because that was a common language at the time. He worked from his own experience as a disabled person and also the common experiences that he knew all disabled people would share – it gave everyone something to identify with.

He thinks Shakespeare could have made a successful career as an actor or comedian. But Shakespeare packed it in after five years. 'I was OK but not great,' he said.

His experience of being a 'dwarf' and performing in public made him think about how disabled people are perceived. One of his earliest academic papers, in 1994, was about the cultural representation of disability at a time when little research had been done in this area. He said disabled sociologists were looking at disability through a 'materialist' lens, which emphasised tangible social and economic disadvantage rather than stigmatising attitudes. He was drawn to feminist theories, such as Simone de Beauvoir's view that women are seen as 'the other' and the anthropologist Mary Douglas' ideas that societies try to assert order against 'anomaly'. Shakespeare found these ideas useful in explaining how society sees disabled people not just as different, but as a threat – 'scapegoats for the fears and vulnerabilities of nondisabled people', as he put it later.

In 1999, he also had some interesting things to say about humour and disability, tracing its development from disabled people as figures of fun to disability arts cabaret. He pointed out that the radical disability comedian made jokes about disabling encounters and environments, not about disabled people.

> In the disability cabaret, jokes are about social workers ('What do they have in common with computers? You have to punch information into both of them'); and occupational therapists ('How many does it take to change a light bulb? One to take out the old one, another to explain that you are not entitled to a new one'); and the Tube ('What do London Transport and Jesus Christ have in common? They both make cripples walk').

Disability comedians could also turn standard jokes on their head, he said. He told a joke about a man with a stammer asking for a drink. The barman stammers a reply, but then, to a posh, non-stammering customer, he speaks in a posh, non-stammering way. The disabled man comes back to the bar. 'Ah heard yuuu!' he says, angrily, 'Yu werrr t-t-t-tekking the pitz out of me!' 'No, I wasn't t-t-tekking the pitz out of you,' says the barman, 'I was t-tekking the pitz out of him.'

Shakespeare sums up:

> In moving from being laughed at, to laughing at themselves, to laughing at their situations and at non-disabled people, people with impairments are performing disability in new ways, which challenge the prejudice within our culture and demand the acceptance of disability as an acceptable and respectable dimension of social diversity.

While disability humour has moved on – Lawrence Clark broke a taboo when he ridiculed another disabled person, Christopher Reeve – and there are now more disabled comedians about, it is still rare for them to appear on TV and radio.

In *Should We Be Laughing?* (BBC Radio 4, 2004), a two-part programme looking at comedy and disability from the disability point of view, Shakespeare called for more disabled comedians to be able to make a professional living from comedy. At the same time, 'disability correctness' should not confine disability jokes to disabled comedians – as long as the joke is about the situation, not about a person's incompetence. (He took exception to Gimli, the dwarf in his childhood favourite, *Lord of the Rings*, being turned into a figure of fun in the film cycle.)

In Newcastle, in the early 1990s, Shakespeare threw himself into bringing disability arts and politics to the North East. He teamed up with Geof Armstrong, who had recently arrived from the London disability arts scene, and together they founded the first disability arts agency in Newcastle in 1992. Shakespeare became chair and Armstrong was development officer. Over the next two years they laid the foundations of the Northern Disability Arts Forum (now Arcadea), securing Arts Council funding, starting a newsletter, organising cabarets and exhibitions, involving local disabled people and arts organisations. Shakespeare was the driver, the spokesperson, says Armstrong. 'He would be encouraging, pushing ideas through, saying "Don't procrastinate, don't hang about wondering if this is the best way forward. Let's just get things done."'

Neither of them had any experience of starting organisations and disabled people were thinner on the ground than in London, but their enthusiasm carried them through. A year later they started Disability Action North East (DANE) with a friend from student days, Stuart Bracking. Run by disabled people, DANE was intended as a discussion group for disability theory, but it got enmeshed in people's practical problems and also had to compete for funding with large disability charities. Still, it survived, and made its point. 'A lot of the other organisations changed because of the challenge that Dane represented,' says Armstrong.

Shakespeare became involved with other groups, including the Gateshead Voluntary Organisations Council, and more arts projects, somehow managing to fit them round his job as lecturer. At the same time he was building his career as a sociologist with academic papers about disability, identity, gender and genetics, and writing his PhD thesis. In 1996 he became a research fellow at the Disability Research Unit (now the Centre for Disability Studies) at Leeds University, the hotbed of disability studies based on the social model, headed by Professor Colin Barnes.

There he worked with Barnes and Geof Mercer on a sociological introduction to disability and edited a collection of essays, *The Disability Reader*, which claimed to be the first book to give a broad introduction to disability studies from a social science perspective.

He also took part in some new disability research – finding out how older disabled children see and experience disability. Like the sexuality book, it covered the experiences of 'ordinary' disabled people. The results were surprising, says Shakespeare. While the children experienced prejudice and social barriers in line with the social model, they did not want to be a disabled minority; they just wanted to be with their mates. 'I honestly think most disabled people want that – to be ordinary people, not 24/7 disabled people.'

Just as that research was about to get underway, there came what Shakespeare calls a turning point in his life. In March 1997, the man who was full of energy and never ill slipped a disc and was out of action for six months. He had underestimated how vulnerable he was and he didn't know how to deal with it. There was pain, fear that he wouldn't get better and deep frustration that he couldn't do what he wanted to do – experiences of impairment that he had only read about. It took six weeks for him to stop fighting and come to terms with the situation. He had to rely on friends and neighbours to shop and care for him.

A concrete result of that experience was *Help!* (2000), a mini book which looked at care-giving from a disability studies perspective – that is, it used the social model. It was written in 1998 for the British Association of Social Workers, whose members must have found the sociology jargon heavy going. Shakespeare used his ideas about cultural representation to argue that the culture of care-giving among professionals, charities and parents placed a stigma of dependency on the person being cared for. On the other hand, he recognised that independence could never be total; everyone in society depends on others. Simply dismissing traditional care-giving ran the risk of 'writing out' the role of compassion in providing help. So demanding rights was not enough; humane values were important too. He called for a 'caring solidarity' – mutual respect – between all parties.

In *Help!*, Shakespeare was for the first time writing a book on his own, neither supported nor impeded by the collective ethos of disability studies; indeed, he was later criticised for not mentioning some earlier work by the disability guru Vic Finkelstein. Although Shakespeare still used the social model, it did not seem to meet his needs. 'Look for that of God in everyone' seemed closer to the mark. This was a Quaker tradition, he said, and Shakespeare, after years of spiritual searching, was on his way to becoming a Quaker.

The injury to his back made him take achondroplasia more seriously. He is not sure if it triggered a more radical rejection of the social model. 'It was certainly very difficult to be as blasé about impairment after that. It often is your personal experiences that have the biggest effect.'

From Cambridge days, Shakespeare had had his own view of the social model. He agreed with feminist thinkers who wanted the model expanded to include different impairments and experiences of disability. His paper on the cultural representation of disabled people in 1994 had called for the social model to be 'reconceptualised', to embrace prejudice, not just material discrimination.

Yet, in 1997, Shakespeare and his friend Nick Watson, now Professor of Disability Studies at the University of Glasgow, were still defending the social model against interpretations by mainstream social scientists. They said it was 'vital' to distinguish between impairment and disability; they pointed out how the social model had had a major impact on British society and 'brought major benefits to disabled people'. They did, however, think the social model was still developing; getting the balance right between the experience of physical impairment and the social experience of disability was 'a continuing endeavour'.

More assertively, they did not accept that the disability movement's political goals would be weakened by internal questioning: 'Debates are necessary, and recognising difference within the disability community is overdue.'

At this stage their comments were still acceptable to disability studies; the paper was included in a book co-edited by Mike Oliver. But by 1999 their position had hardened. The social model, they said, had become a 'sacred cow' and they were looking for a 'more adequate social theory of disability'. This was taking criticism of the social model onto another plane – 'sticking their heads above the parapet', as one observer put it.

Shakespeare and Watson believed that 'people are disabled both by social barriers and by their bodies' and that the concept of the social model – by excluding or subordinating impairment and concentrating on the social barriers – created false distinctions. In practice, this led to hypocrisy: disabled people stressed social barriers in public while talking about their physical pains and problems in private. They said that disabled people have many identities and the social model would be easier for disabled people to accept if it allowed for differences, such as the impact of different impairments, rather than lumping everyone together in a common oppression and providing a single solution.

The social model also created a 'them' and 'us' relationship with non-disabled people and they suggested that by accepting 'everyone is impaired, not just disabled people', a common identity could be forged between the two sides, with all sorts of positive spin-offs for social and medical practice.

Their paper, 'The social model of disability: an outdated ideology?', was turned down by *Disability and Society*, the main journal in British disability studies (not for ideological reasons, insists the editor Professor Len Barton). It was published in 2002 by an American journal, *Research in Social Science and Disability*.

David Colley, an ex-chair of the radical umbrella group British Council of Disabled People (BCODP), remembers how disabled activists criticised Shakespeare for attacking the social model. Colley himself disagreed with Shakespeare, but, as a believer in free speech, he thought the treatment meted out to Shakespeare was unfair. 'I did feel ashamed of the movement at that point. We have to be able to accommodate debate, otherwise the movement can't be democratic.'

In 2003 Colin Barnes, who had coined the term 'disability studies', gave a considered response to Shakespeare and Watson. While acknowledging that biological impairment and social disability were separate concepts, he said the social model allowed for interaction between the two. For example, disabled people talking about their impairments had helped identify social discrimination and provided information for better services. As for the claim that disabled people did not identify with the disability movement, that was because society stigmatised disability.

Barnes agreed that impairment was fundamental to the human experience, but as a way of galvanising society, the social model (with its emphasis on the social context) had worked and should not be torn down before anyone came up with a better formula. Better to build on what had gone before.

Conceptually, Shakespeare and Watson overstated their case by saying that the social model *excluded* impairment. They were right to say, though, that the social model played it down – and Barnes would agree. Shakespeare and Watson were also right to see the social model as a creed that could be used to delegitimise other interpretations of disability in the interests of unity.

For some people, Shakespeare's sin was to cross the line between academic discussion, where different points of view should be permitted, and political reality, where a position must be held to keep people together. This distinction was alien to Shakespeare's temperament and offended his intellectual standards. It ran up against his dislike of being boxed in and his enthusiasm for debate, new ideas and branching out.

Shakespeare's criticism of the social model drew on many sources, including postmodernism and the human genome project. For the non-expert, Shakespeare describes modernism as 'all about dichotomy: things are this, not that'. He sees the social model as based on dichotomy – medical model wrong, social model right, for example (a wheelchair user was recently heard to say of another disabled person, 'I've heard he's medical model'). In postmodernism, things are relative, fluid, on a continuum; it offers 'a way of opening things up, and I think we should open things up and consider other approaches'. In 2002 he co-edited a book of essays, *Disability/Postmodernity: Embodying Disability Theory*, which applied postmodernist theory to disability, partly to see what each could contribute to the other and also to help bring disability studies into the academic mainstream. Now he has veered away from postmodernism, mainly because its emphasis on everything being socially constructed, with no reality underneath, does not fit with his view about the reality of impairment, its pain and limitation. He says he is more at home with critical realism, which accepts physical reality but says there are different ways of looking at it.

Shakespeare's interest in the human genome project stemmed from his personal interest in genetic mutation. Like others in the 1990s, he realised that advances in genetic research and antenatal screening were making it easier to detect genetic defects before birth and destroy an imperfect foetus. He aired his concern to a mainstream audience in a TV documentary about the human genome project that was shot in 1995 and screened on Channel 4 in 1997. It was called *Ivy's Genes* after his daughter, Ivy.

The film starts by contrasting newspaper cuttings, which seem to promise a Utopia free of everyday impairments and diseases, with Shakespeare's view of the reality: 'Disabled people have every reason to think that this is a nightmare scenario.' It ends with Shakespeare expressing hope for the future because the disabled people's movement is growing in strength and 'people are increasingly having to listen to what disabled people have to say about what they want'.

In the course of the film, Shakespeare talks to friends and to a sympathetic doctor, Professor John Burn of the Human Genetics Department at Newcastle University (now head of the university's Institute of Human Genetics). But most of all he draws on his family history and his daughter Ivy, then aged seven. In one scene he is walking with Ivy through King's College, Cambridge. He remembers pushing Ivy in her buggy through the quad and hearing later that a Fellow of the college had remarked: 'How could Tom have gone ahead and had a child, knowing that there was a strong probability that she would be disabled?' It felt 'something like a kick in the teeth', he says. 'When you think that you are accepted for who you are, it is a rude awakening to find that people think there shouldn't be more people like you in the world.'

Ivy stole the show. The film ended with her going to sleep in her bunk bed as the folk singer Roy Bailey sang, 'You can be anybody you want to be ... the only measure of your words and your deeds will be the love you leave behind when you're done.'

There was not much love lost between Shakespeare and members of the disability movement when he accepted a job at the new Policy, Ethics and Life Sciences Research Institute (PEALS) in August 1999. Formed from a partnership between the universities of Newcastle and Durham and the Centre for Life in Newcastle, PEALS was chaired by Sir Kenneth Calman, a former government chief medical officer. Its aim was to carry out research and promote debate around the social, ethical and legal aspects of the life sciences.

Disabled people had been intensely suspicious of the Centre for Life, founded in 1996, fearing its genetics research would lead to the elimination of more disabled people, threaten social diversity and renew the medical view of disability. Disability campaigners had targeted the centre's building site with a 'No Nazi Eugenics' banner. Shakespeare himself had been sceptical about the centre. But now he was becoming research development officer at PEALS at the very time when fears of eugenics and euthanasia were running high. In the USA, disabled people had been demonstrating against the appointment of Professor Peter Singer to a senior chair at Princeton University. Singer was the author of *Practical Ethics*, which justified killing severely disabled infants on the utilitarian grounds of securing the greatest happiness for the greatest number.

Shakespeare justified his appointment by saying scientists must not lead the bioethics debate on their own. 'We can make sure our voice is heard and put our point of view where we disagree with things. That is why I am here.' He was also there because he felt frustrated by disability studies at Leeds and, given his back problems, travel to the new job in Newcastle would be easier.

Members of the disability movement hit back. An anonymous comment in *Coalition*, the magazine of the Greater Manchester Coalition of Disabled People, asked for reassurance that 'you haven't sold out and become the self-appointed "expert" you used to ridicule on stage'. In a longer article, Anne Rae, an ex-chair of BCODP, feared Tom might be seen as supporting Singer's views. She, for one, had no confidence in his ability to protect the interests of disabled people. Even some of his friends disapproved.

Shakespeare, whose skin is less thick than many people realise, was taken aback by the virulence of the criticism. He knew he was stepping out of line, but not how unacceptable that would be.

The criticism did not deter him, though. *Genetic Politics: From Eugenics to Genome* (2002) was his next book, written with the sociologist, Anne Kerr. It diverged from the disability movement in saying parents should be able to avoid the suffering associated with some severe genetic conditions: that is, choose to have an abortion. But otherwise the book covered much of the ground Shakespeare had written about before. Among other things, it drew parallels between antenatal screening, embryo selection, and the power of professional influence today, and the old eugenics; it argued that calculating the cost-benefit of termination versus medical and welfare costs was 'immoral'; it deplored the lack of information for parents to make a real choice; and it drew attention to the dangers of commercial genetic testing.

Dr Bill Albert, who represents BCODP on international bioethics committees and is a former member of the government's Human Genetics Commission, thinks that Shakespeare pioneered the bioethics debate in the disability community, and the book has helped frame that debate. 'It was great. I didn't agree with every bit of it, but why should I?' Still, seeing Shakespeare working alongside leading geneticists and knowing how he had been stung by personal criticism from disabled people, he feared that Shakespeare was being sucked into a medical vortex and would lose his bearings in the fight for human rights.

Certainly Shakespeare respects doctors. After all, his father was a doctor. 'They are our friends', he says. 'I know some doctors treat some disabled people terribly. That's wrong. But that does not mean that all doctors are evil.' He thinks disabled people should be working with doctors, educating them, and that the hostility of disabled activists persists because they don't engage with the medical profession.

Words like 'tragedy' and 'cure' are anathema to many people in the disability movement because they smack of the medical model – seeing disabled people as individual medical problems. Shakespeare treats this pragmatically. He thinks severe impairments like Tay Sachs disease, which is terminal, is a tragedy and he supports a woman's right to have an abortion if that is her informed choice. And while he agrees that raising expectations about a cure is wrong, trying to minimise impairment, prevent it, and cure it if possible, are all fine. 'Most people with a spinal cord injury would not be here today had it not been for medical, surgical, or nursing care,' he says.

When *Superman* actor Christopher Reeve died in 2004, still hoping that stem cell research would one day cure his paralysis, Shakespeare defended him against the chorus of criticism from disabled people for whom society was the culprit. Shakespeare thought Reeve's determination to walk again was a triumph of optimism over evidence, but 'his advocacy of hope and perseverance was both admirable and far-sighted. We need campaigners and fundraisers for medical research, as well as for equality and inclusion. The disability community should celebrate Christopher Reeve, not disown him.'

He has been consistently out of line on assisted dying too. He has supported a bill, introduced several times by Lord Joffe, to legalise assisted dying for terminally ill people. 'People should have the right to die if they are nearing the end of life and are suffering unbearably,' he says. 'I think it's an issue of disabled people having control over their lives.' He and Lord

Ashley were the only well-known figures in the disability world to support Joffe in a 2005 *Disability Now* poll.

Anne Rae was right to suspect that, in working at PEALS, Shakespeare would not protect the interests of disabled people in the way she wanted. Instead, he followed an independent line, trusting his own judgement. Some people valued that.

Apart from offering Shakespeare a different, medical, environment, the PEALS job also spoke to the creative and entrepreneurial sides of him. As the institute's only employee in its early days, he was free to do things his way. Between 1999 and 2005 he raised over £1 million for various research and outreach projects, many of which he has led. He helped develop Café Scientifique in Newcastle, where people meet in bars or cafés to discuss topical scientific issues introduced by a leading scientist or science writer, and he extended the junior version to over 50 schools in the north of England. He has organised sci-art projects, bringing together scientists and artists to explore, for example, memory and forgetting, and innovative discussions about the genetics of sexuality with local gay, lesbian and bisexual people, which led to a visual arts exhibition. A website that gives parents antenatal screening information from a disability equality perspective has been developed, and there have been public meetings on genetics and reproductive choice.

One project kept alive Shakespeare's interest in disabled people's stories and the tie between impairment and disability – research that has never been done before, he says, and probably wouldn't have fitted into disability studies. He and geneticist Dr Michael Wright followed the life histories of 70 people with restricted growth, looking at the physical problems they have and the social barriers they face. 'I think it's very difficult to separate the two,' says Shakespeare. 'Most people, when they talk about their lives, say "my back aches and it's made worse by the chairs I sit on", or "I get fatigue and no one takes account of my needs."' He hopes the findings – such as a lack of comprehensive health services and negative reactions among employers and the public – will help the Restricted Growth Association to lobby for improvements. He never wants to do research which does not have spin-offs or benefits, he says.

Since 2000, Shakespeare's career has broadened out. He travels around the world as a visiting speaker, courtesy of the British Council, and appears regularly on television and radio. He was a member of the Nuffield Council on Bioethics' working party (2000–02), which explored the ethics of research into genes and behaviour. In 2003, he won the Joseph Lister award given to 'outstanding young science communicators' by the British

Association for the Advancement of Science and, in the same year, a People of the Year award from the disability network, RADAR, for furthering human rights for disabled people in the UK.

He has been involved with numerous arts committees and workshops, and is now chair of Arts Council England, North East and a member of Arts Council England (ACE). As such, he was at the heart of a row over cuts to disability arts groups, imposed by ACE between 2007 and 2008. £29 million (35 per cent) was sliced from overall funding to help pay for the Olympics, and in disability arts the sword fell on six organisations, including the London Disability Arts Forum. Many disabled people were furious. Shakespeare says he investigated the decisions and 'was satisfied they were appropriate'. He thinks ACE is still committed to disabled artists and disabled-led initiatives.

Creative writing is not new to Shakespeare, but he believes more and more that it can reach and influence people who might not otherwise think – or feel – about the things he cares about. 'I'm interested in showing how attitudes to disability are a product of our culture and the times we live in; that means they can be changed.' Helped by a three-year fellowship from the National Endowment for Science, Technology and the Arts (NESTA), he has been working on all sorts of projects and taking part in literary festivals. The humorous monologue, *No Small Inheritance*, is being turned into a book. Among other things, he completed an MA in creative writing, and an artwork called *Look*, which gave people an insight into what it is like to be stared at.

At home in Hebburn, near Newcastle, he likes cooking and gardening and used to keep up with the adventures of Harry Potter. For five years he was married to Caroline Bowditch, a disability equality trainer from Australia, but they separated in 2007. Bowditch, who has *osteogenesis imperfecta* (brittle bones), encouraged him to take up modern dance, which became a new Shakespeare enthusiasm. 'I loved it,' he wrote on the BBC website Ouch! 'I think one reason was because in most of my life I use my voice or my brain, not my body.' His inhibitions dropped away and before long he was partnering disabled and non-disabled women in the tango.

Ivy and Robert, Shakespeare's children, are now at university. He acknowledges the immaturity of his student years, but says he has never been the absent father. He is proud of his children's academic success and their sociable lives.

Shakespeare is now 42. If the paraplegia becomes permanent, not only his lifestyle will change. Already he has acquired a new respect for 'rehab' and the medical nuts and bolts of impairment.

Father and son: Tom Shakespeare and Robert Brown at Chesters
Roman Fort, Hadrian's Wall, Northumberland in 2006. Photograph taken by Tom Shakespeare

So how does he rate in the disability firmament? As an academic, he hasn't had one 'big idea', like the social model. But he has pushed disability research and thinking into new areas. He has helped to bring issues of disability and bioethics to a mainstream audience. And he is trying to build bridges between doctors, scientists and disabled people.

'Renaissance man', he has been called, and certainly his many interests and abilities transcend the role of a conventional academic. He is also stimulating to work with, not prickly like some disability activists. He makes an attractive role model.

But his success causes irritation, even jealousy, among disability scholars and others. He is seen as academically flawed on one level and a political traitor on another. He is 'dilettantish' because he does not have a proper respect for orthodox disability studies research. ('I don't follow recipes when I cook, and I'm not keen on following imposed rules when I research,' he has said.) He is 'precious' in elevating individual freedom, including his own, over the collective good. He is 'dangerous' because he cannot be trusted to keep to the party line. By drawing attention to what he sees as the imperfections of the social model, he may turn disabled people off before they have been turned on; he may give succour to doctors and geneticists who, deep down, still adhere to the medical model.

'Tom is a fantastic communicator,' says Bill Albert. 'He's superbly articulate, engaging, supremely intelligent, and for all those reasons he needs to be more careful. And for all those reasons, he isn't.'

Nor could he be. As a man of multiple identities, Shakespeare cannot understand why the disability movement does not pay more respect to differences between disabled people – differences of opinion as well as impairment – within their common identity. When he has said this, though, he could be seen as letting down the side. And, given his obvious impairment, he can be taken to be a spokesperson for the disability movement. Like the baronetcy, he cannot avoid it. A form of discrimination, you could say, a curtailment of his freedom of speech.

Moving on is key to Shakespeare's personality. He sees the potential of an idea or a project, grasps it, shakes things up or helps create something new. Then he loses interest or sees the flaws. He has discarded many an old toy in favour of a shiny new one.

The downside of this temperament – impatience, carelessness, sometimes arrogance – he knows only too well. He tells a story about his great-grandfather, Dr John Howard Shakespeare, general secretary of the Baptist Union, who wanted to amalgamate the Union with other churches. But the members were dead against it. 'He was convinced he was right...and marched straight on. He led from the front and left them all behind.'

The difference between the two is that Tom Shakespeare respects debate.

# PHIL FRIEND:
# ENTREPRENEUR

*Photograph taken by Graham Bool Photography*

Making a net saving of £50,000 a month is enough to whet the appetite of any big business. No wonder a large public company used the disability and diversity consultancy Minty & Friend (M&F) to run a 'reasonable adjustments' service for its disabled employees. Besides helping the company meet its obligations under the Disability Discrimination Act 1995, the service was estimated to increase productivity, cut absence and management time, and avoid legal charges and tribunal awards.

High street bank and insurance group Lloyds TSB has also used the service, operating as a hotline. When disabled employees, including those who had become disabled, needed adjustments to do their job, the manager would ring M&F. M&F worked with the employee, the manager, internal departments such as IT, and the government's Access to Work scheme to get the necessary aids, adaptations or support, and supply education and training. Over 2000 Lloyds TSB disabled employees have benefited.

The service was Phil Friend's idea. For him, the biggest problem is not recruiting disabled people but keeping people in work when they become disabled. 'So for me it was about civil rights. It was certainly a way of making money, but it was always squaring the circle – we could make money *and* keep people with disabilities at work.'

It all started with some induction training he did in the mid-1990s for a group of Trustee Savings Bank (TSB) equal opportunities managers daunted by the disability side of their brief. Friend arrived in his wheelchair – a cheerful, energetic man with his trademark moustache, who lived up to his name. He told stories about himself and other disabled people who had experienced discrimination, made the managers laugh, and gave them practical advice that increased their confidence. Andrew Wakelin, now senior manager for group equality and diversity at Lloyds TSB, found Friend 'one of the most inspiring speakers I had come across'.

After Lloyds and TSB merged, Friend was asked to meet top managers and explain the advantages of having a policy for disabled customers and employees which not only complied with the DDA but made business sense too – how 10 million disabled people offer an £80 billion market for goods and services and a major source of work skills. He helped persuade them that being positive about disabled people would pay off. He then went on to assess Lloyds TSB's work practices, finding many weaknesses. On the employee side, he talked to 150 disabled staff individually and in groups. Besides the horror stories around reasonable adjustments, like a two-year wait for a textphone or a different kind of chair, he found managers who just did not know their responsibilities and disabled employees who felt isolated and disempowered, often stuck on the bottom rung of the promotional ladder. By the beginning of 1999, his solutions were in place. Lloyds TSB underwent 'a huge cultural change', says Wakelin, one that put it ahead of other major companies and public sector bodies.

Alongside ideas you might expect, like a company action plan, management training and a disability resource tool kit, came new ones. Besides the reasonable adjustments service, Friend introduced a newsletter and website for disabled staff, and a personal development programme – four days of small group training and a follow-up – devised with disabled employees. More than 250 people have taken the course. They have shared their experiences, sometimes amid tears, drawn up work and personal action plans, and found new confidence and motivation. 'We have loads of success stories where people feel that Phil Friend is the one person who has got them out of the bottom grade after maybe 30 years,' says Wakelin. 'It is the one event that has changed their lives more than anything else.'

That kind of individualised concern for disabled employees has made M&F special. It goes hand in hand with understanding how employers and suppliers of goods and services think about regulations, profit, and being seen to do the right thing. To help them, Friend co-founded Dining with a Difference, so that top managers could meet key disabled professionals over dinner. In a relaxed atmosphere, managers learn about disability legislation, the business advantages of employing disabled people and practical solutions that open the way for them to make changes in their own companies. With the diversity consultants Schneider-Ross, Friend has now expanded the idea into The All Inclusive Dining Club, which covers all aspects of inclusion in the workplace.

Friend's consultancy and training takes account of the needs of each client, so 'off the shelf' solutions are out. The company has always been small and personal. By mid-2008 it had a maximum of 40 employees, mostly freelance associates, 90 per cent of them disabled, and operated from a modest office near London Bridge. Then there was a staff buyout of the 'reasonable adjustments' side and the London office closed. M&F, with some new staff, now operates as a virtual company that meets weekly. Acknowledged as the leader in the field of disability consultancy, the company has a string of big-name clients past and present, such as Accenture, Barclays, BSkyB, BT, Buckingham Palace, Goldman Sachs, LexisNexis, Royal Mail and Transport for London.

In the mid-1980s, Friend, aged 40, out of work and on his uppers, realised he could make a career from his disability. 'I found that I was sitting on my biggest asset!' He rode the wave of disability awareness that crested with the Disability Discrimination Act in 1995, leaving new duties and responsibilities in its wake that are still being worked through today. Like others, he exploited the opportunities afforded by the Act to help businesses comply with the law, but he also encouraged them to look beyond the burdens to the possibilities. His own business thrived. The company's twentieth anniversary party in 2006 summed up the style of Friend and his partner, Simon Minty: an illustrious and accessible venue, the Treasury, treated with informality – jokes, cabaret by a deaf artist, and Chinese fortune cookies with a disability theme. James Partridge, chief executive of the charity Changing Faces, spoke of the 'soft bigotry of low expectations around disability' and how Friend and Minty were about changing the attitudes of employers, schools and disabled people themselves. 'I see the power you have to change people's heads,' he said. For the boy who reacted violently to that 'soft bigotry' and left special school skilled mainly in rug-making, it must have been a sweet compliment.

Friend was born in Bermondsey, London, in November 1945, the oldest son of Albert and Vicky Friend. Life was difficult from the start. His father developed multiple sclerosis while serving in North Africa and was discharged from the army shortly before the end of the Second World War. Soon he was using a wheelchair, so the family moved to accommodation for ex-servicemen beside Chelsea football ground. Then Friend caught the polio virus in 1949 – the same year as Bert Massie – supposedly during a stay in the local hospital to have his tonsils out.

The three-year-old was whisked into isolation and from there to Queen Mary's Hospital for Children at Carshalton in Surrey. Paralysed and unable to breathe without support, he was put into an iron lung, then the only form of artificial ventilation. His body was inside the machine, his head outside. He lay there for two months, listening to the whoosh of the bellows, his only diversions a frieze of alphabet letters around the wall, which he learned by heart, both ways, and the trains steaming over a viaduct outside that he could see in a tilted mirror. The child in the iron lung beside him died. He remembers the first solid food he ate when he was taken out of the iron lung – baked beans on toast – and the Mars bars and bananas his mother brought on her very occasional visits. He stayed in hospital for three years, by which time he had learned to swear 'like a trooper', according to a friend's mother.

He came home to share a bedroom with his father. 'He was paralysed and in bed and I was paralysed and in a bed-chair.' They played draughts together. Albert smoked 40 Old Holborn cigarettes his wife rolled for him each evening and got his son to masturbate him – a service also required of

Friend's younger brother and sister. Eventually his mother found out and Albert went to the Royal Star & Garter Home for ex-servicemen in Richmond. The family moved to Essex, and Friend did not see his father again. 'My life has been a series of chapters and once one's over I don't go back to it.'

His parents divorced, and after various liaisons, his mother remarried when Friend was 14. The stepfather, a postman, brought in a regular wage, but he was a heavy drinker and often violent when he returned from the pub. 'It was only when me and my brother got big enough that he stopped doing that because we would sort him out if he tried to.' On one occasion, after he had left school, Friend came in to find his mother distressed. He couldn't get into his stepfather's bedroom, so he sat outside with a carving knife, while the terrified tyrant, barricaded in, spent the night beside the door. In the early 1960s the couple divorced. Friend's mother had a mental breakdown and the children were taken into care for a while.

This turbulent home life took its toll on Friend's dearly loved younger brother, who was in and out of trouble, relied on alcohol and cigarettes, and died prematurely. His sister, Vicky, the youngest, felt anger and hurt too, but went on to become a British speed skating champion. Friend thinks that if he had not been disabled he would be in jail. He escaped the family in term time because he was sent away to special schools from the age of six, though he had to bear the separation instead. Despite her physical and emotional absence, he still regards his mother as his champion. He remembers how she worked for the family as a bus conductor, then selling mobile groceries – she had learned to drive in the Ford Prefect given to ex-servicemen –and finally as a telephonist for Thompson newspapers. Her hard work, engaging sense of humour and ability to tell vivid stories have all been inherited by Friend; perhaps also the sharp tongue he admits to, and the 'out of sight, out of mind' trait noticed by colleagues and friends.

Friend's schooling was typical of many physically impaired children in the 1950s and 1960s, when local schools were inaccessible and rehabilitation seemed more important than exam results or job skills. Unable to walk at all to begin with, Friend got around on a tricycle, pushing the pedals with his hands. After trying the local school, he was sent to Hesley Hall, a special school near Doncaster, where he lasted a term. By now he was turning violent, hitting people. When another boy abused his mother, he tipped a big bath on top of him, which caused considerable injury. He thought he had been expelled until his mother said she had withdrawn him because the school was for children with learning difficulties. It was a mismatch of convenience by the then London County Council. In contrast to his limited mobility, Friend was already at ease with words and reading so fluently by the age of seven that teachers used him to read to the rest of the class.

Back home, he was returned to the local school, unsuccessfully. Friend's mother was reported to the National Society for the Prevention of Cruelty to Children because her son had been seen gazing out of the window, seemingly alone, although his father was there. Eventually he was sent to another residential special school, Hatchford Park, near Cobham in Surrey, where he stayed until he was 16, intellectually marking time in beautiful country. One day, aged 11, he was called out of his class by the deputy head and told to report to the snooker table with a pencil, paper and a ruler. 'I sat at the snooker table and did my 11-plus and duly failed. There was no rehearsal, no preparation. I didn't even know what I took until perhaps a year later, when I was told I hadn't got into grammar school.'

The teaching, with one or two exceptions, was very poor. He remembers learning about St Paul's journey from Tarsus to Damascus in the first year. The following year, with a new intake, the lesson was repeated. By the time he was 16, 'I knew his shoe size. I knew the restaurant he ate in. It was an absolute joke.'

He resents the waste of time. 'If I've got any anger, and I have some, it's about that. Because I could have done so much better.' While other bright teenagers were preparing for O levels, he was tracing maps of the world, making ready-cut rugs, doing raffia work, receiving physiotherapy, which helped, and taking long breaks in hospital, which often did not. The school tried to give him some individual work, but it led nowhere. He left without any qualifications. But then, as he points out, his brother and sister had no qualifications either.

What the school did offer was stability. It provided regular routines, disciplines that promoted self-sufficiency – like making your bed or cleaning your shoes – and the opportunity for long-term relationships; people you met aged 9 were often there until you were 16. There was old-fashioned harshness but also caring support. Friend respected the assistant headmaster and he soaked up the kindness of his housemother, who told exciting stories and had a black Labrador beloved by the boys. He never forgot 'Miss Foster'; he has a Labrador now.

He enjoyed the extra-curricular activities. Over the years, he graduated from wolf cub to boy scout and then to Queen's Scout. But there were not enough challenges, so he vented his anger and frustration on things and people. He ripped down the 30-foot curtains in the main hall; he partially sawed through his hated callipers time and again so they broke and had to be sent away for repair; he hurled a typewriter at Graham Bool, nearly two years his junior, and pinched his sweets and magazines. (Later, they became lifelong friends.) He says he was vicious, spiteful, and a bully; though he was small, he was strong and good at sport. What seems to have saved him from himself and expulsion was the school's decision to go co-educational. A group of girls arrived when Friend was 14. He fell in love. 'It was a magical romance,' he says, which didn't get beyond kissing, but gave him a new confidence in himself.

Another event made a lasting impression on him: he held off a gang of schoolmates from attacking a clever boy they had already sent to Coventry. He protected the boy, not because he particularly liked him, but because he thought the odds were unfair. 'I have always tended to open my mouth when I see injustice – I don't care what it is,' he said later. He expected a thumping from the group, but when no one dared to hit him first, he felt a surge of power and confidence. In his final year his leadership qualities were officially recognised. He became head boy, team captain and scout quartermaster. It looked as if he would leave on a high, but then he cheeked his form teacher, the headmaster demoted him, and he spent the last few weeks back at the snooker table doing maths on his own.

By now his home was on a council estate in Roehampton, Surrey. His mother was determined he should get a job and took him off to interviews. He was 16 and had no skills except 'a gift for the gab' and the sympathy card, which inevitably worked with women and made him feel special. He played up his disability at an interview in a local hospital and was turned down. When the male interviewer stood up, Friend saw that he had only one leg. Still, the habit ran deep. It nearly cost him his first job as a clerical assistant in a local office of the Ministry of Pensions and National Insurance, handling grants and benefits. Floundering in a world of desks, filing cabinets, forms and phones, 'I looked pathetic and the women looked after me.' But the manager, who had hired him and became a mentor, called Friend into his office and gave him until the end of the week to start working. That shocked him into getting to grips with the paperwork.

He was sent on a day-release course and used it to acquire English language and maths qualifications, though he failed the clerical officer exam. He also built up his communication skills. He most enjoyed being on counter duty and calming down distressed or angry people; he realised that taking them to a quiet place would help and he knew his disability would make them reluctant to hit him. He stayed in the job for four years, until better pay and prospects, and annoyance at not being permanently graded because of his disability – which at the time he did not realise was discrimination – propelled him to Hammersmith town hall. There he moved from dealing with refuse bills, which he hated, to grave maintenance, where at least there was contact with relatives and trips to the cemeteries in his Invacar, the three-wheeled vehicle leased to disabled people by the Ministry of Transport.

He found office work boring and wanted desperately to get away from it. Mortified at not getting a job as a night duty information officer, he was unexpectedly offered another, as a trainee welfare officer. It was the break he had looked for. He was 22. Suddenly he was visiting 16 elderly people a day, organising meals on wheels and home help for them, 'drinking endless cups of tea and being a companion. I loved it. I absolutely adored it.' He cared about them, and they, of course, reciprocated. He would visit them on Christmas Day, staying for an hour with the most isolated ones. Some gave him sherry. 'I'd come back quite squiffy.'

Drinking was a favourite pastime, especially at weekends. Friend says he missed out on many adolescent activities, but not this one. After they left school, he and Graham Bool and others used to go to a pioneering riding school for disabled people at Chigwell in Essex on a Saturday, where they also met the girl grooms and stayed overnight in the changing rooms after visiting the pub. They 'corrupted' a shy public school boy from up the road, who also had polio and went riding. David Bonnett would sneak out of school and join them in the pub. He remembers Friend as 'abrupt, loud, rude, but hearty, who turned out to be a thoroughly good pal. But first impressions – you think how on earth can anyone accommodate this personality?'

Bool remembers how the three of them would gatecrash parties: 'We would end up taking the girls home and, of course, Phil always got the best-looking one.' But for a long time Friend hid his fear of having sex behind the principle that it wasn't right before marriage and he respected the girl too much, etc., etc. In reality he was scared of showing his legs, being rejected, and not being a competent lover. He said later: 'The question I had about my sexual life was different from able-bodied men. It wasn't that I was more or less secure; it was, could I physically do it?' In the end, a disabled lover showed him he could.

Friend would transport a girlfriend and cans of beer in his single-seat Invacar. He pepped it up with a motorbike engine so it could reach 70mph, but he had to put back the original engine every time it went in for a service. When Bonnett was at Newcastle University, Friend would drive up to see him several times a year, arriving at the end of the day so stiff he had to be levered out. The weekends involved getting plastered with Bonnett and his friends, but they also showed Friend a way of life that he wanted a slice of.

He applied for a childcare course at what was then Manchester Polytechnic, but after an interview he received a letter saying they did not think he could live away from home – in other words, they had no accessible accommodation. Accepted by the then Polytechnic of North London, he started a two-year course for a social work certificate. One of his work placements was in a secure unit, where he was locked in with a member of staff for 12 hours a day, looking after children who had committed serious crimes. He was good at wheelchair basketball, good enough to train with the national team, so he took his wheelchair along and played with the children in the gym. Again, he loved the work. 'I felt at home with them. I knew what they were about, these kids. I also enjoyed the drama of it. Anything could happen.'

His career as a social worker took him to Southwark, the City of Westminster and Barnet, working increasingly with young offenders. Along the way he acquired a certificate in psychotherapeutic group work.

VW camper: Phil Friend on a weekend break at Wichling, Kent, circa 1973.
Photograph taken by Sue Lisney

In 1973, aged 27, he at last left home to share an Islington flat with Bonnett, who was now practising as an architect. They had to negotiate slippery steps and three flights of stairs on their crutches, but they had their own place and their freedom. Friend went hippy; he had long hair and smoked 'all the wrong kind of cigarettes', he says. A year later they teamed up with Bool and another school friend, Ron Morris, to buy a house in Haringey, thanks to a Greater London Council (GLC) mortgage scheme for first-time buyers who could not get funding elsewhere. Bonnett remembers: 'The "four crips", as we called ourselves, knocked on the door of the GLC and said we'd like a mortgage, and they didn't even blink. Had four other disabled people done this? I doubt it.' Nor, perhaps, had four disabled men undertaken major renovation, including digging out a clay floor.

Hard up they might be, but their confidence was growing. Friend had a foot on the property ladder; he had graduated from a second-hand MG Midget to a new Volkswagen with oversized wheels and a tuned-up engine; and he was doing a job he loved. Disability was not important to any of them, claims Bonnett. 'That's the honest truth. And where it was a problem, we would either blather our way around it or beguile the opposition.'

The anger Friend felt as a child dissipated as he took control of his life. He still cared about social justice. It took a more intellectual turn in college, where he encountered Marxism and began to understand oppression. It found a practical outlet in Southwark, when, as a member of the National and Local Government Officers Association, he became one of the first shop stewards in social services. But he did not make the connection between social justice and disability.

One day, when Friend was reporting union news to a team meeting, he was defended against somebody's criticism by a young social worker. It was a new experience for Friend. He thought: 'I'm not used to this; I can look after myself. And then I saw her. I really saw her.' He had met Sue Lisney before, but this was the moment she arrived on his radar. There followed a fraught, on-off courtship before a moderately tamed Friend entered the married state in 1976, aged 30. They went on to have four children.

By this time he was a principal field social worker, but he opted to take a lower status, residential job, managing a reception centre for 20 adolescents awaiting court appearance or placement in a home. As he went through the door, he thought, 'Yeah, this is where I want to be.' He and Sue lived in a house across the garden. He knew how to manage a caseload; now he had ten staff, rotas and the accounts to think about. 'I learned very fast how to run the unit', he said. 'That's where I cut my teeth in management.' From there, he joined a great friend from college days, who had been appointed principal of Maynard House, a new, purpose-built assessment centre in Barnet. He himself became principal in 1978.

The key to Friend's success was his instinctive empathy with troubled adolescents. 'He was a natural,' says Steve Regis, a colleague at Maynard House. Friend had learned the importance of respect from his assistant head-master, and, although he was on crutches, he could restore order and focus to turbulent situations. Later, former pupils told him they had been unnerved because 'you seemed to know before we had done it what we were going to do'.

He made new ideas happen in the creative climate of Maynard House. For example, he built on an innovative programme that tried to keep children out of residential care by working with them at home. A contract was drawn up between the child, the parents and the social worker aimed at improving the child's behaviour; it included penalty clauses – for the social worker as well as the child. 'If we let the child down and the child brought it up and we were culpable, we'd usually take them away for a pizza or something,' says Regis. When Friend became principal, his ideas sometimes ran away with him, leaving the staff panting behind. Faced one day with a girl who was very violent and a habitual absconder, he decided to 'contain' her in one large room, attended by two staff 24 hours a day, until she agreed to change her behaviour. The beleaguered staff thought this was cruel. 'It was all sanctioned, but these days you would be locked up for what I did,' he says. At last the girl capitulated, and after he sent her to a therapeutic centre to have a cleft palette repaired, she blossomed.

Friend could be innovative about staff management. At the reception centre, he started fortnightly supervision sessions for residential social workers. He made conditions easier for his deputy by instituting time off and moving him from a small room close to the boys to the ground floor of Friend's own house. But the children always came first. Still, Friend admits he failed some people. 'It was probably because I wasn't tolerant enough. When I can't see where you're at, I'm not very tolerant. So I make my decision and that's that.'

In 1984 he moved up again, to head the long-established St Christopher's Community Home with Education (formerly an 'approved school'), Hillingdon. In his care were 40 boys housed in four units, supported by 50–60 staff. It was here, he says, that he met his Waterloo: resistance to change among the staff, a culture of theft and dishonesty, and falling child referrals as care in the community replaced residential care and Conservative government cuts impacted on local authority spending. To top it all, Friend tore a shoulder ligament, leading to six months off work. In 1986, he was told to close the home, making all the staff redundant, and then himself – 'horrible', he says.

A self-confessed workaholic, he had a young family to support and no full-time job. He did not seek sympathy from his friends. 'He can be very private over things like that,' says Graham Bool.

But by the end of the year, and after some false starts – selling clay flower pots being one – he had found a niche for himself delivering staff support and disability training to occupational therapists. A partnership with Steve Regis did not pay enough so he left Regis (who felt abandoned) and teamed up with business consultant Phil Churchill, a close friend from Roehampton days. The new partnership, Churchill and Friend, focused on disability equality training for businesses and other organisations.

Three people prompted the move. His wife, Sue, told him he must believe in what he did and, if he was an expert, people would pay him. Disability campaigner, Marilyn Loosely, of the Disablement Association of Hillingdon (DASH), asked him why he was pretending to be normal when he was disabled and why he did not accept his disability and do something about it. And Susan Scott-Parker, who was just setting up the Employers' Forum on Disability (EFD), introduced him to Dr Stephen Duckworth, the only disabled person then running his own disability consultancy business. Duckworth generously let Friend observe him at work and borrow ideas. 'I knew there was a huge market out there,' Duckworth said.

Friend started in the area he knew best, the public sector, just picking up his phone at home and asking contacts if they wanted stress or disability training for their staff. His first big job was for City University, and from there he was recommended to the BBC. By this time, it was evident to him that the disability training market wanted disabled trainers. Churchill, who was not disabled, pursued his own business but remained an adviser.

Susan Scott-Parker was mainly responsible for introducing Friend to private companies. She needed him to help persuade reluctant employers that they could and should be employing disabled people. She built bridges via face-to-face meetings.

> When you are creating what has never been done before, so much of what I was doing, and still am doing, hinges on my ability to persuade a senior business leader that this issue is real and that there are real people involved with real talent, who are getting a raw deal; that they aren't scary; they are honest; and you can have lunch with them. The business leader leaves the lunch thinking, 'I didn't have any idea —we've got to do something about this.' Phil was always part of that process with me.

He became one of the Forum's associates, alongside Duckworth. With Duckworth, he did equality training for Boots in Nottingham, Telethon and, later, the Court Service. Each was a foil for the other – Duckworth in his business suit, Friend dressed informally. Duckworth found Friend easy-going and fun. 'He's particularly astute at reading people's body language.' He appreciated how Friend could lift the mood of a group with a joke and a relevant anecdote.

Both trainers responded to the needs of the commercial market, rather than expecting the market to conform to them. In this they differed from the only other training scheme at that time, run for local authorities by the London Boroughs' Disability Resource team. Its trainers, such as Jane (later Baroness) Campbell, were 'full on' disability campaigners, inspired by the social model theory that people are disabled by social barriers not by their own impairment. They reflected a new militancy and anger among many disabled people who began campaigning for equal opportunities and anti-discrimination legislation in the 1980s. In the early 1990s, Campbell became co-chair of the British Council of Organisations of Disabled People.

Friend knew Campbell and other activists. He found the social model, as they did, 'incredibility liberating'. He and Duckworth used it in their training programmes. Friend was also chairman of DASH for several years and involved with the Association of Disabled Professionals. But neither of them were active members of the disability movement and their association with the Employers' Forum, an organisation run by non-disabled people, marked them as 'establishment'.

When Scott-Parker, financed by ITV's charity fundraising event, Telethon, commissioned Friend and Duckworth to run a disability awareness training programme for independent television producers and presenters in 1992, they found themselves on the wrong side of a long-standing 'Block Telethon' campaign. Telethon was anathema to disability activists because it was seen as perpetuating the stereotype of disabled people as recipients of charity. In fact, that was the very message Friend and Duckworth were taking to their clients, says Friend. 'Many of them began to have real, serious doubts about being involved with it at all.'

On the day of the Telethon, Friend was due to be interviewed by Michael Aspel. He arrived at London Weekend Television studios to find over 1000 protestors outside. Having pushed his way through verbal and physical abuse – he was pinned against a wall and spat upon – he got into the studios and argued, on camera, that people are disabled by society's attitudes and actions, rather than their medical conditions. But the campaign organiser Alan Holdsworth (also known as Johnny Crescendo) said: 'These people are traitors to the disability movement, who co-operate with Telethon for the money and to advance their own careers.' Duckworth responded: 'It is much better to work from within ITV to improve things, rather than shout abuse from the outside.' The campaign finished Telethon, but the stigma attached to Friend and Duckworth remained. A few months later, some disabled people left a course when they found Friend was a co-trainer. It was about ten years before Campbell told Friend she had forgiven him. By 2005 she was saying she loved him. Friend was eventually accepted, but he still regrets crossing the picket line and underestimating the offence that caused.

The Disability Discrimination Act 1995 was greeted as a compromise piece of legislation. Still, it did place legal duties on employers and providers of goods and services not to discriminate unfavourably against disabled people, and this gave disability equality training fresh impetus and a bigger market. Many disabled people became access consultants. For equality consultants already in the business, there were some rich pickings. Scott-Parker introduced Friend to Kay Allen, then head of the diversity team at B&Q. They were soon laughing together over their gin and tonics. She challenged him to roll out disability equality training to 23,500 B&Q employees over six weeks. He accepted. 'How the hell are we going to do this?' he asked when he got home – a familiar question. The planning took six months, but the training was, indeed, rolled out in six weeks. Friend devised a distance-learning workbook for each employee and enlisted Grass Roots, a business improvement company, to handle the administration and evaluation. B&Q became a major client. Together Allen and Friend developed a strategic plan and convinced the directors of the business case for making disability integral to B&Q's activities. She said he was 'superb' with the board, dispelling their preconceptions about disability with talk of his business, his family, his car, his salary.

> Phil, like me, believes that business is part of the solution not part of the problem, and you have to get employers to grab the solution. Phil is a great unpacker of problems and he helps businesses to find a way through, but in very practical steps.

Mary-Anne Rankin joined Friend at this time, working on the B&Q and Barclays Bank contracts and helping to bring order to the office. They had known each other for some time: he had been involved with her charity, the Understanding Disability Educational Trust, and through her, aided by luck, he had landed a ten-year job, providing equality training for Marks & Spencer staff.

Rankin saw how Friend operated from the inside. Besides exploiting his humour and charisma ('We have all flirted with him a bit'), he was down-to-earth, irreverent, habitually swearing. He empathised with directors – not to the same degree as he had with adolescents, but enough to understand and overcome their reluctance to change. 'He has an amazing ability to influence and motivate and get people to buy in who really don't want to,' says Rankin.

'This bloody Disability Act is in the way and we've got to address it.' In comes Phil with his f'ing and blinding and they listen and they hear and he makes it OK; he takes the fear out of it for them. People felt they could say it was very bewildering. 'It is bewildering, but that's what I'm here for. I will work with you.'

Ironically, behind this sophisticated salesman lurked the lad from special school who felt out of his depth. It was a diffidence that has never left him.

I find it incredible that a board of directors actually think I know about anything very much. I am still working class when I go into that scene. They never know it, but I am. Even after all these years it is still not the comfort zone for me. The comfort zone for me is a room full of disabled people.

To help companies comply with the DDA, Friend devised a customer service audit. Physical access audits existed, but there was nothing that measured customer service at every stage of a disabled person's contact with a company or organisation, whether on the phone or website, in the office or shop, or making a complaint. Rankin's audit report – Friend has never liked writing reports – would be 'topped and tailed' by Friend, who added options for the client to adopt –'essential', 'recommended' or 'desirable'. He would then discuss them with the client. Rankin remembers the vivid, easy-to-understand, arguments he would use to drive home the business advantages of accommodating disabled people: for example, how he, his wife and family get through so many pairs of shoes a year, but neither they nor the rest of his family would go into a shoe shop that was inaccessible to wheelchairs, on principle. 'Yet always this humour was bubbling under the surface. They never felt they were being lectured.' Churchill and Friend did customer service audits for many clients, including Buckingham Palace and the Natural History Museum, and trained staff in customer service too.

As Friend brought in more business, he had to take on more help. He moved his office from his home near Hatfield to business premises in Welwyn Garden City in 1998. The number of associates rose from two to fifteen. They were all disabled and most of them were freelance, such as David Bonnett, who had established himself as the leading disability architect. They could be working on several contracts at the same time. 'We were always laughing, enjoying ourselves, but working very, very hard,' says David Sindall, one of the associates.

Friend was not your typical businessman. Being a pioneer and from a social services background, he did what he liked. There was no long-term strategic planning, no financial forecasts. Even by 2000, the products of the company's away-day thinking were stuffed in a drawer until the next time, though they stayed in his head. There were cash flow problems. Rankin remembers how Churchill and Friend charged much less than Duckworth's larger business, Disability Matters. When his own associates charged £475 a day, Friend would take only £75. Told he should be taking more, he would say, 'Well, we can't charge more to the client and I'm not going to ask the associate to work for less.' He did some work free of charge. Essentially, he was not out to get rich. What has always driven him is the desire to make a difference and to do it better than other people. Fortunately, Sue is also 'about rights'. He may have ended up making a very good living in the mainstream, but he has used his skills to improve job opportunities and life chances for disadvantaged people – chances he himself had lacked.

Friend is also choosy about his clients. His business has been built on relationships and good will. Life is too short to work with people he does not like, he says. He has been known to turn down clients, not because he has too much work – his inability to say no is a well-known weakness – but because he distrusts their intentions. 'I don't want to be with people who are playing a game. This isn't a game. We are talking here about human rights.'

A third characteristic of Friend, which makes people blanch, is his habit of attending an important business meeting or making a public speech without notes. Apparently, it almost always works. Many times, pitching for a job, he would say, 'We'll just wing this one.' A few years ago, the apogee of his public speaking was reached at a black tie event in Ireland, where he was the after-dinner speaker. He admitted afterwards that he could not think of a theme over dinner and it was only as he wheeled on to the platform that the phrase 'meaningful activity' came into his head. He talked for 20 minutes, with examples, about how there was no point in setting up work schemes for disabled people unless they led to real jobs. At the end, he got his first standing ovation.

More recently, he shed some light on his idiosyncratic method of preparation; the occasion was the launch of a disability network and programme at the Ministry of Defence, attended by army bigwigs, officials and disabled employees. Interviewed shortly before it, he explained:

> I have for the last day and a half on and off been thinking about this afternoon. It's important. So I am preparing mentally. I don't know what will come out of my mouth when I start. But the minute the first words come out, I'll know what the direction is and I shall take it. Some of that will occur when I see the people.

Unlike most of us, he is nervous not about what he will say, but about whether he will deliver what is expected of him. That is why he always asks for feedback or to see the speaker evaluations. He is looking to get the top score; that shows him he has delivered.

Although Churchill and Friend remained a small company, Friend's reputation as a business leader was growing and he subscribed to the Institute of Directors. By the mid-1990s, he was a member of the Prince's (Prince of Wales) Trust disability advisory committee and a trustee – later a consultant – of the Disability Partnership. He was still an associate of the Employers' Forum, whose membership had grown to 177. In the campaign for a Disability Discrimination Act, the Employers' Forum had helped confound the Conservative government's belief that employers would oppose the bill by working with the Confederation of British Industry to actively support it. The Act called for a National Disability Council to advise the government and, in 1996, both Scott-Parker and Friend were appointed to it. Although the council was derided by disability campaigners as a substitute for an independent commission, it did draw up a code of practice for customer services and produce 'good practice' guides for small businesses and others. It ended in 2000 when Labour set up the Disability Rights Commission. The following year Friend received an OBE.

Friend's interest in the impact of disability law on small businesses took him to the USA on a Winston Churchill Fellowship in 1999. He found that the Americans with Disabilities Act 1990 and generous funding were offset by bureaucratic red tape and federal-state tensions. The unemployment rate for disabled people was no better than the UK. What worked, Friend saw, was a grassroots scheme that matched the requirements of the employer to a disabled job seeker. His findings reinforced his belief in the business case: 'Policies have their place, but employers have businesses to run. We must show how we can improve their profits by placing disabled people who can provide great job performance. It can be done.'

Friend was now in his fifties and planning to retire at 60. His was not a business that could be passed down to a non-disabled offspring; he needed to find a disabled business partner who could eventually take over. He decided against joining Stephen Duckworth, who was now into other areas, such as insurance claims and return-to-work programmes. His hopes were pinned on David Sindall, a freelance associate who worked almost full-time from 1998 to 2000 and became his right-hand man. When the plan fell through and Sindall departed to the Disability Rights Commission, Friend took it badly. Sindall thinks he let Friend down, but he saw himself as forever number two. 'It was always going to be the Phil show. Phil would always be calling the biggest shots on the work.'

Friend, who sets great store by loyalty, thinks disloyalty brings out the worst in him. 'I invest hugely in people,' he says. 'I see myself as a swan – it's for life.' In fact, he himself has been known to let people down – not following up on a promise, putting down a colleague in front of another professional, seeming to abandon his first business partner, Steve Regis. But most of the time he is there for family, friends and work colleagues. He was a mentor for Graham Bool when Bool was starting up as a freelance photographer. He stood by Simon Minty, then a freelance associate, at a time of crisis. Minty, a former trainer at Barclays Bank and a media professional, who loved being in front of a live audience, succumbed to various pressures, including incessant questions about his impairment (restricted growth), and started having panic attacks before a training course. He took two months off, but when he came back it happened again. 'I phoned up Phil and said, "I can't do it." It was all overwhelming. And he said, "You don't have to do it, that's fine. But I would ask that you go in and speak to the client."' Once Minty had been let off the hook by the client, seen the room and checked the delegate list, he was able to do the job. Gradually, his confidence returned. Now, after years of experience and watching Friend, he can comfortably convert a 10-minute keynote speech into a 35-minute one at a moment's notice. Still, Friend might have fired him. 'He could have said, "Sorry, mate, you've let me down two or three times, you're too much of a risk," but that didn't happen.'

When Sindall left, Friend turned to Minty. They trusted each other; they shared jokes; they updated each other every day, and on Friday afternoons after work they often debated disability issues. One of their ongoing arguments stems from Minty's background in business and Friend's in social services: 'Are we a social firm that makes money (Friend's view), or are we a business with a social purpose (Minty's)?'

With work pressure getting him down, Friend negotiated a sell-out to Grass Roots, the business development company. Driving back from a meeting with Grass Roots in Birmingham one day, Minty felt angry because he had been marginalised in the conversation. He did not want to work for a big company, even if they would have him. He thought the turnover of C&F could be increased fairly easily. Was Friend serious about selling, he asked. When Friend said yes, Minty suggested there was an alternative: he could buy Friend out. The car swerved all over the road, according to Friend's version of the story. By the time they reached London it had been agreed that Minty would buy half the business now and the other half in five years' time. They celebrated the formal agreement in August 2001, drinking apple juice from plastic cups. (Seven years later, to Friend's disappointment, Minty had still not bought him out.)

In the meantime, the Friend-Minty partnership brought swift results. With tighter business management, expansion of the reasonable adjustments service and regular growth in training and consultancy, turnover increased rapidly. 'Simon has brought rigour and discipline,' Friend acknowledged.

On a personal level, the partnership has run well, lubricated by affection and humour. Friend, ever the performer, encouraged Minty's broadcasting and performance side. Abnormally Funny People, the comedy group Minty directs, has performed for merchant banks. The company has also staged 'disability dialogues' in which disabled people interact with each other and the business audience. But, inevitably, there have been tensions. It was difficult for a forceful founder to take criticism from someone nearly 25 years younger. And in the early days Minty had to fight hard to be treated as co-director and not *de facto* number two – 'Oh, Simon can pick up that and write some notes for you.' He used to physically prevent himself from holding a pen at a meeting. He also objected to Friend doing *pro bono* work on the grounds that good professional work should be rewarded. Most seriously, they disagreed over how to manage an employee with mental health issues.

The company was restructured and renamed. Churchill, Minty & Friend remained the training and consultancy side of the business; CMF Management Services, with Minty in charge, became responsible for the reasonable adjustments service. Lloyds TSB, the original client, was joined by BT and Royal Mail, bringing some 300,000 employees under the CMF umbrella. Nearly 80 per cent of employees who became disabled have stayed in their jobs. Other companies joined and the service was modified to include one-off cases. All this expansion required more staff and more office space. At one point there were four different offices in Welwyn Garden City, before the reasonable adjustments service moved to London and the training and consultancy side followed in 2006.

New disability legislation brought fresh opportunities. Public sector bodies, such as local councils, government departments and hospitals, now have a duty to promote disability equality, which means drawing up an action plan and involving disabled people. CMF, renamed Minty & Friend, has been on hand to help. It also advises employers on how to manage long-term illness and disability, and it has moved into complex work, such as reviewing how the National Blood Service operates.

Relieved of sole responsibility, Friend has had more freedom to pick and choose what he wants to do. He concentrates on high-level consultancy, keynote speeches, and work which keeps him in touch with disabled employees. He has advised the government, worked with the London Development Agency, and sat on committees of the employers' group, the National Employment Panel, seeking to ease the path of disabled people into work.

His Dining with a Difference idea, started with James Partridge in 2000, had a mixed reception. Eating high on the hog while talking about disability dismayed some disability professionals, but many top managers have left a dinner thinking differently. Royal Mail and Barclays Bank are among the companies that have changed their policies. John Varley, group chief executive of Barclays, started consulting his disabled employees and acting upon what they said. He has become a key figure in the Employers' Forum, which now represents some 25 per cent of the UK workforce. 'We softened him up,' Friend boasted.

Kate Nash, then director of the disability network, RADAR, and a disability campaigner, helped host some of the dinners. She thought the way Friend was not afraid to share his experiences of impairment was a lesson for other disabled people. By chance, Friend heard from Nash that the chair of RADAR would soon be vacant. He applied for the job and got it, in February 2005. 'The idea of being involved in a major charity was in my head, so the opportunity comes and I grab it.' He wanted new challenges. He understood the connection between social justice and disability and RADAR could give him a platform for challenging disabled people themselves to be 'more assertive' about their rights.

A small organisation, RADAR has always punched above its weight because of its influence with MPs and Whitehall. In tune with Friend's career, RADAR is active on the employment front. Its current chief executive, Liz Sayce, is a member of a government commission looking at ways of increasing skills, productivity and employment, 'particularly for those from disadvantaged backgrounds'.

There is still a long way to go, even without a recession. According to the Department of Work and Pensions, the proportion of disabled adults of working age who were in jobs rose from 1998 to 2006 compared with static or falling percentages in other countries, though less than 48 per cent of disabled adults are employed compared to almost 75 per cent overall. Yet a think-tank supported by the Joseph Rowntree Foundation reported at the end of 2007 that 40 per cent of disabled people aged 25–retirement were in work, little different to the late 1990s. Friend thinks that a lot has been done to change employers' attitudes, but the people who are left unemployed are those with severe impairments or 'socially unacceptable' ones like learning difficulties or mental health issues.

> James Purnell [former Work and Pensions Secretary] says he wants 1 million people off incapacity benefit and I say to him, 'All the good disabled people are already in jobs, but the people you are trying to get off IB are the most profoundly disabled, and that's your real challenge.'

A minor stroke in 2005 set Friend back temporarily and necessitated moving house. He is winding down his workload, though he plans to spend more time on RADAR. He claims credit for strengthening the charity, getting rid of debts and appointing new trustees. RADAR sees itself as 'the leading pan-disability charity'. Its aims for disabled people – securing the right to independent living, reducing poverty, increasing the number of leaders in their own communities, and helping people manage their money – correspond with Friend's. 'The challenge for whoever works alongside Phil is being able to take his huge energy and distil it down into workable solutions and keep him excited about things as well,' said David Sindall in 2005. Friend is into his second three-year term as chair, proof that RADAR has done better than other charities in keeping his enthusiasm on board and taming his impatience.

In 2007 Friend became a Fellow of the Royal Society of Arts. He has impressed the business community by creating a successful business from scratch. 'He's certainly established a niche market and delivered a very successful brand, one that is synonymous with excellence in training, one you can trust,' says Kay Allen, now head of social policy and inclusion at the Royal Mail. She saw proof of this consistency at the annual Business in the Community awards, where Friend habitually sat at the winners' table.

He has used his disability and his selling skills to change attitudes in a hard-nosed sector. 'Alongside Steve Duckworth, he's proved there's a legitimate role for a disabled entrepreneur who makes a career business out of helping institutions to become disability-confident in delivering rights,' says Susan Scott-Parker. 'In most countries, there are no such entrepreneurs. They just don't exist.' She adds: 'What people don't know is how many behind the scenes encounters this man has had with senior men and women in business. He has never left a business leader untouched.'

Simon Minty sees Friend's imprint wherever he goes. When he says he's from the company, 'They go, "Ooh, I know Phil Friend. He did this speech and he completely changed the way I thought about this. He really made me think."'

From an unpromising start, Friend has done well for himself by doing good for others. This is important to him. 'I say to my own children, "Did you leave it better than you found it?" And that's what I think I've been able to do.'

# PETER WHITE: BROADCASTER

*Photopraph taken by Sam Frost*

'Longevity is expensive,' said Peter White, the BBC's disability affairs correspondent, introducing a debate about the crisis in social care.

> And before you think, 'Nothing to do with me, then, I'm young and in bouncing good health, and my parents and relatives are fit as fiddles,' the chances are, whatever method the UK chooses to fund social care, most of us will end up paying something towards it or becoming a carer ourselves.

His voice, familiar to BBC Radio 4 listeners, was authoritative, relaxed, with a hint of a twinkle in it. He touched the right buttons – heart and purse – to attract his listeners.

The debate, in May 2007, was the first of seven planned around the UK by such eminent organisations as the King's Fund. White wanted *You and Yours*, Radio 4's consumer affairs programme, to be in at the start, giving social care the attention it deserved. Eight months later, in January 2008, there was a month of follow-up programmes, building on published reports and ensuring that politicians heard the views of consumers. Goaded by widespread concern, the Government launched a consultation about the funding of social care.

The May debate was a carefully choreographed mix of statistics, experiences and comments from panellists such as Sir Derek Wanless, author of a key report on care funding, and the disabled comedian Liz Carr. The audience asked questions too. White held the reins, keeping everyone focused on how to bridge the gap between a spiralling demand for services and not enough money. Later he pressed the Care Services Minister, Ivan Lewis, for a spending commitment.

Nothing strange about all that, you might say; another in-depth Radio 4 programme, whose professionalism can be taken for granted. But what a new listener would not know is that Peter White is blind. If you point him at a window, he can see only a faint variation of light and dark, and if you switched on the electric light, he wouldn't be able to tell. He uses a white cane when he travels from his home in Winchester to London, or anywhere else (a cane is 'so uncluttered', he says, compared to a dog or a navigational device). At Broadcasting House, he accepts the arm of his broadcast assistant to steer him round office furniture, through the swing doors and into the lift. For many years he relied on personal readers and a heavy Braille typewriter to do his job. Now he uses a portable Braille Lite machine, which is fitted with a Braille display and keyboard, and a voice synthesiser. It allows him to download documents procured by his assistant on a personal computer, send his written scripts, or send and receive messages. Once, standing on the

Great Wall of China, looking for a flat surface for his Braille Lite, he was heard to say, 'Ah, yes, now is there a bit of wall round here?'

White has particular assets that help him as a journalist and broadcaster. What he calls, disparagingly, his 'grasshopper mind' can pick up all sorts of information, including dates and mobile phone numbers, and store them away. It helps him win pub quizzes – though he has been known to forget less important appointments. 'You could give him a brief five minutes before an interview and he'd go in and it would be fantastic,' says Cheryl Gabriel, producer of Radio 4's *In Touch*, the programme for blind people White has presented for over 35 years.

White's hearing and intuition can record what his eyes don't see, so he will notice, for example, that someone has fallen asleep in a meeting – 'At what point did we lose Jessica?' – or judge someone's attitude from their voice and body movements.

He also reads Braille very quickly, using two hands simultaneously; they run down a page transferring two sets of messages to his brain at the same time. Blind people who read Braille usually use one hand. A few use two, but hardly ever concurrently. This isn't dexterity, thinks White, because, apart from playing the piano, he is clumsy with implements. He ascribes it to brain–finger coordination. 'I'd be just as good at reading with my elbows. What I obviously have is something up there sorting stuff out quite well.'

White's weekly workload is heavy, varied, and often stressful. Fortunately, he needs only five hours sleep a night. One Monday in June 2007, for example, he was preparing for his phone-in programme *Call You and Yours* and his special guest, Sir Menzies (Ming) Campbell, then leader of the Liberal Democrats. He had to mug up on Campbell and Lib-Dem policies, write an introduction to the programme, the script for the interview, and three different trailers (he disapproves of presenters who make do with the same trailer). That day, he also helped to plug an unexpected gap in *In Touch*, talking with Gabriel and making phone calls. Travelling home on the train, he wrote a rough script for the programme to be handed to her next morning. On Tuesday, he presented *Call You and Yours* around midday, politely questioning Ming's age for the job and whether his style was old fashioned, before moving on to policies. After the routine post-mortem, it was back to working on *In Touch* with Gabriel, hurriedly amending the script on his Braille Lite. By 2.30 they were in the studio to record the 19-minute programme, which included two guests, and then into another studio by 4pm to finish the editing, ready for the programme to go out that evening. On Wednesday, he prepared for *You and Yours* and on Thursday, as the BBC's disability affairs correspondent – a job virtually created for him in 1995 – he co-presented the programme. He interviewed Lord (Patrick) Jenkin (a former Secretary of State for Health and Social Services under Margaret Thatcher) about how contaminated blood came to be used in the NHS, leaving some haemophiliac patients with AIDS. He suggested Jenkin had been giving evidence to an independent inquiry because he felt a 'bit of guilt' that it had happened on his watch. Then there was a studio discussion about the government's strategy on energy and waste and, finally, a mention of how the Teasmade teamaker was back on sale – White recalled trying to find one for his mum when she was old and frail. Also on Wednesday and Thursday, he scripted and recorded voice-overs for two programmes based on his interviews with 30 children who had attended London's Olympics bid in Singapore. On Friday, there was a party to celebrate his sixtieth birthday.

Of all the TV channels and radio stations White has worked on, he is most at home on Radio 4. He feels 'extremely passionate' about its right to exist. It produces quality programmes that are probably unique in the world, he thinks, and it gives him room to spread his wings. Apart from his regular slots, you may find him presenting mainstream programmes like *Pick of the Week*, or a series he has devised himself, such as the award-winning *Blind Man's Beauty*, or the long-running *No Triumph, No Tragedy*, where people like the writer John Mortimer, the actor Christopher Reeve or the commentator Rush Limbaugh have discussed the impact of their disability.

As an interviewer, 'he can get people to tell him anything', says writer and producer, Kevin Mulhern, who is visually impaired himself.

> I've heard some of his interviews and thought, 'My God, Peter, how did you get that?' Because he doesn't ask. Somehow they offer. He gives more of himself in an interview than I ever would. Sue MacGregor does the same thing. And Eddie Meyer does it. You feel they are being a bit vulnerable.

This ability to communicate with people and make compelling programmes has brought him several Sony Radio Academy awards and an MBE (Member of the Order of the British Empire). In 2007 White and Gabriel won a One World Broadcasting Trust award for a documentary in their *Unseen China* series, about a domestic worker in Beijing who returned to her village to see her children for the first time in two years. White was named Sony Speech Broadcaster of the Year in 2001, beating the *Today* programme's John Humphrys.

Of all the things he does, White is happiest presenting live phone-ins. He is interested in how people form their ideas from their experiences, he respects what they say, and he can draw out a point if they get muddled.

Colleagues may flinch at the lack of structure, but for White it brings freedom and risk. 'I love phone-ins. I grew up in local radio and I got used to swinging by the seat of my pants.' There are forms of radio, he says, where you should not know what is going to happen next. 'You've invited people to call. You don't invite people to your house and then tell them exactly what they are going to do.'

White never says no to work. 'I often think "How the hell are you going to fit all that into one day?"' says Gabriel. When he's not broadcasting, he is writing articles, chairing a disability conference or travelling round the country as a guest speaker. It's the mindset of a lifetime freelance. The pressure that goes with the independence suits him and he prides himself on his good health.

How did a blind man get to this? White was a pioneer way back in 1971 and, even now, there are only a handful of visually impaired people in broadcasting. His story is not of a disabled man who found a purpose, but a man who was hooked before he even knew it.

White was born into a working-class family in June 1947. His parents, Don and Joan White, lived in a prefab in Winchester, which they later exchanged for a house on a council estate. Don was an impulsive man, witty and convivial, though he also had a nasty temper. Clever, and independently minded, he acquired many interests and unorganised bits of information. He wanted to be a printer, but had to make do with being a carpenter, which he said he hated, even though he acquired a reputation as a fine craftsman. Joan, who had been a secretary in a magazine company before her marriage, was level-headed, organised, house-proud; given to common-sense solutions and silent resistance if remonstrance failed.

It was a one-in-a-million chance that White would be born blind like his older brother, Colin; there was no history of blindness in the family. For his parents, he thinks his diagnosis was more of a disappointment than a shock, because they had guessed already. Ignoring the meagre help of 'professionals', the admonitions of family and friends and the social expectation that blind people turn into basket weavers, living at home or in an institution, they just got on with bringing up their children. 'They somehow contrived to give us a normal, stable, happy home life,' says White in his autobiography, *See It My Way* (1999). 'If there was a trick in it at all, I think it was that they saw us as children who happened to be blind, rather than blind people who happened to be children.'

So the boys were not spoiled or overly protected. They got cuts and bruises like other kids, White perhaps more because he was hyperactive, with a strong need to explore and take risks unmatched by his navigational skills.

Even at home he found it bewildering: 'The map in my head somehow never corresponded with the ground beneath my feet.' Colin, on the other hand, who had a little more sight, could navigate really well and perfected his independent travel so that he could go from home to town, and ultimately anywhere he wanted. White was torn between the desire to do it too and the embarrassment of failing. But his brother's achievements drove him on. He said later that having someone four years older than himself, who set the standard and knocked aside obstacles, was the best bit of luck in his life. 'For many blind children, the brake on them is not their own low ability but the low expectations of others.' In this case the expectations were high. If Colin could do it, why not Peter?

Colin also excelled at anything that required coordination, such as Meccano or tying his shoelaces. Peter did not. Indeed, at primary school, Peter was threatened with an extended stay in the infants because tying your shoelaces was the condition for advancing to the juniors. It took a summer holiday of repeated showing and practice – and tears and tantrums – before he succeeded. When his father gave him a tricycle, he couldn't get the hang of pedalling. His father gave up, saying the kid would never ride a bike. But at lunchtime next day, he came home to a hurtling shape, hunched over the handlebars. Peter, determined to succeed, had been practising all the morning. Later, the same pattern was repeated with a bike.

This stubborn determination could also work negatively. In the 1950s blind children, like other disabled children, were sent away to segregated schools that were supposed to cater for their special needs. Colin had been sent away, aged five, to a 'Sunshine Home' in Newton Abbot and then to 'big' school in Bristol. His parents acquiesced in the official decision, probably persuaded that it was 'for the best'. Colin would return for the holidays with lurid tales of childish cruelty – boys immersed in water tanks and girls' heads forced down the loo. Peter, aged four, was frightened. He already had a vivid imagination – he would pretend for days that he was away, travelling on a train, or he would impersonate people, or even Sally, the Alsatian. He was upset by the house move and missed Colin, and he realised his turn would soon come to be sent away. He started exhibiting anxiety symptoms – following his mother round the house, getting her to return on various pretexts after he had been put to bed, recoiling at the last moment from a practice stay with his favourite aunt and uncle, vomiting in the car as it approached Bristol, when they all went to visit a sick Colin. Of course he couldn't prevent the fearsome thing happening. On his last night at home, in September 1952, as he was tucked up in bed, he asked his mum if there was a god. She said they would explain all that to him at school. 'The following day I was to discover that if indeed there was a god, he regarded the Bristol Royal School of Industry for the Blind as a no-go area.'

Braced up: Peter White, aged nine, with his older brother,
Colin, and their mother, Joan, in 1956. Photograph by Don White.

He was thrust into a Dickensian world of starched, hard-voiced nurses, long corridors, rough-textured school uniform, insufficient food and that mostly horrible, barely existing hygiene (he once returned for the school holidays with undiagnosed and untreated impetigo) and an army regime. 'How would this nervy, mouthy, emotional, manipulative little boy manage?' he asked in his autobiography. Even when he had established himself, the beginning of term always brought on tears and vomiting, and the odd visits from his parents created a fever-pitch excitement and anxiety. The propensity to vomit when upset, uncertain or excitedly happy remained well into his secondary school. Today he still cannot smell mothballs without shedding a tear – when his 'private clothes' mysteriously appeared on his bed at the end of term, they smelled of mustiness and mothballs.

He found solace in his mouth organ and ingratiated himself with an older boy under whose wing he could shelter (Colin being a far-off junior). He also wheedled himself into the affections – and on one occasion the bed – of the only kindly nurse, though she left soon afterwards.

Best of all, he found he could escape to happier worlds through reading, an opportunity he wants all blind children to have, hence his passionate support now for the Right to Read campaign. Once he had mastered Braille, which he did in his second term, he was off, ordering as many as 40 books at a time from the National Library for the Blind after 'Miss Miller' signed his application form. Not needing a torch, he read illicitly under the bed-clothes after the rest of the dormitory had gone to sleep and then woke at 5am to continue. He also read when the others were doing handicrafts, at which he had rapidly shown zero aptitude. He ran through *Bambi*, *Doctor Dolittle* and *The Wind in the Willows*, discovered Enid Blyton, and then Big-gles and Bulldog Drummond. The Mallory Towers series was a surprising favourite. Not so Bob Morris, the blind child detective, who encompassed all the myths of blindness and was hated by everyone. In the precious holidays he also read, especially when Colin was not there to battle at cricket or share crazes like Bagatelle, which they made into a game of precise skill, or Monopoly, using home-embossed cards and money. Later, stuck at home because he feared to explore outside, he also tinkered on the piano and cre-ated complicated mental games involving cricket scores and Braille dice.

The fact that White could read Braille so fluently, using two hands at the same time, became his passport to fame as well as knowledge. The school entered him for the National Braille-Reading Competition when he was seven, and he took the prize for his age group, as he did for the next three years. It brought him into contact with famous trophy presenters like the Queen Mother or T. S. Eliot, whose presence ensured media coverage. White found himself on BBC Radio Newsreel and the *Today* programme in 1958, unwittingly fulfilling a dream he was yet to have. Radio was already important to him, both at home and as another refuge from school. By the time he was seven, he was listening to almost anything – sport, music, plays, comedy, even political discussions. By giving information to everyone, radio helped to even the score for blind people. Today he still believes radio has been more important for blind people than anything specially invented for them.

Another success in his early years at Bristol was acting. He had talent – including the ability to get the best part. 'I soon learnt that there was a subtle art to this, which involved pushing yourself forward to the extent that you weren't overlooked, but never so much that you annoyed the teacher in the process.' He played the title role of Rumpelstiltskin on his sixth birthday, and then Prince Charming in *Cinderella*, his manner making up for deficien-cies in the beauty department – White was short and had buck teeth. After that, he usually managed to get the lead. Being centre stage held no fears for him; he enjoyed showing off, whether it was in a school play or performing feats of memory at home.

The school, for all its faults, did not, he thinks, undermine self-respect. Everyone was blind to some degree, yet they all sat exams, took part in plays and competed at sports days. No one had to apologise. 'I just wonder how much self-respect blind children at mainstream schools have when they have to sit out games because there's no provision for them, or when they're constantly described as having "special needs".' He goes further, challenging the inclusive thinking that now pervades government policy and has brought the closure of many 'special schools'. Given the small number of sight-impaired children in the UK, about 25,000, he backs special education – the modern, enlightened kind – arguing that in a mainstream school there must inevitably be a shortage of expensive equipment, Braille books and trained teachers. If there was an ideal, local, inclusive school, he would choose that, but, meanwhile, he is not prepared to give up the advantages of special education for an inferior type of integration. When he learned, years later, that the blind, seven-year-old child of a colleague was learning Braille at mainstream school from a teacher who was also learning Braille, he wanted to scream. 'That's not integration. That's not inclusion.'

Aged 11, White exchanged one special school for another. Worcester College for the Blind (now New College Worcester) was a hotbed of intellectual talent, drawing boys from all over England and giving them a free education with public school pretension. Colin had already gone to Worcester so the pressure was on Peter to follow. He was one of two boys put in by his school for the entrance exam that year and at the three-day residential test which followed, his enthusiasm, sociability and strength in English subjects – perhaps also his reputation – weighed more than his clumsy eating, untidiness and ignorance of decimals. A new world opened up for him; already he could discern the light and space at Worcester compared with the dank darkness of Bristol.

The competitive, academic atmosphere was in some ways just what he needed. He had 'reasonably' well-qualified teachers, 'who seemed to know a little more than I did', and a big Braille library he could explore endlessly. His class had only nine pupils and he found people who could 'even' beat him in an argument. On the negative side was an intellectual arrogance he unconsciously acquired himself and bullying prefects. Exam results took precedence over social skills; no one ever thought of preparing blind boys for job interviews. Contact with girls, sighted girls, was limited to weekly dancing lessons or sex-charged school balls. White admits he was 'well behind the door myself when sex appeal was dished out'. His teenage years were mainly given over to sexual fantasies of an ill-informed kind – probably not so very different from many sighted teenage boys in single-sex schools.

Yet Worcester offered new freedoms. There were oceans of spare time to spend in the library and no limits to roaming outside the school. It was only when White and a lorry collided on the main road that the school instituted gradations of freedom, much to the irritation of everyone, including White. But he had made a mark, in a way, and he started to make others. The prefects vied with each other as to who could give out the most punishments, so White's year formed their own fraternity to break the rules. For a time, White held the title of most punished in one term; his total of 45 represented three punishments every four days. As they worked up the school, his group gravitated from dumb insolence interspersed with escapades to a refusal to dish out punishments themselves. Hauled before the headmaster in his final year for issuing only one punishment, White argued that there was something wrong with the school if you couldn't keep order without punishments. His year, he felt, was the first to have grasped that the world was changing.

Questioning authority became White's hallmark, developed, he thinks, when he could no longer be best at everything and needed something else at which to excel. But it ran deeper than that. Worcester's rules and customs nurtured a rebellion that became a cornerstone of his life. 'My instinctive reaction is that as soon as something seems to be accepted without question by any group of people, I want to question it.' Like his father, he sought his own answers.

He became editor of the school magazine, jettisoning the usual fare for features about politics, sex and religion. The one opposing compulsory chapel attendance had to be cut, but he got away with the rest, quadrupled the circulation and won that year's prize for citizenship.

White's atheism brought him into conflict with the headmaster. The head had cleverly outflanked the prefects' plan to liberalise school traditions by giving them permission to go to the pub. But, led by White, they still held out for free worship. In the end, White stood alone, unexpectedly losing the argument when his atheist father came down in favour of school rules. Still, in his final term he was allowed to withdraw from chapel. Not realising this included daily assembly, he went along as usual. The headmaster turned him away. White asked: 'What if I have a sudden conversion, sir?' The head barked, 'Then you see me first.'

Intellectual victories like this came comparatively easily to White; life choices proved more difficult. Armed with A levels including an A grade in History, he went from Worcester to Southampton University to study law, which held out prospects, rather than his real love, history. The grasshopper mind soon rebelled. Add to that the shock of no longer being a big fish in a small pool, wanting to be accepted, having to do everything for himself – including getting to lectures a mile away with the right books – having to find readers, and using a non-Braille typewriter – it all proved too much.

He began to miss lectures and hand essays in late. Official help for disabled students barely existed in those days and anyway he wanted to be independent. To friends he kept up his bubbly facade. Then he flunked his first year exams, mentally freezing in front of his typewriter. During the summer vacation he agreed to retake them and scraped through. But the same pattern recurred in the second year and he left the university. Back home in the summer of 1968, seeing his parents disappointed and bewildered, and with few friends to talk to, he hit rock bottom. 'I have never experienced before or since such despair.'

At last, an officer at the Royal National Institute for the Blind introduced him to Community Service Volunteers, who asked him to run a project in York that recruited disaffected teenagers to help the community by repainting a room or building an adventure playground. When White arrived in the scruffy, smelly, basement office, there were no volunteers, no jobs, and one other organiser, Lynda. From this unpromising start, Youth Action York, surprisingly, prospered. White found he had a way with all sorts of people. He offered the teenagers beer, darts and freedom from adult restraint, and they joined up. He persuaded local social services and voluntary organisations to produce projects and funding. And he enjoyed chatting up elderly customers and hearing about their life experiences – it was history. The local newspaper exploited his blindness on its front page and he built brand recognition by cycling round with Lynda on a tandem. The year restored his self-respect on one level, though he had still not got laid.

In the autumn of 1969, he returned to university to embark on a politics, economics and sociology degree at Kent. Some things were better this time: he was three years older, socially more at ease, and he made some good friends. One of them, Godfrey Davis, alerted him to his self-pity – the blind man who wanted to be treated like everyone else, yet exploited his disability to get help or avoid unpalatable chores.

Nowadays, Davis remembers White's independence, even belligerence. One night, they were walking down the high street in Canterbury, three abreast, Davis, his girlfriend and White, when ribald comments about three in a bed issued from a dark alley. White turned into the alley and shouted, 'Why don't you fuck off?' Out of the alley emerged a small gang of Hell's Angels, ready for a punch up. One grabbed White by the collar. Undaunted, he demanded to be put down. 'I'm blind. I don't have my white stick with me, but if I did, I'd stick it right up your fucking nose.' The Hell's Angel turned to Davis for verification. 'Is he?' 'Yes.' The Hell's Angel let go. 'There isn't a copper in Kent who won't kick your arse if you don't fuck off,' persisted White. And without a word, they did. Davis thinks White would have done the same thing had he not been blind; he never minded getting into a fight in those days. 'He just didn't want to be treated as disabled.' And no one was going to make him do what he didn't want to do.

The trouble was White did not know what he did want to do. So the square peg kept forcing itself into the round hole. There were cheerfully outrageous moments at Kent, but failure dogged him. He dated Davis' girl-friend, not having one of his own. And, most importantly, the work was grinding to a halt. Alcohol helped to drown out reality, until one evening in the summer vacation his self-respect took a final battering: he vomited in the garden of his parents' friends. Back home, the truth came tumbling out with the tears. What he really wanted, he said, was to get into radio. Not that he had any idea how to do it.

The only bright spot in that vacation was meeting a student nurse in the local pub, Jo Daley. He remembers her as 'a girl who was as awkward, shy and as out of place as I was and, most miraculously of all, a girl who seemed to like me without wanting either to mother or nurse me'. Out of place he might have felt with girls, but he was in his element at the pub keyboard, a foaming pint beside him, belting out old numbers and trading quips with the customers. From his father, also a pub pianist, he had learned how to handle an audience, gaining experience from surreptitious trips to the pub in his Worcester days. On another pub trip, he plucked up the courage to ask Jo for a date. Once they started talking, they never stopped.

Drifting miserably in his second year at Kent, White had a stroke of luck. He heard on the radio that the BBC was opening more local stations, including Southampton, which was only nine miles from Winchester. He set off to doorstep BBC Radio Solent. Turned away by an unsympathetic receptionist, he was saved by his white stick. A pioneer producer of local radio, Ken Warburton, was planning a weekly programme for blind people, called *Link*. He phoned White and the upshot was that White joined Radio Solent on its second day, 1 January 1971. Untried, ignorant of pretty well everything, from blind politics and interviewing technique to operating the heavy Uher tape recorder or editing a tape, he became a freelance journalist. He was paid, at most, £3 a week (about £30 today). It was not the 'real', mainstream, broadcasting he had envisaged, but his disability had given him a toehold and he could live at home.

Local radio was interactive, involving the community. The audiences were small, but grew after 1974, when Solent started broadcasting on a me-dium waveband. Because there were amateur broadcasters needing training, it was easier for White to be accepted. His two main problems were control-ling modulation on the tape recorder via a circular control, and cutting and splicing tape. He solved the first by running a trial tape every time; as for the second, lacking the dexterity to edit tape, he made sure someone else would do it for him.

The great advantage of local radio for an unqualified beginner lay in its small, over-pressed staff and low budget. Programme ideas were welcomed and sooner or later you could get a 'break'. White's first non-disability interview involved an army captain who wanted to promote a recruitment day. The captain's appointment had been forgotten and there was no one available to do an interview, so White offered, little thinking he would be asked to do it live, with no preparation. Nevertheless, he carried it off without mishap. Then, after a training day in London, the BBC realised his publicity potential and BBC Television South made a programme about him. At one point he claimed he kept a hand on the green light that cued him to speak so he could feel the heat when it came on. It wasn't true, but it made a good story and no one exposed the fib. Out of the programme came more opportunities.

White needed the work. Jo was pregnant and after they married, in 1972, the rent for their flat was £8 a week (about £80 today). They couldn't make ends meet. Playing on the pub piano five nights a week brought him more money than radio journalism. Still, he had always wanted a family of his own. Having children, he later wrote, showed he was 'normal'; it also allowed him to give and to feel needed. He and Jo went on to have three children and foster another. His family has always been very important to him.

The combination of having Jo, a job that required travel, and little money did wonders for his navigational skills. He started hitchhiking alone, save for his charm and his white stick, and pulled off some remarkable coups. Once he arrived at a Cornish weekend cottage by car, coinciding with Jo and some friends, who had come by train and a taxi. When he started commuting to and from Waterloo, he became a familiar figure, clattering down the escalator with his Perkins Brailler (a Braille typewriter) swinging round his neck – like Mrs Thatcher's handbag, thought Robin Worman, another local radio pioneer and Solent producer. Worman would try to coincide with White on the rush hour platform so they could both get a seat. 'We worked out a system. I would hold Peter's arm, and Peter would produce his white stick and we just walked to the front of the queue. "Hello, Peter", people were saying.' Many years later, White's advice to anyone who had lost their sight was, 'Always go out with a smile. You get more help that way.'

In the early years at Solent, White still needed help. His idea for a *Talk About* programme was accepted, so Worman ferried him around Hampshire villages in the car to interview people. Faced with tongue-tied villagers, White developed his own technique for putting them at ease. 'When they suddenly realised he was blind, and started to fuss about, he just let them sit him down and then waited, quietly and calmly,' says Worman. 'They relaxed while they fussed about him.'

Within two years, White had a second mainstream series. His love affair with pubs spawned *In Time Gentlemen Please*, which sought out the best pub sing-song. Gradually, he made himself indispensable. He interviewed all sorts of people, from politicians and priests to starlets and actors, including the two Ronnies (Barker and Corbett) in their prime. He contributed humorous titbits, arts reviews, news and sports stories. His excellent general knowledge, ability to listen and grasp the gist of something, plus his pleasant, unplummy voice and sense of humour made him both versatile and reliable. While he could stand his ground against a producer to the point of stubbornness if he thought something important was being edited out, he also accepted advice. As he settled into the team, he got teased; Worman and Warbuton used to throw sugar on his Braille notes to confuse him.

Even so, it was not until 1983 that he was invited to present Solent's daily current events programme, a blend of high-level political interviews, combustible studio discussions and potentially libellous callers. Soon afterwards, he started presenting four hours of live sport on Saturday afternoons. He was in seventh heaven. He loved all sport, especially cricket, and he proved that a blind person could handle a control panel and four sound sources. Long before these jobs came along, though, low pay and a growing family had forced him to strike out into network radio. Perhaps blindness did delay his promotion in local radio; or, as he says himself, he may have feared failure and not pushed hard enough. Worman saw no signs of discrimination.

People who worked on *In Touch* recall it with great warmth. Started in 1961, it had become, by 1973, a 15-minute weekly programme for blind people, many of whom were elderly. It gave practical information and comment on products and services. Thena Heshel, its producer for 30 years, was both a street fighter and a mother hen. She would take on BBC bosses if their new ideas or time-tinkering threatened the programme. As an ex-journalist, she expected high standards, but she also fostered an unusual family atmosphere among her small team. Not blind herself, she still recognised the value of a radio forum for blind people and used reporters with visual impairments. When White sent her a tape of *In Time Gentlemen Please*, she invited him for an interview, expecting – as she said afterwards – to meet a boozy middle-aged man. Under her guidance he learned to produce a three-minute tape; he also developed his own strategy for getting focused answers, which he later passed on to blind trainee reporters. Heshel appreciated his ability to travel and his equable temperament. But what impressed her most was his ease at the microphone. Within a few months he became an occasional presenter of *In Touch* and then its main presenter. Once again his blindness had opened a door, and the freelance pay rates impressed him, but he still hankered after mainstream presenting. 'The last thing I wanted was to be seen as a blind man broadcasting to "his own kind",' he said.

In the early days of *In Touch*, Heshel had made the occasional controversial programme. Now, with White, two other young, visually impaired reporters, a benefits expert and a researcher, *In Touch* began to go for the jugular. They questioned how the big, powerful charities 'for' blind people spent their money and revealed the second-rate services and patronising attitudes of both blind and non-blind decision-makers. They helped to launch user-led groups. They took the government to task for inadequate and inconsistent benefits, fought for deaf-blind people to receive a mobility allowance, and played a leading role in securing the Disability Living Allowance (DLA) in 1992, which, for blind people, was their first disability entitlement. White rates DLA as the most important gain for disabled people in the past 30 years, notwithstanding civil rights.

He enjoyed the chase. His faintly amused disrespect for the blind establishment gave the younger Kevin Mulhern, also a rebel at Worcester, the confidence to campaign too. 'It was like a stockpot boiling in the background. The rest of the world was saying "These marvellous charities," and Peter was saying "Uh uh?" long before it was fashionable.' White's report in the early 1980s about the rich charity, Guide Dogs for the Blind – 'a dog orientated rather than people orientated organisation' – set off an almighty row. Eventually a representative from the charity came on the programme to deny the allegations, but over the years most of White's proposals were implemented. Heshel says:

> It was quite revealing to see how people who would bluster their way through an interview with a sighted reporter asking awkward questions were quite thrown when equally thrusting questions were put by somebody like Peter. He was extremely good.

*In Touch* was not all pulsating politics. They had fun doing quizzes. An off-air phone-in was introduced. White wove in his two loves, sport and family, and he made Braille, and the lack of access to it, a big issue. He began to understand how difficult it was for people who had become blind. It angered him that only 25 per cent of blind people of working age had a job and those that did were often victimised. Blind people, he also found, were not alike, which coloured his view of the 'disability movement'. '*In Touch* cured me forever of the myth that there is solidarity in disability.'

He started to travel abroad on his own for *In Touch* – to France, Belgium and then the USA. One conference in Washington elicited a relationship with a blind librarian that lasted several years. Today, far from being shy with women, he is thought to be quite a flirt.

By the mid-1980s, Heshel felt that someone with White's talents should be moving on, but she got nowhere when she suggested him to other pro-gramme makers. 'There was such prejudice at that stage,' she says. So White never got to chair a chat show like *Mid-Week*. Still, he had had news stories on *Today* and the *Six O'clock News* and, ironically, in the year after his father's death, the opportunities started to roll in. Heshel helped him with a series about sport in literature and secured him a slot on BBC Radio 4 for his first series of autobiographical talks. They were so funny and so successful that others followed and he was commissioned to write an autobiography.

Long before Heshel retired in 1994, White had found another source of income: television. It started when Martin Davison, an independent film-maker with a burning desire to improve the lives of disabled people and break into television, asked White to work with him. The plan was to make a series for Channel 4 Television that would prove the channel's commitment to disability as part of social diversity, and rival *Link*, the long-established ITV programme for disabled people. Davison, who was not disabled, would be the producer, while White would front the programme as presenter and editor. White had reservations. Presenting another disability show was not the direction he wanted to go. He was wary of disability politics, which was gaining strength in the 1980s as the call for civil rights legislation became more imperative. While he supported direct action on the streets, he disliked what he called the 'trendier aspects' – promoting solidarity by driving a wedge between disabled and non-disabled people, and wrong-footing non-disabled people with 'a tortuous debate about terminology'. Finally, he had no real experience of television. However, £300,000 of funding came through and the plan went ahead. He found he liked the discipline of ed-iting his copy to fit the pictures and he adapted quickly to being a presenter on television. But being editor was never realistic: he was not the boss and, although he could set up shots, he could not evaluate the result.

*Same Difference* set out to be interactive, employing disabled people to answer the phone lines and feed back views and experiences. White pro-duced many ideas himself. He used to arrive from Winchester carrying a supermarket bag of Braille notes, saying he had had an idea on the train. Together, he and Davison made three series of eight, weekly, programmes between 1987 and 1989. It was a strenuous time, but also a creative one. During a series White would be doing *In Touch* Monday to Tuesday and then *Same Difference* Wednesday to Sunday, for the half-hour transmission on Monday. From a glib start, said *Disability Now*'s television reviewer, Chris Davies, the programmes became 'hard-nosed and provocative' – sometimes more provocative than strictly honest. Davison remembers how White quizzed the operations manager of the Post Office about lack of access, declaring that 70 per cent of post offices were inaccessible. It was a guess. Afterwards White said, "He didn't gainsay me, did he?"

Davison and White had their differences. Davison wanted the programme to reflect the anger of disabled people; he wanted a blind Jeremy Paxman. White liked to delve, but antagonism was not his style, just as acquiescing to a party line was not his philosophy. Indeed, he would have preferred more humour. He came to see Davison as a 'control freak'. With relief, he decamped to *Link* when he was offered a full-year contract.

*Link* had been the thinking person's disability programme for many years, 'our voice', as Chris Davies put it. Davison called it 'worthy'. Mulhern, its producer, agreed. He had set up his own film company to employ more disabled people but, by 1989, he admits the programme was 'dreadful', too much in thrall to the 'disability lobby', and the life had gone out of it. White represented salvation. 'I just fell on Peter.' White could work fast compared to other disabled people, and he had the stamina to deliver, day in and day out. What he delivered were personal stories that made *Link* come alive again. He interviewed the blind veteran jazz pianist, George Shearing, who, like himself, had eked out a living on a pub piano; he talked to Sir Robert Winston about genetics before he had become a household name; and he asked religious leaders, like the late Cardinal Hume, what they thought about disability. Some members of the team resented the quality of White's work. Mulhern regrets now that he failed to deal with them.

In 1991, White became an occasional presenter of *Link*. For the first time in 20 years, there was a glitch in his freelance career. He still had *In Touch*. He picked up the Solent morning job again and got another, on the television station BBC South, where he could be seen every Monday night reading his Braille script. He churned out ideas, producing the quiz series, *It's Your Round*, and a prescient series for Channel 4, *Seeds of Discontent* (made with Davison), which tracked the UK disability lobby and compared it with other movements. He concluded that for the UK to copy the USA's anti-discrimination law would be a fatal mistake because it did not include support for the most vulnerable disabled people. He also launched the first of the now famous series *No Triumph, No Tragedy* exploring, among other things, what he saw as the hypocrisies surrounding disability. 'One of the most obvious ones is that whatever you say about your rights or what you can or can't do, all disabled people need various kinds of help. And it colours their lives.' He has little time for the social model, the disability movement's central belief that social barriers disable people rather than their physical or mental impairments. 'I've never met an intelligent disabled person who really believed in the social model,' he says.

He also questions the blanket rejection of euthanasia by many disabled people, who fear that others may make the decision for them. Disabled people have fought to control their lives, he argues. 'So is there not an inconsistency if the movement baulks at perhaps the most important right of all?' Surely, a framework of legislation and safeguards could be worked out, he wrote on the BBC's disability website, Ouch! Remarkably, the movement has never taken revenge on White for his unorthodox views – as it has on others – perhaps because he does not broadcast them.

In 1995, the year of the Disability Discrimination Act (DDA), White became the BBC's first disability affairs correspondent. The timing was no coincidence. Disability had been making headline news in the run-up to the Act, so a case could be made for having a designated reporter funded by BBC Radio 4 and BBC News. This was how Dave Harvey, a newly appointed chief producer at Radio 4, sold the idea to Radio 4's controller, Michael Green, and Today's editor, Roger Mosey. 'Peter personally made an impact by his tenaciousness combined with genuine charm and diplomacy,' remembers Mosey. He was disabled, but not politically 'chippy'.

Both Harvey and White found it frustrating that news stories of interest to a wide audience of disabled people never reached the mainstream news. Harvey's proposal to Green was bolstered by a two-month survey showing how many disability stories could have been used on mainstream programmes. White himself hesitated about the proposal, wary of losing his independence. 'He has a twinkly, almost poker-playing way of saying "tell me more,"' says Harvey, 'and he said a lot of encouraging things without saying yes.' But in the end he wanted the job, and got it. It gave him a route into mainstream news – he was the first blind person to produce reports for television news – and it opened up more opportunities for him as a freelance. But being a correspondent was always an anomaly. Correspondents are daily news reporters; White covered both news and magazine programmes, and when most of his funding moved to Radio 4 in 1998, so did most of the work. Geoff Adams-Spink is now the BBC's 'age and disability correspondent'.

In the early days, though, White was covering news all over the place, until the excitement of the DDA died down and airtime decreased. Getting ordinary disabled people on air was another problem. At a national conference in 1997 he urged disabled people to risk being interviewed. 'You have to get your hands dirty,' he said.

He himself made the most of 'Labour's first banana skin', as he called it. Having won the general election in 1997, Tony Blair was trying to cut the benefits bill, which, in the case of disability benefits, had doubled in less than ten years, and stamp out fraud. The plan included means testing for the Disability Living Allowance (DLA). Disabled people were checked without their knowledge; there were cases of people going to the post office to find their DLA had been cancelled. Outraged disability groups organised a protest and the Disabled People's Direct Action Network threw 'Blair's blood' over the gates of Downing Street. The role of an informed disability affairs correspondent came into its own. Other networks copied the BBC, says White. In March 1998, the Government backed down over DLA.

In 1998 James Boyle, the new controller of Radio 4, shook everyone up with a major rescheduling of programmes. *In Touch* survived, on the grounds that it had a distinct audience for which radio was crucial, and Peter White, though its time was cut. *In Touch* needs 30 minutes to do things in proper depth, argues White. 'What other programme can you think of on Radio 4 that has 20 minutes?' *Does He Take Sugar?* the sister disability programme, was axed, but Boyle transferred its content to an extended *You and Yours*, bringing disability into the mainstream and reaching 3 million listeners a week. White became a presenter, covering more than just disability stories, as did his new phone-in segment, *Call You and Yours*. Chris Burns, now executive editor of factual programmes, built up the links between disability and mainstream broadcasting and recognised the ability of people like White to bridge the two.

In many ways, the arrangement has proved ideal for White. Still freelance, he has the freedom to roam on other subjects and in other series, yet retains a base in disability journalism. He can go on being his own kind of campaigner, influenced not by dogma, but by the imperative to get a story – like the social care crisis – on air. 'I've always seen my job to tell people what is going on. They can decide what to do about it.'

His preference for specific campaigning, plus a crowded work schedule, helps explain why he has not been more active in trying to change the BBC's attitudes to portraying disabled people or recruiting more disabled employees. Also, head-on confrontation is not his style. He undermines prejudice by showing the job can be done. 'He sort of infiltrates,' says Geoff Adams-Spink, who is also chair of the BBC's Disabled Staff Forum.

White certainly wants to see disability portrayed more widely – he argued successfully for the Paralympics to be taken in-house and treated as an important sporting event, and has enjoyed covering four of them – but he is wary, as ever, of the fashionable view. 'I don't think you can force portrayal and I don't like the idea of writers being told what to write.' Writers write from experience, he says, adding with some exasperation, 'If disabled people want there to be a good series and good portrayal, they better bloody write it.'

For him, more jobs are the answer. He went out to bat for Gary O'Donoghue – 'Me, but 30 years younger' – arguing that if the BBC did not confirm a blind man with his skills and experience as a permanent po-litical correspondent, their commitment to equality would be shot. They did, in 2007, but then blotted their copybook a year later by not allowing O'Donoghue to report his lead story on the Ten O'Clock News (he later recieved a five-figure payout).

Like others in the BBC, White regrets that there is no longer a Disability Programmes Unit to train beginners and only two specialist programmes left, *In Touch* and *See Hear* (on BBC Two for deaf people) to nurture them. *In Touch* has no training budget; it cannot even fund its own researcher. The savings and staff cuts imposed on programme makers over the years are now worse than ever as the BBC struggles with a £2 billion shortfall in its licence fee income up to 2013 and tries to make itself more efficient and relevant in a digital age. Like other public bodies, it is now bound by the Disability Equality Duty of the Disability Discrimination Act 2005 to actively promote equal opportunities for disabled people. It managed to overshoot its target of 4 per cent of disabled employees by March 2008, but it never set a target for disabled managers – who could make all the difference – though there were management targets for women and people from ethnic minorities. White wants a 'realistic' target of 7–8 per cent of disabled people across the whole workforce. Properly supported, he thinks, they would change the ethos of the BBC, legitimise the public portrayal of disabled people, and offset the young employees in BBC News who have little experience of disability.

At the other end of the age spectrum, older BBC broadcasters have been made to feel insecure. White, with other presenters, was fired from Radio Solent in 2006 – although he was soon back with two series of celebrity interviews. He has no intention of retiring; having felt the despair of unem-ployment and found a job he loves, he has always kept himself impossibly busy. Not generally a man for regrets, he does wish he could have presented

*Today* or been a political correspondent like O'Donoghue. One of his latest ideas is a mainstream series that highlights books, now forgotten, which reflect the interests of their time. It would be his legacy, 'something that was mine, and when you thought of it, you thought of me'.

But his real legacy, even if he would not have it so, is to have been the BBC's first blind broadcaster. He has blazed a trail for disabled broadcasters – though not an easy one to follow if you are blind and don't have his Braille skills or his lack of dependence on technology. He has influenced the people he has worked with at the BBC, from Mark Thompson, the Director-General, downwards. Dave Harvey, now political editor at BBC Points West, says:

> I know an awful lot of jobbing reporters, presenters, editors, etc., who are now more senior ten years later, whose understanding of what it's like to be disabled, what the politics of disability are, and so on, were changed for the good by him.

Beyond the BBC he has made people think twice about the abilities of blind people. If you saw him reading his Braille script on BBC South, or caught him on *Link* as you waited for your children's programme, or noticed him negotiating Oxford Circus tube station, or recognised his voice over a wide range of programmes, you learned the lesson.

People talk of the 'steel' behind his benign manner, but that should be no surprise – he hasn't got to his level without knowing what he wants and how to get it. Sometimes his genial tone comes across as smug. But to people who know him, he is a good friend and a loyal colleague, supporting producers who get into scrapes, and giving generous help to younger broadcasters. Wherever he is working, he tries to get back home each night to Winchester, to his family and his pub. Their affairs, with everything else, must be packed into his day. His former colleague, Ian Macrae, says: 'If you are briefing him, it can be infuriating, because as soon as the phone rings, he'll say "Do you mind? I'll just get this."'

# MAT FRASER:
# ACTOR/PERFORMER

*Photograph taken by JW Evans*

*The Bill*, ITV's long-running police drama, is listed on the CV of many actors, an accepted part of their career trajectory. For Mat Fraser, it didn't happen. Born with short arms and flipper-like hands that have no thumbs – the result of his mother taking the drug thalidomide in pregnancy – Fraser was a former rock musician, carving a place for himself as an actor, writer and presenter. Exuberant, ambitious and sexy, he had kicked his way out of the passive, 'can't do', 'shouldn't do' expectations put upon disabled people, flouting many social conventions along the way. When his agent sent him to audition for *The Bill* in 2000, he was no stranger to mainstream acting and well known in disability arts. 'I had a long audition,' he remembers, 'and the guy loved me, he really loved me. He said, "Mat, you've got a very *Bill* voice. We'll call you."' The call never came. When Fraser's agent checked, she was told he had not been offered the part because they needed someone who could drive. Yet there, on the front page of his CV, was the information that he had 20 years' driving experience and a clean licence. It was the same old story. 'I had been turned down for a disablist reason,' he says. 'But we exposed their lie.'

Fraser went on to prove himself in theatre, film, radio and television, culminating in the role of Chris in *Every Time You Look At Me*, an award-winning, 90-minute drama for BBC Two. The BBC broke new ground by commissioning a full-length film starring two disabled actors – the other was Lisa Hammond (Denny in *Grange Hill*) – and going beyond the love story to explore their own prejudices: 'Every time you look at me, you see yourself.' The love-making was also a first, and so was the manner of it. 'She's kissing my most disabled bits and that's another benchmarky moment, innit?' says Fraser. 'Normally the person playing opposite me would go "Ooh, what muscular legs you have, Mat" – i.e. you may be weird up top but you're still a good lad down there, aren't ya? And I love the fact that we're not doing that.' It was also the first BBC film to be shot on high-definition digital video. Widely praised for the quality of its acting, it won the highest audience appreciation for any BBC drama in 2004. Fraser had arrived – or so he thought.

Given that acting was in his blood, it should not have been unexpected. His parents, Richard Fraser and Paddy Glynn, were all-round actors, singers and dancers. His mother started her career as a Bluebell girl in Las Vegas, one of a troupe renowned in Paris and the USA for their beauty and high-kick dancing. His father became the black sheep of the family when he opted for acting; his own father was an RAF wing commander.

In 1961 the couple were touring the UK in a version of the 1950s musical, *Salad Days*, when Paddy became pregnant and was prescribed thalidomide for morning sickness. Fraser was born the following January with phocomelia (literally, 'seal limb'). He was one of about 460 babies born with limb damage in the UK between 1958 and 1962, when the drug was withdrawn. His mother thought he had died, so when she heard he had short arms, she said with relief, 'Oh, is that all?' As he grew up, she did her best to protect him by trading stare for stare. His disability was not discussed. Anything Fraser wanted to do, he was encouraged to, though when his impairment allowed him to beat the other children at collecting 'a penny for the Guy', he had to be retrieved. The Frasers were not among the parents who waged a historic campaign for adequate compensation, though they did attend at least one meeting.

To begin with, Fraser was not worried that he looked different from other people. He could not tie his shoelaces or do up his top button, but he learned to cope with routines, like going to the loo or using a pencil. Everyday objects, such as a drawer knob, could help him lever clothes on or off. At his posh primary school, Sheen Mount, near Richmond Park, he played football like the other boys, shone at English and History, took part in school plays and enjoyed singing. People were ready to help him, especially girls. He had his own group of friends, who never mentioned his disability; only once did a boy allude to his 'screwed-up arms'. 'I was as much as one can be, as the only disabled kid, a regular member of the school.'

Aged about seven, he had an assessment for compensation. He remembers going into a strange room without his mother and seeing three men behind a desk. They asked him to retrieve a bag of sweets from the top drawer of a three-drawer filing cabinet. He dragged his chair to the cabinet, climbed up, took out the sweets, and dragged the chair back. When he found out it had been an assessment, he was angry with his mother for not telling him; even then, he says, he could have made it look a lot worse. He received a lump sum of £15,000, and an annual payment of about £4000 that today has risen to £12,000 (though not price index linked). The lump sum went into a trust to accrue until he reached 21. Fraser has never been eligible for Income Support (IS) because of that lump sum. He finds this unfair: compensation money is designed to reimburse you for a specific loss, so it should not be counted in an assessment for IS.

Seeing a cine film of a birthday party when he was about eight brought home to him his difference; he was shocked at his short, flapping arms. Then, a year later, his father came out as gay and went off to live with 'Gerry', a dancer, in Colchester. Fraser remembers six months of turmoil before he and his mother left for Auckland, New Zealand, where they stayed for 18 months. He went to the Kowhai Intermediate School, for children aged 10 to 12, which seems to have given him some welcome stability.

> They had a very liberal, proactive attitude to my disability. They made me a prefect and put me in the softball team, because they thought that would give me some responsibility and make me do a sport that would push me physically. And I did it and it gave me great confidence.

Back in England, Fraser and his mother settled in Canterbury, where Paddy worked at the Marlowe Theatre. Fraser's education had taken a nose dive, academically, in Auckland; while he could weld metal and make dovetail joints, he had no idea of long division. So he was sent to Kent College, then a direct grant school.

Money was short, so Fraser's school uniform came from the second-hand uniform shop. But that was of little consequence compared to being a day boy in a school where the boarders reigned. He became not just 'a weed', but a disabled weed; somebody who could be mocked for being different. For the first time, he was called 'flid' and 'spastic'. He did his best to join the pack. He won over one tormentor by helping him with his maths. He found he could earn respect by entertaining the class, so he became the comedian, the one who dared to cheek the teacher. It made him both a rebel and a conformist. He was obeying his father's admonition to 'Be a social chameleon. When you are with Dave the builder, be like Dave the builder.' Good advice for an actor, maybe, but dangerous for a small boy trying to be true to himself. Fraser accepted it on both levels. For him, the actor should be able to absorb any kind of character.

> When one learns to communicate with people on their level, one accesses an openness from them and that's a very useful thing. It makes people like you more and I've always had a desperate need to be liked. I think all performers have that.

A highlight of Kent College was the day he made a favourite English teacher laugh. He was 13 at the time. The class had to write a little play about narration and miming and Fraser allowed one of his characters to exclaim, 'fuck with the form'. The teacher bellowed with laughter. 'That must have been the first moment I got pleasure from someone liking what I had written,' he says. His ability to shock could win approval from the teacher as well as the class. Shortly afterwards, the teacher disappeared, perhaps, thinks Fraser, because he had a mental breakdown. Fraser missed him.

Two years later, he found himself in a very different environment, a comprehensive school at Tregaron in rural Wales. His mother remarried and they moved to the village of Bronnant, near Aberystwyth.

Fraser acted bravely on his first day at the new school. A huge boy challenged him to a wrestling match in front of a group in the playing field. He accepted, and was thoroughly beaten. Afterwards the boy said, 'He's all right, that guy; he had a go.' There was no more bullying.

Another English pupil, Dan Jones, was assigned to look after Fraser. He had never seen anyone with a physical disability before. 'I was very shocked. It took me a week before I could look at him comfortably.' But then Fraser burnt a Bible, and Jones thought that was cool.

Both outsiders in a Welsh school at a time of militant Welsh nationalism, the teenagers were drawn to each other. Music cemented the relationship. While the other pupils liked Elvis Presley and the rock band Status Quo, Fraser and Jones discovered punk and made it their own. They wore the clothes, spiked their hair, swore and spat, and most of all they copied the music. Fraser taught himself drumming, while Jones played the guitar. Fraser led the way in mischief-making. On one occasion he suggested they should go to the village youth club in their punk gear and play a record of the national anthem. The result was spectacular. The Welsh kids chased them out of the club and threw stones at them. Jones still laughs at the memory of Fraser trying to run away in his mother's high-heeled boots.

Punk was a stroke of luck for Fraser. It confirmed him as a rebel and gave him an alternative label. He and Jones were the only punks in Dafydd, he says, and attracted a lot of attention. 'I convinced myself they were staring at me because I had spiky hair, because I was a punk. Being a punk meant I could not call myself disabled; it meant I could call myself something else.'

Difference gave him a sense of power; it even allowed him to transfer the pain, sometimes quite sadistically. One day, when a group of kids were waiting in the sports pavilion to play cricket, Fraser asked who would like to have his sunglasses. Jones recalls: 'The Welsh pupils said, "I'll have them, I'll have them."' So Mat took them off, put them on the ground and just smashed them to pieces.' On another occasion Fraser took his short-legged dog, Brutus, into a stream and told him to sit in the cold water. Jones still remembers the dog's imploring eyes.

Jones eventually walked out of school before the end of the year. Fraser stayed, but failed his O levels. He spent the summer holidays in his room, listening to music and reading girly mags. Determined he should get some qualifications and discipline, his mother sent him back to Kent College, as a boarder, to retake the O level year. He says he bullied the younger people in the form, joined the 'cool' set, who smoked marijuana, and played in the punkier of the two school bands. A new headmaster, a former social worker, introduced a more liberal regime and the pupils were allowed to organise a rock concert at the end of the year. The girls played their part, screaming at the front, and the boys played theirs helped by cans of lager. Fraser loved being on stage and performing. 'I was totally hooked. I knew that's what I wanted to be, from that moment.'

But, for the time being, armed with five O levels, he went off to further education college in Colchester, where he lived with his father. Somehow or other he achieved an A level in Sociology after two years, but all that came way behind gigs, alcohol, drugs and girls. The alternative label was becoming the alternative lifestyle.

Many years later, when Fraser was starring as someone with his own disability in *The Flid Show*, an off-Broadway play, he remarked on the nude love scene: 'It's the first time you see this character actually his real self, without all the brick walls on him. That's one of the things we are not allowed to be traditionally – sexual.' From his teens on, Fraser threw himself into proving he was a full-blooded, heterosexual male, drowning out the knowledge that his impairment could repel some women. As a 13-year-old on a mass date, he had seen its impact on 'the very nervous, polite and acutely embarrassed Vicky. Her look of determination overcoming revulsion convinced me something was wrong.' He was one of the first people in the class to lose his virginity. Sexual experience with disabled girls was available on the foreign holidays organised for teenagers by the Thalidomide Society, but that led to no relationships; having a disabled girlfriend would have underlined his own disability.

Through punk he found non-disabled girls willing to flout convention, 'though always in a private, darkened room'. He looks back on them as revolutionaries. 'I had sussed out that only girls who could reject the confinements of society's values would reject the negatives of disability and find the person inside.' As his musical career developed, the rock star phenomenon kicked in, giving Fraser sexual opportunities he could exploit, a way to relieve the anger and frustration of being different. 'He fucked it out of his system,' says Julie McNamara, friend and colleague on the disability arts scene.

In his second year at Colchester, Fraser joined up again with Dan Jones, who had enrolled at the art college. They formed their first band, A Fear of Sex, composed of a drummer and two guitarists, with Jones doubling as singer. There was no bass player, which they thought was radical. 'For the first time we were playing our own songs and doing our own thing,' says

Fraser. 'It was an extraordinarily rich time in Colchester – everyone was in a band – there was so much going on.'

He wanted to move out of his father's house and, luckily, he could draw on the lump sum compensation: £12,500 went into buying a house for him in Colchester, at 66 South Street.

> I was a drug-addled youth so I just made it the party house. How it stayed standing I don't know. We used to rehearse in the dining room, blaring out the music. People would walk in and out and know there was always a party going on. LSD entered the scene and pretty soon we were a bunch of people just staring at the ceiling for hours, tripped out of our heads, doing that whole thing, shagging around a lot. I was on first-name terms with the staff of the sexually transmitted disease clinic.

Fraser was happy. He never talked about his disability, so no one mentioned it.

A Fear of Sex morphed into another band, North, which included two people on bass and keyboard, and a singer – a pretty girl, who caught the eye of the rock reviewer on the *Colchester Gazette*, ensuring they became the biggest band in town. Fraser had his own methods of publicity. Jones was walking along a main road in Colchester one day, when he saw what had been an empty billboard now advertising North in enormous purple letters. He followed a trail of purple paint, which led to a paint-covered broom standing outside 66 South Street.

Eventually, Jones moved to London with the rock band Living in Texas, while Fraser joined The Reasonable Strollers. Here he found serious musicians experimenting with complicated rhythms, which for a drummer used to 4/4 time were challenging and exciting. But his taste was always one step ahead; now he was into post-punk and the band Theatre of Hate, and he was outgrowing Colchester. When Jones phoned to say his band was doing a gig and needed a drummer, Fraser filled in, and stayed. Pleased to be working with his greatest friend in a band that he thought was going to 'happen', Fraser moved to London in 1983, to the first of many squats. His drumming won widespread respect. 'It was very good, very inventive,' says Jones. 'The rhythm section was strictly Mat.'

Over the next eight years, the band toured all over Europe, made four albums, reached Number 4 in Italy, and ended up being signed to EMI in France, where it appeared on lunchtime TV. Fraser was recognised on the streets of Paris, which delighted him. But they made little money from their records, partly because they were too disorganised to secure good contracts. Even at the height of their success, when they were being flown over to

France, Fraser was paid only £100 a week (about £200 today), which was supplemented by £6000 a year from his thalidomide compensation and by his activities as a 'black market commodity broker', which he later sold on.

One day in 1991 he decided he had had enough. Jones had already moved on, facing up to the question of what to do next. Fraser, now into his cocaine years, joined Joyride, a 'full on' speed metal band. But he knew his days in rock were numbered. The following year he bought a flat in Brixton, overcoming his embarrassment about having money when his friends, who were left-wing, did not. Now, aged 30, he was putting down roots. Shortly afterwards, he met Patou Soult. A French percussionist, she shared many of his interests – Reggae, fetish clubs and martial arts. Brixton was the place to be for Reggae, and within a few weeks they had set up The Grateful Dub, a new age Reggae band that lasted three years. It was, he claims, the 'toast of Brixton' in 1994.

Fraser discovered fetish clubs in the early 1990s. He had never felt comfortable in more conventional clubs. One day, he saw a box of used fetish gear in a shop. He bought it for £30, dressed up at home, and went off with a friend to 'try rubber'. As soon as they walked into the club Submission, he felt it was 'Welcome, weirdo'. He loved it all – the secret venues you accessed by phone, the kinky dressing up, the freedom to be a voyeur himself, the 'anything goes' culture that made his disability irrelevant, or at times attractive. The only other disabled person he remembers seeing was the broadcaster and DJ, Mik Scarlett. Fraser had found himself a scene and a community; he even picked up work from meeting TV producers. Patou joined in. After a few years, though, it was time to move on. Fetish had got too commercial, says Fraser. 'Rubber's expensive. A new outfit's 200 quid.' But he kept up with the Sex Maniacs' Ball, now renamed Night of the Senses, run by Outsiders, the club for disabled people, and still comperes the Erotic Oscars, which raise money for the club. A few years ago, after he and Patou were married, they took her mother along to one of the balls.

Cycling round Brixton in the early 1990s on a converted bike with high handlebars and a back pedal brake, Fraser was an eye-catching sight, 'distinctive, even by Brixton standards', says the writer Allan Sutherland. Caroline Parker, a deaf actress and cabaret artist, thought he was 'yummy' when she met him at a pub in north London. 'He looked cool and very sexy. With dreadlocks going down to his arse and being over six feet tall, he stood out from anyone else around.'

But bubbling under the cool was the issue of his disability. For all his adult life he had smothered it in the noisy, drug-saturated life of a rock musician. Now his immune system was buckling under the drug abuse; boils

Fetish years: Mat Fraser agonising pleasurably with, from left, Naughty Nicola, Grindcore Ginny and Jo Tighthutch. Photograph taken by Patou Soult.

on his legs kept recurring and he was growing resistant to antibiotics. He made a decision to give up hard drugs and rethink his lifestyle. He also had to accept that his impairment, phocomelia, was part of the whole of him, man and artist, if he was to move forward. The conversion happened over a couple of years, in two stages.

In 1992 he went to the first international thalidomide conference in the Netherlands, where he heard Mary Duffy reading her poems. Duffy's mother had also taken thalidomide. Born with no arms and a hand attached to one shoulder, she grew up rejecting the social values that saw her as incomplete and needing prostheses to make her 'normal'. She set out to communicate the reality and validity of her life through poetry, photography and perform-ance art, using her own nudity to shock audiences into seeing disability differently. Her poem about wholeness struck a chord with Fraser: 'When one is born, that is what one is; one doesn't think of having a bit missing,' he says. He was also impressed by Duffy's professionalism. After talking to her, he felt somewhat manipulated into feeling shame about his denial of disability, but she introduced him to a liberating idea: people are disabled not by their own impairments but by society's negative attitude to them and the physical barriers around them (what he came to know later as the 'social model'). She also suggested he should check out the disability arts scene and contact Alan Holdsworth (aka Johnny Crescendo, the singer). He did, and it opened up for him a new field of live performance that took in arts festivals and cabarets all over the country and brought him to the notice of a new, young, audience. Years later he repaid Duffy by suggesting her as a disabled actor for an American movie.

The disability arts scene had grown rapidly through the 1980s as disabled people sought to tell their stories and present their images against a backdrop of increasing demands for political rights. Regional disability arts forums and then a national forum were set up to encourage people and promote events. Into this vibrant, supportive, minority world, Fraser leaped. With all the energy of the newly converted, he drummed, he sang and he performed rap poetry, pouring out his pent-up anger at the ignorance and prejudice of non-disabled people who stared at him, rejected him or saw him as a sexual conquest – though that could work both ways. On his first CD (there were three altogether) he included 'Verbatim Vomit'. Against the sound of someone being sick, he relayed people's comments about him, 'A lovely long lascivious list/Of the words of oppression that still exist'. *Survival of the Shittest*, the title track of that CD, was a rap lament for caring, honesty and difference. He had seen an old woman knocked over in the scramble for a bus, the hacks making money from Princess Diana's death and two disabled men trying to face down the stares in a pub by bonding on sexual anecdotes which demeaned women:

> Why's he ashamed of himself and his crowd?
> Survival of the shittest.
> When you're hurt why d'you hurt the next one down?
> Survival of the shittest.
> How do we obey the System's rules?
> Survival of the shittest
> What's the cream that makes us fools?
> Survival of the shittest.

He also lambasted disability's familiar baddies: politicians, doctors, non-disabled actors who played disability parts and television charity shows that perpetuated the status quo.

Not only did Fraser perform his poetry before disabled people, he also took it to mainstream poetry events. His impact on audiences was 'amazing', says Geraldine Collinge, director of the performance poetry organisation, Apples & Snakes. Through him, other disabled poets found a wider audience.

On the disability circuit, he scattered expletives like cinders, shocking some, attracting others. His most extreme performance was as 'an obsessive avenger, a Thalidomide Ninja'. Wearing a black balaclava and brandishing a gun, he exploded on to the stage with a giant dropkick. It titillated the women, even as it scared them, and fed the aspirations of young disabled men. 'They had never seen a positive role model, so passionate, so angry, so active out there. His show was dynamic,' says Julie McNamara. Now a playwright, actor and arts administrator, she shared many gigs with Fraser in the 1990s and later co-hosted disability events with him.

It was McNamara who defended Fraser when he offended elements of the disability movement. Two occasions stand out. In 1999, he took a paid-for role in a government poster campaign called 'See the Person', which tried to combat discrimination by emphasising individual people, not their disability. It ran foul of disability activists on several counts, including that, since society was responsible for discrimination against disabled people, discrimination was a government matter and nothing to do with disabled individuals. For his *faux pas* Fraser was disinvited to an Independence Festival in Manchester, which he missed anyway because he was in the USA.

The following year he co-presented the Channel 4 Television comedy series *Freak Out*, in which disabled lads behaved badly. The final straw, in the eyes of some activists, was when Bernard Manning, notorious for his seemingly racist jokes, was invited on to the show. Fraser was labelled 'a media whore'. Even Mik Scarlett thought Fraser had been naive to get involved.

Fraser says that he should have asked more questions about the poster campaign before taking the money. But he has stood by *Freak Out*, arguing that politically correct eggs may get broken in the battle for integration. 'I am carrying on with my agenda, which is to get disabled people on telly, radio and stage,' he declared at the time. The Disabled People's Direct Action Network (DAN) retaliated by picketing another Independence Festival, refusing to join in unless Fraser was excluded. Barbara Lisicki, from DAN, wanted to make an unscheduled speech, but McNamara, the compere, refused. McNamara also tried to get Fraser on stage as a guest and dedicated her band's last piece of drumming to him. 'I thought, we are so punitive and, yes, Mat had made mistakes. But I had to speak out for a fellow activist, a fellow human being.'

Fraser tried to take control of his image, working with unconventional artists who were keen to explore the connections between freak, beauty and art. The photographer Manuel Vason included images of Fraser in *Exposures*, a book devoted to contemporary live artists in Britain. The sculptor Marc Quinn, known for his dramatic statue of the artist Alison Lapper in Trafalgar Square, made other sculptures in white marble of limbless people. His version of Rodin's 'The Kiss', now at the Graves Art Gallery in South Yorkshire, has Fraser standing naked with the performance artist, Catherine Long, his right hand resting on her left shoulder, where her arm would have been.

Fraser explained, 'I've increasingly used my own image in more and more confrontational presentations, and now find that "telling the truth", rather than being a painful realisation, is in fact fuelling me with outrageously ostracised power.' He went on, 'I feel no need to beautify or uglify, to qualify. I, we, disabled artists are the real fucking deal; we are porno, blood, titillation, revulsion, failure, success, beauty, ugliness.' But even Fraser could get out of his depth. Appearing for the first time in the *Freak Show* in Coney Island, USA, he was welcomed as a freak and it shocked him. Now he goes back regularly and feels quite comfortable in that world. It is certainly parading difference to make money, he says, but he controls what he does on stage; he's treated with respect and, as a 'born freak', he gets top billing.

Over the years he has deliberately exploited 'freak' – to shock and make a living, as well as explore beyond the disability to the person inside. His CV is full of it, from *Freak Fucking Basics* (1996), funded by the British Film Institute, through *Freak Out* (2000), and his own play, *Sealboy:Freak* (2001), to *Born Freak* (2002), a multi-award-winning Channel 4 documentary about the history of disabled performers.

Interwoven with disability arts was, of course, political action. The early 1990s was a time of intense activity among politicised disabled people who wanted a civil rights act, accessible public transport and an end to ITV's patronising Telethon fundraiser. Frustrated by Tory government inaction and determined to force change, they took to the streets, led by Alan Holdsworth. In those days, Fraser was a DAN man. He threw himself into demonstrations on behalf of disabled people's rights as ardently as he had thrown himself into demonstrations against the Poll Tax in his punk days. 'I was standing there defying the might of the evil state. But now, flanking me on either side, my co-warriors were disabled people. I was about as happy as you could be.' Disabled people were cool. Still, it did rile him that no one was charging the police and he wasn't allowed to throw a brick.

Later, thoughtless of his acting career, he would rebuke people he thought were demeaning 'my people' or being flippant about disability. He once confronted the reviewer, broadcaster and programme maker Victor Lewis-Smith over a review in the *Evening Standard,* and another time he took Channel 4 to task for casting a non-disabled actor as a wheelchair user in their *Book Club* series. He also warned film-maker Mike Leigh against the disability version of 'blacking up' – using non-disabled actors for disabled parts.

In 1994 disabled people were furious when the Government blocked a civil rights bill in favour of a compromise anti-discrimination bill. At one of the protests, Ewan Marshall, artistic director of Graeae, the UK's leading disabled-led theatre company, watched Fraser's impact on a party of posh schoolgirls in Parliament Square. The sight of Fraser, eye catching as usual in short shorts and long dreadlocks, had literally freaked the schoolgirls out, but his charm and directness soon won them over.

> He was turning them into disability activists as they went into the Houses of Parliament. I remember thinking, if that guy can do that with those kids in about two minutes, he should come and work with us.

Seeing Graeae perform *Ubu Roi* was a defining moment for Fraser. He had set aside acting as a career ever since he had been laughed at during an audition at Kent College. Now he was 'blown away' by the Graeae experience. At first he could not understand what Jamie Beddard, an actor with cerebral palsy, was saying, and yet the audience around him was laughing. Eventually he tuned in. The play showed him that disabled people could act; they could entertain; and they did not embarrass a non-disabled audience. At the next open audition, he bullied his way in, probably stinking of marijuana, he says. He sang a song and delivered a Shakespeare soliloquy, forgetting two lines. Marshall had little to go on, but the memory of Parliament Square was indelible. Fraser was accepted.

Graeae offered only on-the-job training and occasional workshops run by an established actor, such as Richard Wilson; drama schools were closed to disabled actors in those days. Fraser learned the Forum technique, a type of interactive theatre from Brazil, which tackles issues, such as social oppression, by setting up conflict scenarios and working with the audience to find solutions. Actors have to be flexible, good improvisers and good listeners. With Caroline Parker and Jamie Beddard, Fraser toured schools around the country. Acting held no fears for him and he appreciated the comforts of a regular job.

> I got my own hotel room. I got paid. I got meals every day. People were moaning. I said, 'You want to get in the van that I've been in for the last ten years, smells of sick going up the M1, sleeping in sleeping bags on people's floors – that's rock 'n' roll.'

At an audition for Joe Orton's farce, *What the Butler Saw*, Fraser proved himself a natural, helped by an impressive physicality – he could express surprise with a standing jump on to a table. He won the key role of Dr Prentice, and a national tour, but the dreadlocks had to go. Marshall now regarded Fraser as a core member of the company. He enjoyed working with an actor who listened to what he was told, learnt quickly, had ideas and dared to try new things. Fraser says Marshall has taught him more about acting than anyone else.

The year 1997 brought him more firsts. He made a pioneering commercial for the Co-op bank in which a disabled man describes being called a wanker by a non-disabled man for chatting up his girlfriend. He had a small part in the First World War drama *Unknown Soldier* (ITV) and he auditioned so well for a minor part in *Inmates*, a BBC Radio 4 comedy-drama about life in a long-stay institution, that he got the lead. He also acquired an agent – the unobtainable Holy Grail for most disabled actors. A disabled friend working with the agent Hetty Churchill argued, successfully, that she should have a disabled actor on her books. Churchill saw Fraser in *What the Butler Saw* and signed him up. He started in unpaid fringe theatre to gain experience. Again, he proved his competence in auditions and had a favourable mention in the *Evening Standard*. He was beginning to feel like a jobbing actor.

On Radio 4, he became one of the regulars in *Yes, Sir, I Can Boogie*, sending up able-bodied attitudes to disability in comedy sketches that sometimes offended even disabled people. Then came *Metrosexuality*, a six-part comedy-drama for Channel 4. (His mum had a part too.)

> Rikki Beadle Blair, this huge lion of a camp, black man, brought me up to his gym one day and said 'I want to cast you as the heroin dealer…but I don't want to talk about your arms. Are you up for that?'

He was, so long as there could be a 'jacking up' scene – 'I knew it would make a good shot.' But reviewers panned the pop-video style, sex-engrossed trip round Notting Hill, so there was no follow-on series. Some viewers saw the characters as tokenistic, with Fraser providing the disability interest. For one youngster, though, it hit the spot. Ade Adepitan, now a CBBC presenter and star of the wheelchair basketball drama series, *Desperados*, saw a disabled actor on TV and found that inspiring.

Apart from his setback over *The Bill*, Fraser's TV career was going strong and the money was rolling in, enough to take out a mortgage on a house in Teddington and buy a Volvo automatic. An extended steering column was standard on a Volvo, so he no longer needed to get a car adapted. From 2000 to 2003 he did lucrative voice-overs for three series, *Lost* (Channel 4), *Trouble at the Top* (BBC Two) and *Living by the Book* (ITV). He made another commercial, for Virgin Mobile. He became a regular on *The Heaven and Earth Show* (BBC One). Despite this success on TV, his disability still defined him; most casting directors and producers could not see beyond it. For Channel 4 he was a documentary presenter; after *Born Freak* came *Unarmed and Dangerous* (2003) and *Happy Birthday Thalidomide* (shown April 2004).

A documentary on cage fighting, the fast-growing, no-holds-barred mix of wrestling, boxing and martial arts, appealed to Fraser. He had been into martial arts ever since a gang of kids scared him 16 years earlier and a Tae Kwon Do advertisement offered him the chance to fight back. He kicked so hard in his first lesson he went straight through a block of wood. 'It gave me a feeling of aliveness that I got from some drugs, but the quality of that feeling was better.' He had tried other disciplines, before settling for Dynamic Self Defence and working up to a second degree black belt. The practice dummy in his back garden is for kick-boxing, 'the flashy stuff'. Given his impairment, he says, the most effective defence is to kick the legs of an antagonist from under him. Not that an occasion has arisen yet.

When he discovered cage fighting, he was hooked; why, he wasn't sure. Animal instincts, he suggests. 'I think we should celebrate the sex and violence in our lives and not suppress it.' He is also suspicious of regulation.

> I think a lot of it is about social control of the masses and not really about what is right and wrong. And I don't care to live like that a lot of the time. So I think watching fighting is fine.

But he also wanted to do it, to prove that he could. He even accepted the mutation of his original idea, a two-minute practice session in the gym, into a film centred on the first disabled man to enter a cage. He got away with only a bruised rib, but he was criticised for setting himself an impossible task, only to have the rules relaxed. As the promoter pointed out, 'Not wishing to be disrespectful, but the guy has got no arms.'

The award-winning *Happy Birthday Thalidomide* (April 2004) is considered by some people to be Fraser's best piece of TV work. The film contrasts the evil reputation of thalidomide after 50 years with its new status as a wonder drug that relieves the pain and symptoms of diseases like leprosy and cancer. Fraser goes to Brazil to meet people with leprosy. It becomes a personal journey too, his emotions recorded on camera. Holding a packet of thalidomide for the first time and wiping away a tear, he has to accept the good it can do. He is frustrated when he cannot communicate with a deaf, thalidomide-impaired teenager, who beats him at chess yet watches TV all day. And he can barely restrain himself from hitting her father, who is building himself a swimming pool funded by his daughter's compensation.

In 2002, Fraser challenged Channel 4, which he thought was probably best at representing disability, to go further. 'I want to see disabled people's issues explored in drama. I want to see disabled actors being used as a lawyer here, a housewife here, a cut and thrust drug dealer there in dramas. Why not?' Channel 4's disability adviser, Alison Walsh (disabled herself), acknowledged the weaknesses. 'In the end, it is down to the production company,' she said. 'The pool of disabled actors is very small – it's often hard to find exactly the right face for the part.'

Ewan Marshall, now a producer and director for BBC television, saw it the same way. That year, he produced three ten-minute dramas based on two strangers meeting, one disabled, one not disabled. He matched three good disabled actors with three good writers, who then worked together. 'The most important thing was to write something inspired by the actor rather than go on a trawl for an actor that might fit a preconceived part,' he said. One of the dramas, the award-winning *Urban Myth*, which he directed, covered the familiar ground of boy-meets-girl again and will it happen this time? It starred Fraser, who had lobbied hard to be included, and Saffron Burrows, coincidentally the stepdaughter of disability activist Richard Reiser. The three 'shorts' went down so well that the BBC Drama Department asked Marshall if he would like to develop a longer film. *Every Time You Look At Me* had funding of £1.2 million and an experienced scriptwriter and director, so the only risks were Fraser and Hammond. They proved that two disabled leads could carry the plot.

For Fraser, this was the highlight of his acting career. He may have had the less feisty part, but people thought he did a good job, and he touched stardom. A car collected him; he and Hammond had the biggest dressing rooms on the set; dressing and make-up routines were adapted to his needs, and his whims were attended to – 'Usual veggie breakfast is it, Mat?'

As luck would have it, *Happy Birthday Thalidomide* and *Every Time You Look At Me* were transmitted in the same month in 2004. What with press interviews and breakfast TV appearances, Fraser became quite a celebrity, recognised on the streets of London. Not for the first time, though. *The Big Issue* had run a front cover picture of him a few years earlier, sporting a short, knitted jumper with the slogan 'Short armed and dangerous'. Inside, a *Big Issue* vendor had commented: 'He's cool, yeah, he's cool, and he's got short arms.'

Given such a successful BBC 'special', Fraser expected to be offered a part in a returning TV series or featured in an episode of a series. That is what usually happens. For Fraser, like David Bower, the deaf actor in *Four Weddings and a Funeral*, it didn't happen. Yet Paul Henshall, who was drama school trained and uses that symbol of disability, a wheelchair, succeeded a year later in BBC One's *Holby City*.

Why Fraser was dropped is hard to pin down. With 90 per cent of non-disabled actors out of work, if people don't want to cast an actor with thalidomide in a part, they don't have to, says Hilary Salmon, a BBC executive producer of drama, responsible for *Every Time You Look At Me*. She agrees there could be an attitude of 'We've done Mat Fraser' among casting directors and producers; like so many people, they see the disability before the person – or the actor. 'It's a very hard cast of mind to change, that sense of difference,' she says. Perhaps, in a Catch-22 situation, Fraser's acceptance of the 'freak' label, which brought him some success in television, contributed to his short shelf life.

No one doubts his professionalism, but he can be unpredictable. Salmon remembers with amusement how he had the gall to tackle Jane Root, then Controller of BBC Two, about why she hadn't yet scheduled *Every Time You Look at Me* for transmission. Root organised it then and there, as Salmon stood watching, open-mouthed. Fraser was transgressing the rule that actors should be amenable. As he himself has said, 'When you're the ambassador for disability, you don't moan about the state of the crips' bog until you've signed the contract.'

Apart from playing a social worker in one of the BBC Two *If...* series, in 2004, Fraser had no more work in television. 'My television acting career is lying belly up in the water,' he says, bitterly, in 2006. He was forced to look elsewhere for work and recognition.

Parallel with TV, Fraser was building a career in the theatre. Marshall directed his one-man show, *Sealboy:Freak* (2001) in which Fraser wrote about and acted two people, a contemporary actor with phocomelia striving to be taken seriously for mainstream parts, and Stanley Berent, known as 'Sealo, the Sealboy'. Berent also had phocomelia, though not caused by thalidomide, and made a good living as a sideshow act in twentieth-century America. *Sealboy:Freak* posed tricky questions. Is the lot of a phocomelic actor or performer today better than it was 50 years ago? Has the advance of political correctness – closing down freak shows – made it harder for him to get a job? Can a disabled performer ever be seen as anything but a freak? Fraser laid himself bare, and that made people think. Simon Minty, disabled comedian and businessman, remembers how the play made a great impression on his non-disabled parents, while he himself was so engrossed he forgot he was watching a friend. 'It was the best piece of work I had ever seen him do.' The show was funny too, and full of Fraser energy, even to a blast of drumming and rap at the end. It won considerable praise, toured the UK twice, and took in the 2001 Edinburgh Festival and disability arts festivals in Adelaide, Auckland and Chicago.

Meanwhile, he had some limited success in mainstream theatre. One part he secured at the Young Vic after a gruelling audition allowed him about five minutes on stage – not enough time for people to get over their initial shock and connect with the character. He learnt a lesson from that: he would never again take a small part. 'Half the reason I became an actor was for the politics as well. So what was the point if they did not go home thinking, "You know, he was really all right. We should look at disabled actors differently"?' Again, the tension between Fraser the jobbing actor and Fraser the disabled activist.

But how many directors were going to be impairment neutral and give him the kind of bread-and-butter parts he wanted? It hadn't worked with *The Bill*. What he needed was someone to write a show around him, as Marshall had done for him in television. One day, stranded on the sofa, recovering from an operation on his knee, he decided to do it himself. By 2004 *Thalidomide!! A Musical* was taking shape.

Once again he mined the subject he knew best, producing a mix of historical fact about the thalidomide drug scandal, his own experiences of growing up, and a love story. It was, he says, a 'comedy horror pastiche musical'. He wrote and composed the songs, such as 'I can be his arms', or 'It's hard to hitch down life's highway with no thumbs'. In went salsa, tap and tango dance routines, and puppets. He shared the parts with actress Anna Winslet. To play non-disabled people, he wore broomstick handles adorned with gloves, which he could waggle.

'I want to see new territories used to explore disability – violence, aggression, speed…and musicals,' he said. He was confident the time had come for disability to be the subject of sick humour, for people to be shocked out of their received notions, for disabled people – who knew the reality of flippers and 'monster' babies – to joke about them. After all, mainstream theatre and TV was now more risqué. He called the genre 'cripsploitation'.

Many disabled people loved the show and found it very funny. Geoff Adams-Spink, the BBC's age and disability correspondent and a fellow thalidomider, saw it four times. It had two successful national tours and a fortnight at the Battersea Arts Centre in London, in 2006. The *Daily Telegraph* hailed 'a sharp and highly original musical that deserves a wide audience'. But most London-based critics gave it the thumbs down, confused, perhaps, by a plot which allowed Fraser to become a surgeon cutting off deformed limbs, and allowed true love to flourish only after the heroine had lost her arms in a car crash. Lyn Gardner of the *Guardian* wrote: 'Perhaps if the show was less clumsy in its staging and the writing sharper and funnier, Fraser would get away with these oddities, but this tale of people with short arms is badly in need of more legs.'

Fraser was bruised. 'They didn't get it,' he said. 'I adore horror films, "B" movies, really shitty musicals and crassness and bad taste. I put it all into one thing and it was far too much for most people.' But, more than that, his confidence was shaken. His earlier plans had worked: he had starred in a BBC 'special'; he had written *Sealboy:Freak* and toured it successfully. This time he had misjudged. All he could do was sell some albums, hope to make a radio or TV adaptation, and move on.

As far as his acting was concerned, *The Flid Show*, produced off-Broadway in 2005, gave him reassurance. He played a self-pitying, phocomelic, lounge singer who comes to terms with his disability after ghostly visitations and a sexual relationship with a woman doctor. The play itself had mixed reviews, but Fraser's acting was widely praised. The *New York Times* talked of 'a seasoned and charismatic actor'. *The Village Voice* commented, 'It is a testament to Fraser's acting…that as the show progresses you do see, increasingly, not the arms but the man.' That must have been sweet justification after the Young Vic experience.

But the question remained, where was Fraser's career going? He could remain in disability arts. He could go on compering his saucy sex variety cabarets and celebratory festivals, giving live performances here and abroad, working with student actors, recording music. None of this would produce a BAFTA (British Academy of Film and Television Arts) award.

Ouch!, the BBC's radical website for disabled people, was pioneering a comedy podcast, hoping to reach younger listeners. Fraser now co-hosts that with comedian Liz Carr. They tease each other, make fun of disability, puncture the stereotypes. 'People should be able to laugh with us and at what we experience, including my inability to hold a cup with one hand,' Fraser told *New Statesman* readers. As with *Freak Out*, the risk of offending or hurting remains. On the 2007 Valentine's Day podcast, for example, after a romp through nipple jokes, online dating, and the views of a sex worker, Fraser and Carr reached the podcast parlour game, 'Vegetable, vegetable, vegetable'. They have to guess 'what is wrong' with a disabled caller in 60 seconds, when the caller can only answer 'yes' or 'no'. Fraser had to comfort an Australian caller – 'Don't cry, it's OK, baby, we love you' – when his joke about her multiple impairments threatened to overwhelm her. Balancing exuberant comedian with caring host is tricky; he can tilt either way. 'Mat Fraser is a little worthy at times,' said Dr Paul Darke, the disability and culture critic, in 2006. But the podcasts have proved so successful that they are now permanent. People as far afield as San Francisco download them.

This new wave of irreverent disability comedy is gaining ground. The question is whether it can break into mainstream and take Fraser and others with it. He and Carr are trying their hand at a TV sitcom. Yet Fraser passed up the chance to join Carr and Simon Minty in the comedy troupe, Abnormally Funny People, which took off from the Edinburgh Festival in 2005 and reached the West End in 2008. He says he was too involved with his musical.

On another front, he has written a comedy drama, *A Multitude of Elvii*, about the sad and lonely, but also funny, world of Elvis and his ultra fans. Maybe this will plumb the depths people think he is capable of reaching. 'When he's being quite deep and thoughtful, there's a huge strength there', says Minty, remembering *Sealboy:Freak*. But Fraser still loves acting and, since there were so few parts on offer, no wonder he wrote a disabled one into *Elvii*. Julie McNamara believes he has a lot more to give as an actor, though he needs a strong director to push him. When she asked him to read a woman's part in her latest play, he did it 'brilliantly'.

Fraser's aspirations can be unexpected. He certainly wants a part he can get his teeth into, yet he would be up for a Bond villain, regardless of what other disabled people think about the association between disability and villainy. Then, again, he would draw the line at playing Henry V, following in the footsteps of the black actor Adrian Lester, because he sees that as defying historical reality.

Disabled actors and actors from black and ethnic minorities have much in common as regards lack of opportunities in the theatre and in television. At the BBC, a diktat from its Director-General, Greg Dyke, pushed the corporation into employing more people from ethnic minorities and showing them more on TV, but the BBC has lost ground since Dyke left in 2004. Hilary Salmon thinks Mark Thompson, the current Director-General, should issue a similar directive for disabled actors. Meanwhile, under pressure at a diversity conference in November 2007, the BBC's head of editorial diversity, Mary FitzPatrick, promised that in future disabled actors would be considered for all mainstream roles, not just disabled ones. Fraser remained sceptical: 'I've been going to events like this and hearing the same thing for the past eleven years,' he says.

Various schemes have been devised by the television channels to attract disabled actors (and increase disabled people in programme making), but the pool of trained actors is still small, which is not surprising given there are few jobs to attract them – a vicious circle. No disabled actor has a constant career and the overall situation has changed little since 2001, says Ewan Marshall: 'The complete lack of opportunity for employment, it's just like apartheid.' He thinks the culture would change if more disabled people were employed in arts administration. The Independent Theatre Council has begun training deaf and disabled people for middle-ranking theatre management. But it needs top administrators to acknowledge their responsibility. Michael Lynch, chief executive at London's South Bank Centre, who had polio as a child, already does. 'There is discrimination in various forms, some of it quite unwitting,' he admits. 'We will do our very best to be seen as a leader for change and to make credible improvements.' He is backing Sync, a new leadership programme for disabled people in the arts.

Public bodies, like the BBC and Channel 4, are now bound by the Disability Equality Duty of the Disability Discrimination Act 2005 to actively promote equal opportunities for disabled people. But no anti-discrimination law or well-meaning strategy can prevent casting directors and producers rejecting a disabled actor on grounds of their ability or suitability for a part, when behind that decision may lurk ignorance and prejudice.

Meanwhile, Fraser drives on, his revamped website talking of diverse projects, though the events are mainly striptease and cabaret with an element of freak show. Kaos Theatre company, which toured a controversial version of *A Midsummer Night's Dream* in 2007–08, gave him a chance to play Puck, before succumbing to funding cuts by the Arts Council. Its director, Xavier Leret, has written a 'tough gangster' feature film for Fraser, called *Kung Fu Flid*, to be released on DVD. In 2009, Fraser's TV career may be looking up. He is in an episode of *Holby City*, and one of six disabled *Cast Offs* in a Channel 4 series.

As he advances through his forties, the contradictions become sharper. He's a middle-class man, who shares his house in Teddington with his ex-wife, notices cat hairs on the carpet and wishes *Disability Now* readers for 2007 'love in your life – real, unselfish love'. Yet he's 'the sex icon of the disabled people's movement,' current holder of the Erotic Award for best male striptease artiste (he collected his flying gold cock and balls trophy in 2008) and his website offers links to erotic burlesque performers. He's the committed professional, hardwired to achievement, who can be humble, vulnerable and 'soft as a bunny'. He's the disability activist whose anger is being channelled into humour and whose respect for the 'movement' has been eroded by a stronger respect for free speech. He's the martial arts devotee, who practises Ashtanga yoga, eats vegetarian, worries about the environment, celebrates Beltane and votes Green. No wonder he intrigues so many people and demolishes the traditional stereotypes of disability.

Dan Jones pays tribute to Fraser's grit in the face of many setbacks: 'He hasn't let anyone grind him down.' Furthermore, through the power of television, he has been inside people's homes and won them over. 'Now, when he walks down the street, it's not "Look at that freak," it's "Look at that guy from television." He's forced people to accept him, which is wonderful.'

No one doubts he has been a trailblazer. Does he see himself as a role model for other disabled people? 'No, I bloody don't. I'm in this for me,' he barked on his old website. Nowadays he has come to terms with it, though he thinks it was a matter of being the right person at the right time in the right place. 'I never had anyone to aspire to be better than,' he says. And then, in an unexpected gesture to the next generation of disabled actors and performers: 'I'd love to feel the tyre prints running me over as somebody gets more than I've got.'

# ANDREW LEE:
# ACTIVIST/CAMPAIGNER

*Photograph taken by Hugh Hill*

'People with learning difficulties' (or 'learning disability') is how people who used to have a 'mental handicap' choose to be called. Abandoning the old label has been easier than changing people's attitudes. Up to 1.5 million people with learning difficulties want to throw off the stigma that has traditionally separated them from the rest of society – even the disability community – and allowed them to be treated differently. It has been acceptable to shut them away in long-stay hospitals, run their lives, dope the difficult ones. It has been acceptable to ignore their physical and sexual abuse, miss out on the regular health checks and specialist care that other NHS patients receive, and even let them die. In 2007, three reports – from the Healthcare Commission, the Disability Rights Commission and the charity Mencap – showed that these things were still going on.

All this is far removed from the aspirations of many people with learning difficulties. Statistics are shamefully patchy, but 65 per cent of them want a job; only 11 per cent have a job; 94 per cent have no choice about who they live with; 50 per cent or more of parents who have learning difficulties do not live with their children. The idea that, given the right support, they could be citizens, with all the human rights that most people enjoy (such as life, liberty, privacy, education, marriage, freedom of expression – including receiving and imparting information – free movement and protection against discrimination) has for years seemed unthinkable and unaffordable. It still does to some people. When *Community Care* magazine launched a campaign in 2007 calling for people with learning difficulties to have 'A life like any other', among the questionnaires it received back was one from a woman with learning difficulties who said she wanted to have a job and live independently. Alongside, her carer had written 'not capable of this'. The carer could see only the difficulties, not the solutions. Back in 2001, the Labour government produced a policy to close the last long-stay hospitals and ensure that people with learning difficulties could 'live full and independent lives as part of their local communities', but the political muscle was soft and the money was never ring-fenced. Now they are trying again, egged on by a trenchant report in 2008 from the Parliamentary Joint Committee on Human Rights.

Andrew Lee, director of People First (Self Advocacy), knows the everyday reality. At the launch of the *Community Care* campaign, he said:

> Life for many people with learning difficulties is like being taken to watch a football match and never being allowed to play – we get to see other people take a full part in life but we never get the chance.

Lee, himself, was lucky to get some chances; others he made for himself. There is a deep determination behind his boyish appearance and cheery manner. Since he was 19, he has lived in his own home. He's been married twice and looks forward to having children. And for nine years he has had a paid job, an increasingly influential one.

Some people, seeing his political awareness and hearing his speeches, think he doesn't have learning difficulties, which he finds intensely annoying. They do not see the time-consuming work that goes on behind the scenes. Lee's difficulties involve reading and processing information, particularly if there are complex ideas or long words and they are coming thick and fast. He employs non-disabled 'supporters', as People First calls them, who are partly funded by the government's Access to Work scheme. They summarise documents or emails, put them in context and present them in an accessible way, so he can respond. They turn his ideas into speeches or correct speeches he writes himself. They present him with options from which to make a management decision. When he goes to meetings he usually has a supporter with him. He and the supporter have worked out techniques, like a nudge or a note, for dealing with his propensity to talk for too long, repeat points, or go off at a tangent. Part of this is sheer exuberance, and people who know him well can tease him or tell him to shut up.

People First (Self Advocacy) is London based but has over 100 local member groups around the UK and many more individual members. One-third of its management committee come from outside London. It represents the views of people with learning difficulties on a growing number of important committees and argues for money and services to give them more control over their lives. As its first director with learning difficulties, Lee has been a figurehead, helping to build the confidence and skills of his members in speaking up for themselves. From being out on the street with a placard, he is now more likely to be seen at formal meetings of politicians and professionals. Two of his proudest moments were challenging Tony Blair about the Mental Capacity Act 2005 in Downing Street and telling the Queen about People First.

In 2007 he gave evidence to the Parliamentary Joint Committee on Human Rights, which was looking into the human rights of people with learning disabilities. It gave him a chance to lay the issues on the line, shocking committee members. Behind the barriers facing people with learning difficulties, he said, was the idea that 'we are less good and less worthwhile than other people'. It starts from birth, when parents are encouraged to mourn that they have an abnormal child, 'and their disappointment stays with us throughout our lives'. The human rights abuses that happen every day on different levels – in long-stay hospitals, group homes, within the family – come from this culture of disrespect. He gave vivid examples. His first wife had been sterilised at the request of her parents. And a disabled advocate had been forbidden to leave her group home until she had made her bed. When she went, anyway, to meet the Minister for Disabled People, no less, she was reported missing to the police, and ended up in a police car before the situation was resolved. Referring to recent abuses in hospitals and homes in Sutton and Merton, Lee thought one of the most tragic things was that 'staff did not even know they were doing anything wrong'. The abuses went on, he said, because there were 'no consequences'; society had low expectations of people with learning difficulties and carers feared to take risks.

Over-protective carers are one of Lee's bugbears. 'The effect of removing risk from life is removing the chance of a real life,' he told the committee. He also blamed lack of public funding. If the Government is serious about stopping human rights abuses, it will cost money, he said. He urged the Government to pass the Disabled Persons (Independent Living) Bill, which would give disabled people a legal right to control their care budgets, and choice and support in housing and everyday life.

Anne McGuire, former Minister for Disabled People, also gave evidence to the committee. In the late 1970s, she worked alongside people with learning difficulties and saw how even articulate people were not in a position to speak up for themselves. 'Now Andrew is speaking on behalf of people with learning difficulties in a way that is stunningly impressive,' she says, noting how he uses real-life examples to make his point. He is one of the senior people in the disability field that she talked to regularly.

Lee is now at the heart of disability politics, helping to keep the flag flying for disabled people in the Equality and Human Rights Commission, which encompasses gender, race, age, sexual orientation and religious belief as well as disability. The small disability committee, chaired in its first year by disability commissioner Baroness Jane Campbell, met only six times and had an uphill task linking up with the other strands, educating the commission about disability and explaining its role to disabled people. Campbell called for disabled people to make common cause with other groups as the next stage in the fight for human rights. But many compaigners just saw the disability corner languishing. Lee wishes some critics would talk directly to the disability committee, instead of complaining on the sidelines. 'You know who we are', he says. 'We won't bite.'

Lee leads a hectic life. Funding cuts at People First meant he officially worked four days a week in 2007, but he would jump into a train on his no-pay day if he thought the appointment was important. With a funding boost in 2008, he is back to full-time. Saturdays can be taken up with trustee meetings, either his own organisation or other people's. He commutes from Stevenage to a small, open-plan office on London's Albert Embankment, where the noise of trains competes with the conversation. Near his desk is a target board speckled with stickers, reminding him of what he has to do for the quarter and the year – People First's constitution (how to involve younger people, for example), fundraising, business plan, overseeing staff, a lunch for supporters. Two of Lee's trusted supporters left in 2007, so he had to rely temporarily on himself or other supporters in the office. The unanswered emails piled up. Fortunately, he seems able to departmentalise himself, though the pressure shows when he stumbles more than usual over sentences or employs 'actually' too often. His friendly manner when he greets you, his warm handshake and his shirt-and-tie appearance bespeak the charity director. He can laugh at the absurdities of prejudice rather than snarling. Even the message on his mobile phone admonishes you to 'Be happy!' But beneath an essentially positive outlook on life lies what he calls his 'passion' – to campaign against the injustice done to people with learning difficulties and to insist on their human rights. This comes as no surprise once you learn what he has had to contend with.

Lee's early years mirror the experiences of most people with learning difficulties, though his family's persistence was to make a big difference. He was born in a Greater Manchester hospital in August 1969, the first child of Linda and Michael Lee. His mother was an occupational therapist, his father a hospital catering manager, who later became responsible for three hospitals in the Dudley health authority. From his father, Lee inherited a stubbornness that never takes no for an answer, and from his mother a dogged determination to keep going. His sense of humour, he thinks, comes from his mother's side.

From the beginning, he was labelled as having learning difficulties (including, later, dyslexia), along with cerebral palsy and epilepsy. These conditions elicited the usual thumbs down from the medical profession. 'Doctors told my parents I would not walk or talk and I would be a cabbage for the rest of my life. Most new parents would have believed what the doctors said, but my parents did not.' His mother used her professional skills to prove the doctors wrong. Lee sat up and walked. Then he learned to swim and to ride a horse. 'Whenever we heard anyone in the healthcare or education system say "no", we put two invisible fingers up at them and did it anyway.' It helped, he thinks, that his parents knew the NHS from the inside and where to find help if they needed it.

The family moved home seven times as Lee grew up, on account of his father's job or for Lee's benefit. In the early days they lived around Manchester, and later near Birmingham. His brother, Richard, born seven years later, in 1976, sometimes complained that Andrew got the lion's share of his parents' attention. But there was a general feeling of unity. The support at home helped sustain him against the prejudice of the world outside.

> The reasons people gave me for not being able to do things varied – it could be because I was 'disabled', 'a Spaco' or a 'thicko'. I broke down and cried a lot at school and I used to think the whole world hated me and I did not know why.

In his first two schools, he remembers no abuse, just boredom. His father was a Roman Catholic, so Lee was sent to a convent school in Ashton under Lyne, where he sat in his smart school uniform, the lessons passing him by. Next he went to Wordsley infant school, and then to The Brier School in Stourbridge, which was for children with special educational needs (SEN). You would expect that a school geared to disabled pupils would have some understanding of them, but Lee says that from the headmaster down, he was bullied. As well as having learning difficulties, he had epileptic seizures and he also stammered under stress. He became a butt for other pupils. Travelling on the school bus, they called him names.

> When I was brave enough to go into the playground I was kicked and punched on a regular basis, and yet the headmaster denied there was a bullying problem. Sometimes it was safer to spend playtime, as it was known, in an empty classroom.

One day he was beaten up just beyond the closed school gates; the headmaster, on the inside, saw what was going on but took no responsibility for it. Later, children from Richard's school as well as his own set upon the brothers at the local bus stop, which happened to be next to the police station. Lee told a policeman and they were taken home in a police car, but the police took no action against the bullies. Eight out of ten children or young people with learning difficulties get bullied, according to research in 2007 by the charity Mencap; it called on the government to treat 'disablist' bullying as seriously as racist or homophobic bullying. Lee thinks the situation is even worse than it used to be.

Church was a sanctuary for him as a child. He became an altar boy and when he was 11 he joined a group from the church who were going to Lourdes, whether for a cure or not was unsaid, but in fact he had no seizures for three years afterwards.

There were two other distractions from his misery. He loved horse riding and went to a mainstream riding school where he could enter competitions like everybody else. He also loved music. From playing tunes on an electronic keyboard, he moved to a Hammond organ, and his parents arranged music lessons for him. As a teenager he discovered Status Quo and punk rock. He likes dancing as well as listening. Most kinds of music attract him, except jazz.

Reading was a source of frustration because he could not read books appropriate for his age and there were hardly any easy-read books for older children in the library. His mother found him audio-taped versions, such as *Swallows and Amazons*. Nowadays, he argues for publishers to make more books accessible to people with learning difficulties. 'There is a massive community out there that would like to read novels, but there's a perception that if it's in large print and picture format they are only reaching people who can't or don't want to read these things.' More than that, if publishers worked with groups of disabled people, he suggests, they would find storylines based on personal experiences that would attract a readership of disabled people.

If Lee's parents had not hired a private tutor when he was about seven, he thinks he would never have learned to read, write, spell and add up. He had an hour's tutorial in the evening after school. His parents had to go without other things to pay for the tutor. Lee remembers having 'toasted toppers' – toast with various toppings – for the evening meal, and living in a caravan.

His parents complained in vain to the school governors and the local education authority about the ill treatment Lee was receiving at The Brier School. Finally, they threatened to go public. They forced the authority to move him to another SEN school, Penn Hall, near Wolverhampton and moved themselves so that he could be a dayboy. At his new school Lee found pupils could be friendly, and teachers were patient and willing to listen to him. 'It was strange not being criticised for everything I did.' He thinks the switch to Penn Hall was the making of him. Although there was no chance to take external exams, the school offered extra-curricular activities that helped build his confidence. He learned to ski on a dry ski-slope; he steered a motorboat; he took part in discussions about TV programmes. He also took responsibility for feeding younger pupils at lunchtime and playing games with them.

His newfound confidence made him more resistant to bullying, so when a boy – who had learning difficulties himself – started on him, he was determined to deal with it. It happened on a 'visit' day, a few weeks into his first term, when the class broke up into small groups and went out to gather information in Wolverhampton before joining their teacher at a McDonald's. One of his group started verbally abusing Lee in a shop, where other people could overhear. Lee had completed the assignment, so he slipped away and made his own way to McDonald's – no mean feat since the town was strange to him and he has no sense of direction. He got there by asking directions. The teacher listened to his story and the bullying stopped. Lee sees this as a milestone.

> My belief in myself grew that day. For the first time a teacher believed me. It was the first time I had coped with a bully and I did it myself, even though I could have got lost in a strange city.

Another time, when he was staying in the residential unit for a week, he helped a boy, who used a wheelchair, to get up in the morning. This involved learning to use the hoist, which pupils were not supposed to touch. Starting at 5am, the job was accomplished by 6.30. Though they impressed the teacher, the head was less than enthusiastic about the rules being broken. Still, Lee was beginning to make decisions for himself.

His parents 'got some stick', he says, for encouraging this independence. When he left school, they chose not to have him at home, attending a day centre. Instead, they sent him away to Derwen College, a residential college for people with learning difficulties, near Oswestry, on the Welsh border. Lee had never been apart from his family for a long period, and he had to get used to a new place and make new friends. He went with some trepidation, but it worked for him. He learned how to live independently. He had a girlfriend. (One houseparent who tried to stop a couple holding hands got short shrift from the students and was fired by the head.) His grandfather, 'Poppa', encouraged him to sit for the West Midlands Maths Proficiency exam, which he passed. He also learned a language, a form of British Sign Language that was part Welsh, part English, to help a deaf student communicate with college teachers. He left college after a mock job interview, feeling he could hold down a paid job. 'It made me think I could have a future other than one stuck in a day centre putting pens in boxes all day, a place someone put you in and called it a job.'

But finding the paid job proved very difficult. Work experience in one of his father's kitchens exposed him to a mainstream job environment; he saw how fast people worked, and he learned about timekeeping and contributing to the team effort. After that it was a series of jobs in a Youth Training Scheme, all unpaid; he ran a burger bar in a youth centre, fitted carpets in people's homes, ran a sweet shop at a youth centre for disabled people, and swept driveways. But the scheme failed to lead to a paid job. He felt he was going nowhere. In one respect, though, he had taken the initiative. When his parents split up, rather than choose between them, he decided to live on his own. While other friends stayed at home or lived in college, he moved into a bed-sit in Oswestry, aged 19, and took full responsibility for himself. After 18 months of voluntary work and a rather disastrous twenty-first birthday party – he invited 50 people but only three college friends and four relatives appeared – he asked his parents to scout for jobs for him in their areas. His father could find no jobs in Liverpool, so he moved south, to his mother, and lived in a bed-sit in Stevenage. Then, in 1991, with money from his grandparents, he bought a mobile home in Hitchin, where he lived for the next four years.

During this time he tried to find mainstream jobs, usually running into social prejudice. A petrol station owner, who saw him filling in an application form slowly, brusquely showed him the door; hotel staff made fun of the new kitchen porter. He stuck at it, and from a hospital open day came another job as a kitchen porter. He enjoyed this and made friends, but then his epilepsy returned and he was made redundant on health grounds.

Out of a chance encounter, his life took a new turn. His mother passed on to him the phone number of a social worker, who gave voluntary support to a group of people with learning difficulties in Hitchin. Invited to a barbecue in 1994, Lee was welcomed by the chair of the group, 'a burger in one hand and a can of beer in the other', who talked about not being able to access his benefits because his parents had financial control. This got Lee thinking. 'I wanted people in my life who would empower me to do things for myself, not do things for me with the illusion that I was in control.'

He started going to meetings of the group, which later joined up with others to form North Herts People First. Isabella Rutter, who supported Lee, says:

> They all felt, and Andrew felt, that they didn't have special needs. They wanted somewhere to live, they wanted transport, they wanted a partner. That wasn't special; it was the same as anybody else. And with the right support, you can have those things.

Seeing members campaigning on issues he felt strongly about was an eye-opener for him. He saw self-advocacy in action and joined in enthusiastically. Helped by publicity in the local *Comet* newspaper, they persuaded Abbey National to reverse its decision not to allow people with learning difficulties into its offices on Saturdays or to access their own bank accounts. Lee argues that even people with high support needs should control their money; if they cannot communicate, then local authorities should provide them with the technology to do so. He dismisses excuses about cost. 'It's a matter of priorities,' he argues.

They also persuaded Stevenage council to end a rush-hour exclusion on the free bus pass so that people with learning difficulties could get to college in the morning. Then came a big campaign to stop local authorities, which were being financially squeezed by the Thatcher government, from increasing day care and transport charges. Disability groups came from all over Hertfordshire to fill City Hall and Lee spoke on their behalf. He went on local radio too. Rutter remembers his speech. 'He was so eloquent and passionate,' she says. 'He can hit the nail on the head, and he really made people sit up.' Hertfordshire postponed the price hike for some people for a year, and reduced the rate for others.

By 1996, North Herts People First had become 'one of the most active self-advocacy organisations in the country', says David Morris, now senior policy adviser on disability to the Mayor of London. As chair of the management committee, Lee helped to secure Lottery funding. But none of this would have been possible without the initial backing of Hertfordshire social services, which pioneered the development and funding of grassroots self-advocacy groups. With the help of disabled people, including Lee, social services went on to fund POhWER (People Of Hertfordshire Want Equal Rights), an umbrella agency delivering advocacy and other services through seven independent, but allied, groups. Morris, the first chief executive, had to make the idea work. POhWER was run and controlled by people with different disabilities – the first in the country, Lee claims. He was one of the trustees. Tim Anfilogoff, then policy officer for users and carers in Hertfordshire, remembers how Lee stood out from the others – a dapper young man with an Errol Flynn moustache, who insisted that people less articulate than himself should be included in decision-making – that everybody could contribute something.

Inevitably, there were tensions at POhWER between trustees and management over running the organisation and providing services. There were staff problems too. Morris remembers two highly stressful employment tribunals involving disabled employees in which Lee was involved. At one meeting Lee had an epileptic seizure and at another the deputy director had a stroke. Nevertheless, Lee's experiences at POhWER, plus the support he received from Morris at North Herts People First, gave him the know-how to manage an umbrella, user-led organisation. Today POhWER has 200 employees and runs advocacy services in three UK regions.

Lee had a finger in many pies in the mid-1990s. He was a member of Hertfordshire's Community Learning Disability Team, helping to make decisions alongside health and social services professionals. He and five others with learning difficulties trained to become independent lay assessors of residential care homes. On voluntary forums and steering groups, he began his long-term campaign for 'easy-read' versions of minutes and documents; information, he knew, was power. (Easy-read, with its one idea per sentence, simplified words and illustrations, is a welcome relief from bureaucratic jargon.) With Rutter and others, he travelled the country telling people about self-advocacy, undeterred by his epileptic seizures. 'Andrew doesn't let his disability interfere with what he believes is his job or what he would like to see done,' says Rutter. Stevenage MP Barbara Follett, now Minister for Culture, noticed his determination. 'He was quite a remarkable young man, very self-possessed, very focused,' she says. 'He's a born leader, and people looked up to him.'

From time to time Lee joined demos in London. He remembers with glee one held in support of inclusive education, the campaign to educate disabled and non-disabled children together. The rain was pouring down, so they crowded into the Department for Education. 'A man in a white shirt held up his hand and asked, "Is there anybody I can talk to who is in charge of these people?" And everybody said, "We are. Talk to us."' By this time, his interest in the wider canvas had led him to stand for the management committee of People First in London. He was elected in 1996.

Set up in December 1984, People First was the first self-advocacy group of people with learning difficulties in the UK. The self-advocacy idea started in Sweden and then moved to North America, where Gary Bourlet, the learning-difficulties campaigner, discovered it. From the group in London, others sprang up around the country, challenging the accepted view among policy makers and carers that people with learning difficulties could not think for themselves and needed care and protection.

The term 'people with learning difficulties' mystified non-disabled people because it seemed to stress education at the expense of, say, behavioural or communication difficulties. But for members anything was better than the demeaning 'mental handicap'. They turned on Mencap, the charity set up by parents, attacking its patronising image, its posters, and its very name. As Bob Findlay, of the Birmingham Disability Rights Group, explained to readers of *Disability Now*:

> The issue of disability terminology is not merely a question of certain terms or definitions being insulting or misleading, but the *right* of people who are

subject to those terms and definitions to throw them off and *take control* of how they are seen as a collective group.

Mencap declined to change its name, but the Department of Health started using 'learning disability' after the Community Care Act 1990 and that has stuck in government circles. People First members have also rejected specific 'medical labels', such as autism or Down's syndrome. By using 'support needs' instead, they position themselves in mainstream society; everyone, they argue, needs some kind of support, to a greater or lesser extent.

Self-advocacy took off in the 1990s, stimulated by long-stay hospital closures and a growing awareness of advocacy and civil rights. Supposedly managed by people with learning difficulties, the groups relied on non-disabled 'supporters', which led to power tussles. Eventually, at People First, the rights campaigners won the day, hired a consultant and embarked on a reorganisation. Two women with learning difficulties stand out in this period: Carol Dickson, chair of the management committee until 1999, who married Lee in 1997, and Simone Aspis, who served with Lee on the committee. Aspis, urgent and abrasive, urged the group towards political activism. She secured the inclusion of people with learning difficulties in the Disability Discrimination Act (DDA) 1995 and in the Community Care (Direct Payments) Act 1996, which introduced local authority direct payments for disabled people's care. She also shamed the Tory government into making the DDA available in easy-read, the first accessible government document. It was Aspis who made the 'social model' meaningful to Lee and others at People First. Over the years, she has continued to influence the direction of the organisation's campaigning.

The People First plan called for a director with learning difficulties. Lee got the job in 1999 at the age of 30. Even today people are surprised that someone with learning difficulties can hold down a director's post. The support workers at his housing scheme in Stevenage were incredulous when he told them the news. 'You wouldn't be able to do that. Don't be bloody stupid,' was their reaction, says Lee. They even managed to give him wrong information about his rent, which landed him in debt; but he sought advice, difficult though it was to understand some of the information, and successfully challenged them. His parents feared for his benefits (Income Support and Disability Living Allowance). 'It was a big jump to go from benefits to full-time work,' he admits, but he was determined to prove himself. 'It became a personal campaigning issue to change minds.'

More battles awaited him in London. Access to Work officials said the government support scheme did not cover people with learning difficulties;

they had to be reminded of the DDA. That paved the way for other people with learning difficulties to apply. But when an occupational psychologist came to the office in Kentish Town to assess what he could do, she immediately blotted her copybook by announcing, 'We will get on fine. I used to be a nurse.'

One of Lee's first acts was to invoke disciplinary procedure against a member of his team for failing to pass on financial information to the staff and management committee – a matter, he thinks, of someone with physical disabilities distrusting people with learning difficulties. This was not unusual. After People First joined the umbrella organisation, the British Council of Disabled People (BCODP) in the 1990s, Simone Aspis claimed that people with learning difficulties, including herself, were kept at arm's length because other disabled people feared they would all be labelled 'stupid, thick, mental and mad' by the non-disabled public.

Lee has his own take on the relationship: people with learning difficulties usually did not look disabled but they had to overcome a lack of self-confidence before they could begin to fight the system. He tells of a silent drama performed by North Herts People First.

> One person knocked on a door, and someone else closed it. Then more people came to the door, but the door was still closed. Then it got to about 20 people, and the door opened. It showed oppression from a learning difficulties perspective; it meant that you can't ignore us any more.

Perhaps that was true for BCODP too. Certainly Lee's personality – sunny but determined – equipped him to bridge the gap between learning difficulties and other disabilities. Today, he is a trustee of the UK Disabled People's Council (BCODP renamed), while Aspis looks after its press and campaigning. 'He's got a willingness to work with the rest of us and, God knows, it's not easy for him at times,' says Ruth Bashall, an independent consultant and trainer.

In his new job Lee tried to boost People First's profile on a low budget, while running an organisation whose member groups did not take kindly to any usurping of their autonomy. He was on a tightrope, but it was exciting. The Labour Party had won the 1997 general election and was now building on the Disability Discrimination Act 1995. In the surge of legislative activity that created the Disability Rights Commission (DRC), education came within the Act and, for the first time, people with learning difficulties from all over the UK were consulted about what should go into a government white paper, *Valuing People*, about services for them. Lee's wife, Carol, was the first person with learning difficulties to receive an MBE for her work on the advisory group. From the four principles of 'rights, independence, choice and inclusion' came plans for person-centred services, annual health checks, a greater choice of housing, employment services, and so on. Learning disability partnership boards, which included people with learning difficulties, were set up to make the plans happen. Six years on, in 2007, people were fed up with the lack of progress. Care and advocacy services had been cut as cash-strapped local authorities tightened their criteria. The Care Services Minister, Ivan Lewis, promised a revitalised white paper that would make local delivery a priority, and the Government added jobs and accommodation for people with learning difficulties to its targets for local authorities.

*Valuing People* had recognised the importance of self-advocacy. Building on the advisory group, the Government had funded a structure of regional, user-led groups, feeding into a National Forum for People with Learning Disabilities that advised the Department of Health via membership of the Learning Disability Taskforce. The forum was a national voice for people with learning difficulties. Besides elected representatives, three groups were seen as important enough to warrant permanent membership of the forum: Mencap, the DRC and Carol Lee, representing People First (Self Advocacy). This implied that the London-based group was a national organisation – a status not recognised by all the local groups.

Meanwhile, other people with learning difficulties, besides the Lees, were assuming positions of influence, including Eve Rank, as a DRC commissioner, and Nicola Smith, the Department of Health's co-director for learning disabilities.

Rank chaired the DRC's Learning Disability Action Group of which Lee was a member. They helped produce a pioneering easy-read booklet and CD, which encouraged people with learning difficulties to join a political party, vote, and stand for office. Lee also joined a DRC investigation into health services for people with learning difficulties and mental health problems – he was the only person on the inquiry panel to have learning difficulties. He heard evidence from disability groups and quizzed representatives of the Department of Health and the British Medical Association. The report, which also appeared in easy-read, revealed shocking levels of ill-health and widespread discrimination in the NHS.

Working on formal committees like this is not easy for Lee, though when he asks for clarification or time to digest a document, it can be helpful for others. Having a reliable supporter is essential. 'We have to try and work as two heads sharing one brain,' says Lee. 'I see an extra head as a huge advantage!' Still, it is a tricky arrangement. 'When you are supporting, it's quite an intimate thing because you end up knowing what each other's thinking,' says Ellen Clifford, who, with her husband, Kevin, supported Lee for several years. Between them they covered planning, fundraising and campaigns, and Ellen Clifford would also hear about family matters. 'You have to like each other when you are working together, so there was obviously a friendship as well,' she says. Even with her experience and commitment to user-led organisations, she found it difficult not to impose her own views and to work at a slower pace. Supporters have a shelf life, she says, and some find the environment too difficult and the pay too low. All the People First supporters had walked out before she started, and within a couple of months the other four from her intake had gone too. She helped to introduce some assistance for the other supporters.

Self-advocacy has always been dogged by a tension around the supporter's role; there may be obvious intervention or subtle bias, and a decision can be influenced by the way you present the options. Eve Rank remembers the early days of the Learning Disability Action Group, before the Cliffords came on the scene. 'Andrew was occasionally told what to say by his supporter and sometimes he didn't take any notice, which was good.' Nowadays, Lee has a circle of supporters with different expertise, on which he draws as needed; this spreads the workload and dilutes the influence of one person, even if it makes sharing information more difficult. The supporter idea is still evolving. Lee's ideas are appreciated by physically impaired people who use a personal assistant – another bridge between the two groups.

From 2003, the new All Party Parliamentary Group on Learning Disability started giving self-advocacy groups as well as bigger charities the chance to bend the ear of sympathetic MPs and peers and influence government policy. Its appearance coincided with the Mental Incapacity Bill. People First and others feared that, despite its intention to protect people with the capacity to make decisions, the bill would actually enable parents and carers to continue making decisions for those deemed to lack capacity.

Lee was a witness at the Parliamentary Joint Committee on the bill. He argued that the 'general authority' of parents or carers to make decisions on behalf of people with learning difficulties was open to abuse and in conflict with the aims of *Valuing People* and the human rights of people to freedom, family life and privacy. He spoke with authority because People First had held a conference and a workshop beforehand. 'Our members have told us about their relatives and paid carers bossing them about,' he said. 'This shows that it is unwise to put our faith in these people to really allow us to make our own choices.' Also, he said, there was no easy way for people to complain about a decision. His members thought the bill would set the self-advocacy and advocacy movements back 20 years. Asked by a long-winded

MP what he would like, he replied, succinctly, 'There should be a mandatory right to an independent advocate whenever a person's ability to make a decision is questioned.' Lee explained how he had acted as an independent advocate for a friend with learning difficulties and mental health issues because the supporters, not trained in both conditions, saw it as in the friend's best interests, and quicker, to make a decision for him. Lee also called for people unable to speak up for themselves to have a right to aids that would allow them to communicate their decisions.

He had never before given oral evidence to a parliamentary committee and he was proud of it. As the bill progressed, there were more parliamentary meetings. On one occasion, while Lee and others were inside the House of Lords, staff from People First staged a demo outside; one was tied up and gagged, while others, dressed as a doctor, social worker and parent, held the ropes. Although the resulting Mental Capacity Act 2005 disappointed self-advocacy campaigners, it did provide for independent advocates and a maximum prison sentence of five years for the ill treatment or neglect of someone who lacks capacity, which came into operation in 2007.

The year 2005 also heralded a report from the Prime Minister's Strategy Unit that the disability world could welcome, even if there was no new money to pay for the big promises. The Government set itself a target of equality for disabled people by 2025 and a strategy for getting there. People First prepared the easy-read version, and Lee was one of 13 disabled people who advised the Government on the role of Equality 2025, a new advisory network of disabled people – though he did not win a seat on it.

Alongside his political lobbying and government appointments, Lee was becoming an influential spokesperson for people with learning difficulties on the London scene. As a member of the London Equalities Commission – though rarely at meetings – he called for the Greater London Authority (GLA) to use accessible language and for the disabled facilities grant, which pays for home adaptations, to be accessible to people with learning difficulties. David Morris, as the Mayor's senior disability adviser, invited him to speak at two consecutive Disability Capital conferences, the major event for disabled people in London. In 2005, Lee joined Maria Eagle, Minister for Disabled People, and others in a public discussion of the forthcoming 'public sector duty', which would oblige bodies like the GLA to draw up plans for treating disabled people equally and consulting with them. Lee, of course, wanted to include easy-read in the duty and require local authority departments to work with people with learning difficulties: 'If you don't involve us, you are going to keep getting everything wrong… So start talking to us.' He was applauded on both points. The audience also appreciated his call for police officers to have disability equality training; a police officer had told him they were lucky if they got 20 minutes' worth. The following year, discussing the future of the disability movement in London, he urged local groups to work together more closely and deplored the time spent on complicated fundraising.

Behind the suit-and-tie public appearances, Lee has led a hand-to-mouth existence at People First, fundraising a lot of the time. But unlike most groups he has to provide for supporters as well as staff. Bigger givers have included the Association of London Government or the Department of Health, but usually it has been £10,000 or £20,000 here and there for specific projects. The year 2005–06 was a disastrous one, when income fell sharply, necessitating cheaper offices, spending cuts and shorter staff hours; 2006–07 saw a slight recovery and a small surplus, allowing People First to start a much-needed reserve fund. (Meanwhile, Mencap recorded a surplus of over £5 million in 2006–07, with £858,000 spent on advocacy services.)

Nevertheless, things are looking up. In January 2008, People First (Self Advocacy) was one of seven disability groups, led by Scope, to win a £4.2 million grant over three years from a Big Lottery Fund programme. The money is to build the skills of 200 local disabled people's organisations. People First's share, about £200,000 a year, will nearly double its annual income and add 12 people to its team. As part of Disability LIB (Listen, Include, Build), People First will help improve self-advocacy skills and make sure the voice of people with learning difficulties is heard and information made accessible to them. Meanwhile, it continues political campaigning, running conferences, organising training – including sexuality awareness – and building ties with opposite numbers in Europe. It makes money from an easy-read information and contract service, training disability and main-stream organisations and producing guides and factsheets.

One of Lee's greatest achievements, people think, is to have kept his organisation going. He may bounce into the office with a big 'Hello, everyone!' that makes the team jump, but Sue Bott sees the pressures behind the smiling facade. As director of the National Centre for Independent Living, with offices down the corridor, she supports the chair of Lee's management committee, who also has learning difficulties, so that he can supervise Lee. 'The thing about Andrew is that he takes it all on board,' she says. 'He won't leave anything. He can't say OK that's a problem, I'm going to deal with it tomorrow. It's all going around in his head the whole time and he works incredibly hard.'

Friends and colleagues have worried that the stress will get on top of him as it did around the time of his divorce, when his epileptic seizures accelerated and he had to take a month off work. In 2007 he had the excitement and stress of getting married again, after some family battles, but he has had no seizures for three years. His second wife, Olcay Ucurel, who also has learning difficulties, was born in Turkey and raised in the UK. She was a member of People First's management committee until her marriage. Lee won a battle with his local authority to move them to accommodation that is accessible for Olcay's wheelchair.

Signing up: Andrew Lee marries Olcay Ucurel in June 2007. Photograph taken by Berfin Video

He shows no signs of slowing down. Indeed, his public appointments and appearances are growing like Topsy. In 2007 he took People First into the Learning Disability Coalition with 14 other charities, which has highlighted swingeing cuts in care services and called for a strategic review of the trends that affect demand. Older people, of course, are living longer, but the number of people with learning difficulties is increasing by 1 per cent a year as more babies survive, needing high and expensive levels of support. In this climate, self-advocacy groups are needed more than ever.

Lee's enthusiasm to push forward the cause of people with learning difficulties and work with erstwhile enemies like Scope or Mencap has brought criticism from People First insiders. Mencap's chief executive until November 2008 was Dame Jo Williams, who co-chairs the coalition. She and Lee gave their human rights evidence together, often agreeing with each other, and they supported the *Community Care* campaign. Williams saw no conflict between the two organisations and thought the relationship gave them a louder voice. 'Our vision and aspirations are in line, really,' she said. Lee admitted, 'It is unusual for People First to work with non-disabled people's organisations, but in this case I think we are stronger speaking up together and also, sometimes, you have to go into the lion's den to tame the lion.'

Meanwhile the incipient rivalry between the National Forum for People with Learning Disabilities (also a member of the coalition) and People First erupted into a public row in 2007. People First (Self Advocacy) had lost its permanent seat on the National Forum a year earlier and had still not been given an explanation beyond it was 'confidential'. Lee claimed the forum was not user led, blamed the system set up by the Department of Health, and called for change. He also wanted forum members paid like members of the other government advisory body, Equality 2025. He took to the streets withmembers of People First (Self Advocacy) and distributed leaflets outside a forum meeting. Karen Flood, who has learning difficulties and was then co-chair of the forum and the coalition, came to the forum's defence, saying it was user led, that many members would lose benefits if they were paid, and, anyway, they took part for the privilege of being a representative. Andrew Holman, social care consultant at Inspired Services, who helped set up the forum, regrets that People First (Self Advocacy) has lost its seat. 'The forum needs to return to being user led and not being told what to think or do,' he says. He also favours paying national members, in line with Equality 2025.

That self-advocacy groups do not have a national campaigning voice outside the forum is seen as a serious weakness by some people. 'Andrew desperately needs to be freed up to do the job he should be doing, forming a national organisation,' argues Holman. But that would reawaken old fears. Many People First groups want to be independent and not subservient to a national organisation. Eve Rank, now a consultant, says other groups can do government work and need the funding: 'The work should be shared out.'

In practice, People First (Self Advocacy), based in London, is increasingly picking up the invitations to represent people with learning difficulties on committees or on the media, and Lee gets most of the limelight. In 2008, for example, he jointly presented the first TV news programme for people with learning difficulties, and he now co-chairs the coalition. 'He's learned an awful lot about how to work the mechanisms of campaigning and lobbying,' says Rachel Hurst, director of Disability Awareness in Action. Certainly he has grown more canny. When a journalist phoned him recently for a comment about local authorities calling for more powers, he said, cheerfully, 'I'd better look at this before I go into a rant!'

He knows the value of controlled anger too, and it can serve him well, getting the words flowing. In a vodcast in 2007, he was angry about the justice system and the way the media failed to report the abuse of people with learning difficulties.

> 144 people with learning difficulties can get sexually abused in Sutton and Merton – why wasn't that actually reported better? Why is it that people with learning difficulties can get sexually abused and it's a training issue, whereas if a child gets sexually abused, there's a public outcry and people get taken to court?

Over the years, he said, he had known ten friends in the movement who had suffered abuse yet not received justice because, as people with learning difficulties, they were labelled 'unreliable witnesses'. 'Our justice system fundamentally fails people with learning difficulties,' he declared. But attitudes are beginning to shift, thanks in part to a campaign by *Disability Now*, which has logged more than 50 'hate crimes', including murder, against people with learning disabilities over two years. The Home Office has asked the police to collect data, and the Director of Public Prosecutions has told police forces and the Crown Prosecution Service to look harder for prejudiced attitudes that could support a prosecution for disability hate crime under the Criminal Justice Act 2003. So far, there have been very few successful cases.

Sometimes Lee's ideas – and they *are* his ideas, even if they appear through the prism of a supporter – produce rhetoric that soars beyond the practical. He said in a speech at the launch of one campaign:

> A big part of having 'a life like any other' is being able to be impulsive, to be passionate and to act on your dreams. This is all part of being an individual that our current services do not allow for. No wonder people with learning difficulties die earlier and suffer worse health – we are a people who have yet to live.

In 2007 Lee was asked how he would like life to be for people with learning difficulties in 20 years' time. His wish list was, of course, coloured by his own experiences. 'I don't want future generations of people with learning difficulties to carry inside them a feeling of inadequacy, shame or lack of worth, like the present generation,' he said. For himself, he needed to stop apologising for his grammar and speech.

He wanted children with learning difficulties educated alongside non-disabled children so that there was no sense of strangeness – 'If Malta can do it, why can't we?' He wanted real choices after school, though he re-alised this would need a big change in attitude among employers and a serious investment by the government. He wanted individual care budgets, so people with learning difficulties could control their lives, and he wanted them to vote and take roles in public life. He wanted the skills of supporters to be appreciated and properly paid for. And perhaps his warmest wish was that people with learning difficulties should be parents, getting information they can understand and the support they need so that they can keep their children. (The Government is now, officially, on side about this.) Finally, he wanted someone to give People First 'a few million pounds!' (He got a bit of that!)

Raymond Johnson, Lee's Number 2, sums up the achievement of his boss. 'He stands up to some of the most important people, MPs, lot of professionals, everyone across the board, really.' Lee's authority is rooted in personal experience. Liz Sayce, chief executive of the disability network, RADAR, has highlighted the 'acute need for clear rights to advocacy and communication support so everybody can make their voices heard'. That has been Lee's philosophy and his contribution – to make the voice of his people heard.

# TANNI GREY-THOMPSON: ATHLETE

Photograph taken by Graham Bool Photography

A photo of Tanni Grey-Thompson at the Athens Paralympic Games in September 2004 shows her slumped over her racing chair, head in hands, crying. In the T53 800m, she had finished in seventh place.* It was a spectacular failure. The 'golden girl' of Paralympic racing, holder of nine gold medals, who had broken over 30 world records and come close to breaking another in her semi-final the day before, had fluffed her first race. And it had all been shown live by the BBC.

Unlike the shorter distances, in the 800m you are allowed to change lanes part of the way through, so there is more room for tactical error. From a good start, Grey-Thompson allowed herself to be boxed in and never managed to secure a good position. She was honest about her mistake in an interview afterwards. 'I just made a really stupid decision and raced a bad race,' she admitted. 'It was my worst position in a Paralympic final ever and worst time of the season and worst everything, really.' Some of the team thought she should go home and give the rest of the games a miss. Paul Dickenson of the BBC wondered if Athens was a Paralympics too far (it was her fifth Games). She was 35, and the mother of a two-year-old. Time to retire?

Keeping focused under that kind of pressure takes grit. But if you have been out on the road in all weathers, clocking 100 miles a week, 50 weeks a year – not to mention indoor training – and all you want to do is win, you don't give up easily. Fear of failure can bring you down and send you home, Grey-Thompson says, but it keeps her coming back and keeps her training. She had gone into the 800m sensing she would fail; it was the first time she had felt like that and she had to confront it. She had also let down other people as well as herself. So two days later, she lined up for the T53 100m. Her usual pre-race nerves were in overdrive: she had been sick twelve times and her hands were shaking. But she held on to the words of her coach, Jason Bridges, and a generous rival, Francesca Porcellato, who had both told her she was the best in the world. Once she got started, tactics and technique took over, and she stormed to a gold in a personal best time of 17.24 seconds. She took another gold in the T53 400m, setting a new Paralympic record of 57.36 seconds, and just missed a bronze in the T54 200m, which included athletes less impaired than herself. She left Athens vindicated. And with eleven gold medals she had become, as BBC Sport put it, 'Britain's greatest ever Paralympian' (only matched in 2008 by the swimmer David Roberts).

---

*    Of the four wheelchair track categories, T51–54 (formerly T1–4), Grey-Thompson is classified at T53, an athlete who is paralysed from the waist down, with no stomach or lower back muscles or hip flexors, so she does not have the stability to make a fast start.

It's the kind of pinnacle that the media love, particularly when it has been scaled by a pretty, articulate, young woman in a wheelchair – that familiar and acceptable symbol of disability – who projects a friendly, down-to-earth personality and is not afraid of fame. As a result, Grey-Thompson has become a universal 'heroine', the key ambassador for disability sport.

Sometimes that flame is fanned unexpectedly. When she came third in the BBC Sports Personality of the Year in 2000, the first Paralympian to get this far, she was unable to join the rower Steve Redgrave and heptathlete Denise Lewis on stage because the BBC had provided no ramp. 'They just didn't think,' she said, without rancour. But others, who had watched her win four gold medals at the Sydney Paralympics, were furious. They flooded the BBC with complaints and Grey-Thompson was moved swiftly into the interview studios. The oversight did wonders for the profile of disability sport, she admitted later.

Grey-Thompson has been a pioneer, pushing the boundaries back for others, says Phil Lane, chief executive of ParalympicsGB. She is a model for the next generation of young disabled athletes, who competed in the 2008 Paralympic Games in Beijing and are preparing for the 2012 Games in London. She helped promote London's 2012 bid and sat beside Lord (Sebastian) Coe at the presentation in Singapore. Her athletic career drives home the ethic of dedication, high professional standards and hard work – with no short cuts. Well before she retired in 2007, Dame Tanni, as she is now, embraced this motivational role, visiting schools, working with young disabled athletes and the charities that support them. She extended it to the workplace. 'I can talk for Britain,' she says, cheerfully. So she is in demand as a public speaker at all sorts of events, from corporate conferences and seminars to small charity fundraisers, as well as being a successful television presenter. She was on the BBC's payroll at the Beijing Paralympics. All this has given her a niche, a good income, and the opportunity to go on promoting disability sport.

Some disabled people criticise Grey-Thompson. Comments about her hard-won media fame and financial success smack of jealousy; after all, non-disabled athletes do it and she has paved the way for others, if they care to make the effort. But fame and fortune are certainly harder to grasp in team sports, where the team may be aiming for one medal rather than a single person aiming for many.

Disability Bitch on the BBC website, Ouch!, wraps her barbs in humour. Grey-Thompson has 'moved the goal posts' so that disabled people are seen as capable of doing physical education or sponsored runs, she says. 'Being disabled isn't always totally brilliant.' She also mocks the 'noble reaction' of Grey-Thompson in seeming to accept the lack of a ramp at the Sports Personality of the Year awards. It was, as others have said, a missed opportunity to highlight social discrimination and promote disabled people's rights. Tara Flood, gold medallist and record-breaking swimmer at the Barcelona Paralympics, who now runs a campaigning organisation, says: 'Tanni was completely single minded about wanting to achieve – nothing wrong with that at all. I just wish she hadn't been quite so meek about some things.'

If there's one thing that makes Grey-Thompson angry, it is the assumption that she has overcome enormous obstacles as a disabled person to be a successful athlete. In her autobiography, *Seize the Day* (2001), she says she cannot remember getting her first wheelchair – it wasn't important. 'There is this perception that walking is good and not walking is bad. For me that's not true because being in a wheelchair has given me more mobility, not less…it's never stopped me from doing anything I wanted to do.'

She was born with spina bifida at Cardiff's Glossop Maternity Hospital, in July 1969. At that time, Wales and Ireland shared the highest incidence of spina bifida in the world. The cause of it is still unknown, though lack of folic acid plays a part. Spina bifida ('split spine') happens when an embryo's neural tube fails to close, causing a defective spinal cord, and the vertebrae over it do not fuse. Part of the spinal cord protrudes, often covered by a sac of fluid. Below the lesion, nerves governing movement and continence are paralysed to some extent. As a baby, Grey-Thompson had a small lump on her lower back, the size of half a boiled egg. It did not stop her learning to walk. Only if she bumped it did it hurt – like hitting your funny bone. Once, when she was a little girl, she hit the bump coming downstairs and was seen sitting at the bottom muttering, 'My bloody bump, you stupid bugger.' She had learned the swear words from her grandfather.

Her parents, Peter and Sulwen Grey, both Welsh, were not the kind of people to weep over spilt milk. Peter, an architect, later a director of works in the NHS, had learned from his own experiences of childhood illness the negative effects of over-protective parents; he was determined to encourage his younger daughter in anything she wanted to do. While his determination was calm and methodical, Sulwen's could be fast and fiery. Her parents complemented each other, and their united front meant that doctors and education authorities were not going to get away with professional mumbo-jumbo.

There was plenty of professional input in those early years. Not only did Grey-Thompson have regular trips to orthopaedic, spina bifida and neurology clinics, but also her sister Sian, 18 months older, was found to have a dislocated hip and a heart defect that required surgery. None of this was allowed to disrupt everyday life at St Alban's Avenue, in the middle-class suburb of Heath. The girls would play on a log in the garden, which their father had made into a pretend car with a steering wheel and a poker for the gear lever, or they would 'fry' clothes pegs in a frying pan. They shared the same bedroom until Grey-Thompson was 13. Close as they were, they often fought; their personalities were very different. Sian remembers how her sister tried to boss her about. 'I am not as competitive as Tanni and I have always been less extrovert,' she said. But it was Sian who got the upper hand over her sister's name. Looking at the new baby, officially named Carys, she commented how tiny she was; 'Tiny' soon became 'Tanni'.

Grey-Thompson was competitive almost from the start. Perhaps she inherited it from her paternal grandfather, Alex Grey, who was a star of Welsh amateur TT motorcycling in the 1920s. When Grey-Thompson went to the local Birchgrove primary school, she not only worked hard in class, but also tried everything outside, whether it was climbing a tree or swinging along on the monkey bars once she had been lifted up. Her great friend, Sue Roberts, was a spur as well as a support. 'If she did something, I wanted to do it too'. She joined the Brownies and ended up a 'sixer', in charge of her own group. From there, she discovered horse riding, which gave her a sense of freedom, though she didn't understand why she was riding with 'these people', who were all disabled.

As her body grew heavier, her legs needed support. Before she started school she had been walking stiffly and falling down a lot, coming home with bloody knees. By the time she was seven, her bump had grown much bigger, she had lost feeling in her legs and she was using callipers and a walking frame. She tried out the brand new callipers enthusiastically, but the NHS forgot to tell her parents to wash them first and the abrasions produced big, yellow blisters, which took time to heal because of her slow circulation. An operation succeeded in pushing the protruding spinal cord into her spinal column and flattening her back, but it could not improve the paralysis. She started using a wheelchair when she felt tired, and a catheter.

Unusually for the time, the headmaster was positive about having an increasingly disabled pupil in his mainstream school; it probably helped that he knew her already and most of the school was on flat ground. Grey-Thompson was included in everything that went on. In the Christmas plays she started as a wobbly angel, became a magical Christmas tree, decorated under an enveloping green cape, and finally a wheelchair-using Mary. Being popular, she had friends who helped her up steps to the loo and defended her from occasional taunts. Once she was called 'limpy legs' at a meeting of the Girls' Brigade in the local church and refused to go again. She went with a church group to Lourdes – for the trip, not the cure. When the priest asked if she wanted to go into the water, she asked if the water was cold, and was told it was freezing. 'I don't think I'll bother, then,' she said.

As Grey-Thompson grew older, she got more stroppy with the doctors. They never did explain the long-term effects of spina bifida. Like other people impaired from birth, she accepted she had it and might as well get on with it, but she increasingly resented the ineffectual prodding, the aim to keep her on her feet no matter what, and the pressures to look 'normal'. Backed up by her parents, she resisted a complicated operation that would have lengthened her shorter leg without helping her to walk.

Her parents had a long-drawn-out battle when it came to getting her into a mainstream secondary school. The local comprehensive, Llanishen, where Grey-Thompson's sister Sian had gone and her friend Sue was due to go, was out of bounds for Grey-Thompson. The headmaster had never had a pupil in a wheelchair before and turned her down, sight unseen. He claimed the school was inaccessible, and nothing would move him. South Glamorgan Education Authority assumed that because Grey-Thompson was in a wheelchair she had a learning difficulty and needed 'special' education. They suggested Erw'r Delyn, a school for disabled children nine miles away in Penarth. The Greys said no. Peter Grey found a clause in the influential Warnock Report (1978) on special needs education, which said that every child had the right to be educated in the environment that was best for their educational needs. Both parents were ready to send their daughter to a boarding school or educate her at home rather than have her education jeopardised. They argued that she should be assessed in her primary school. At last the local authority gave in. Grey-Thompson was assessed, once by a man who did little more than stand at the door of her classroom to watch her, and then by a psychologist who asked her simple questions, such as 'How many days are there in the year?' All this hassle, she says, 'brought home to me that I was thought of as different'.

Finally, it was agreed that she should go to St Cyres, a mainstream comprehensive next door to Erw'r Delyn. The drawbacks were distance, both for travel and having a social life outside school, plus the rule that wheelchair users must have lunch and do PE at Erw'r Delyn. From feeling very shy in this large school, Grey-Thompson soon made new friends. She rebelled against her callipers and crutches – anyway, the crutches caused havoc in the corridors – preferring to use her wheelchair. And she wangled herself out of lunch at Erw'r Delyn by pretending at St Cyres that she needed help with her work in the lunch hour and lying to Erw'r Delyn that she was in detention at St Cyres. After two years the lunch rule was relaxed, allowing 15 wheelchair users to eat in the mainstream school. Young men were employed to carry them up and down stairs.

The connection with Erw'r Delyn elicited an unexpected opportunity for Grey-Thompson – sports day. Aged 12, she had her first experience of wheelchair racing and disability sport. 'I had done a lot of sports where I competed against able-bodied people, but it was good to be able to compete against others the same as me and not be beaten hands down.' In fact, she came home armed with cups, shields and the award for top all-round performance. From there, things moved quickly. She was one of 12 disabled pupils from the school to be selected that year for the 15-strong Welsh team at the British Wheelchair Sports Association's Junior National Games at Stoke Mandeville. She took gold in the girls' junior slalom and silver in the 100m wheelchair dash. Even in her NHS wheelchair she was already showing an agility that allowed her to accelerate, brake and out-manoeuvre other people. The will to win made her formidable. Sometimes she overdid it and became, she says, obnoxious. As a defender in the Wales junior basketball team she held on to the ball, fouled other players and even fought on court with people bigger than herself. She was better in individual sports, setting her own agenda.

As things were taking off on the sports front, the spina bifida began to nag her. She was getting pain from curvature of the spine. To stop this and prevent further complications, she needed to have a metal rod inserted into her back, with bone grafts to help it knit, and clips at the bottom. It would be a painful operation, followed by six months in plaster, but at least Grey-Thompson had a consultant who could talk to teenagers. 'I didn't have a choice, but Mr [David] Jenkins presented it to me in a way that made me think I did.' She went ahead, in January 1983. One of the worst things was being helpless. By the time the plaster was removed, her neck muscles were so weak she had to hold up her lolling head with her hands for an X-ray, 'which Mum and Sian found hysterically funny'. There was no chance to feel sorry for herself.

She trained hard to get herself back in shape and felt stronger than she had ever been when she competed again at local and national level. In 1984 she set a new British junior record in the 100m at Stoke Mandeville and a year later she became the Junior Sports Personality of the Year at the Rotary Welsh Sports Team Championship. All the time, she was borrowing the school's sports chair.

Beyond sport, her life followed the pattern of most teenagers, except that the local authority still saw fit to assess her ability for mainstream education at 13 and again at 15 after she had successfully taken nine O levels. At this stage a careers teacher offered to get her a place in a secretarial college. When she said no, he responded: 'But you're in a wheelchair.' 'What's that got to do with anything?' she shot back.

The wheelchair did not figure in her thinking about a career or even much in her social life. The sixth form common room was difficult to reach on the second floor, but she went to parties and discos, and to a Penarth club called Marconi, where she was carried up and down the stairs, went on the dance floor, and no one stared. Her wheelchair was not a turn-off for boys. When they were younger, she and her non-disabled friend Jo Dutch used to play a trick on passers-by: she would sit on a bench while Dutch wheeled up and down in the chair, and then got out and walked. It never failed to amaze. She passed her driving test, aged 17, in a Motability car fitted with hand controls, which meant more freedom for her and her parents. Many shops in Cardiff were not accessible to wheelchairs, she found, and sometimes shop assistants would ignore her in favour of her friend. Her reaction was to boycott them – as she does now. Dutch remembered no open complaint in those days. While Grey-Thompson could be sharp with a narrow-minded professional, she was, perhaps, too 'nice' to make a fuss in public. Also, her life had been mainly integrated; she did not feel inferior or oppressed, and she had not encountered disability politics, let alone the 'social model'.

The last year of school, 1987, was a triumph. She passed four A levels in English, History, General Studies and Computer Studies, and an S (Special) level in Computer Studies. Also, the Cardiff branch of the Rotary Club raised funds for her to buy a state-of-the art Bromakin chair. It was the first of 19 racing chairs, mainly acquired through sponsorship deals. As the technology has developed so has the price of chairs, to around £2500. Using her Bromakin, Grey-Thompson took three golds and two silvers at the British Paraplegic Games that year, breaking the British record in the 200m. From there she went to the World Games at Stoke Mandeville, holding her eighteenth birthday party in a field, and then to Vienna – her first plane trip – to represent Britain in a European International. She stayed in a convent, an initiation into the strange places wheelchair athletes could find themselves in. The strangest was probably in Switzerland a couple of years later, an underground nuclear bunker for 150 people with no running water. But at least it was free, an advantage for impecunious athletes who usually had to fund their own trips.

Grey-Thompson had wanted to represent Britain ever since she was 14 and had seen the British wheelchair basketball team in their official tracksuits. Watching Chris Hallam, the flamboyant Welsh wheelchair athlete, winning the 1985 London Marathon on TV whetted her appetite too. But she never dreamed of being a professional wheelchair athlete, because at that time there was no such thing. Paralympic sport, which covered five categories of impairment ('para' means being parallel to the Olympics, not paralysed), attracted none of the status and sponsorship of the four-yearly summer or winter Olympics. From the first meeting in Rome in 1960, where doctors handed out the awards, it had been hampered by a perception of 'crips having a go', supported by charities, rather than serious athletes out to win races and break records. Seoul started a trend for both Games to share the same venue, the Paralympics following the Olympics, but the media still tended to pack up and go home. It was only when the London Marathon was televised in the 1980s, and wheelchair competitors were seen racing for the finish ahead of non-disabled runners, that disabled athletes really attracted public interest.

Given her early successes, Grey-Thompson wanted to go on building up her speed and stamina. So when it came to choosing a university, Loughborough, with its outstanding athletics facilities and famous graduates, such as Sebastian Coe, seemed a logical choice.

During her last year at school she had started training with non-disabled male athletes at the Bridgend Athletics Club – an unusual thing in those days, but a pattern she followed for most of her future training. Her coach, Roy Anthony, pushed her to the limit, as he did everybody. 'I like that sick feeling you get when you push yourself too hard,' she said. But sometimes even he had to tell her she'd done enough. Together they worked out how to tape her thumbs to protect them from unremitting pressure on the wheels. The friendly atmosphere of the club made up for its limited facilities; you either trained on grass, which was hard work, or, in bad weather, in the multi-storey car park.

By contrast, Loughborough had the track and training facilities, but not, it turned out, the will to support a wheelchair athlete. When Grey-Thompson turned up for a full training session, the non-disabled athletes looked askance, and a coach suggested it might be better if she used the track at a different time so the runners didn't get in her way. Once again, she was made to feel different. Through a friend, she joined the mountaineers for training; their group was small and friendly, and their focus, like hers, was on the upper body.

The other disappointment at Loughborough was poor access. Grey-Thompson was the only student in a wheelchair and although she was considerately housed in an adapted bungalow on campus, friends and student facilities were in the high-rise 'Towers', which meant negotiating steps or lifts that stopped at alternate floors. As with her impairment, she accepted the situation and dealt with it. 'I found a way of getting up the steps on my bum and dragging my chair as I did so. Once I'd done this a few times, it got relatively easy.'

As she made new friends, they helped her. And when she was selected to go to Seoul in 1988, aged 19, and came back with a bronze medal and a new British record in the 400m, non-disabled athletes saw her differently. Performance was what counted. Funding for Seoul had depended on five disability organisations raising £250,000 and the Minister for Sport, Colin Moynihan, doing a sponsored bike ride. It was the biggest Paralympics to date, but received little media coverage.

For Grey-Thompson, though, Seoul brought a step into celebrity. Wales recognised her as its own; the *Western Mail*, for example, added a disability dimension to its Welsh Sports Personality of the Year. When she also won the student category of the *Sunday Times* Sportswomen of the Year, which was not disability specific, she felt that disability sport was on the road to recognition.

Then, abruptly, the rod in her back snapped away at the bottom. It probably happened because she climbed one rope too many in the gym and had a fall and then could not resist trying scuba diving. She found herself in the Loughborough medical centre, in excruciating pain. The doctor misdiagnosed the problem and prescribed antibiotics for a bladder infection, refusing to authorise an X-ray or hospital transfer. Warned that their daughter was in the medical centre, Sulwen and Peter Grey drove up from Cardiff and arrived to hear screaming. It was not Tanni, Grey assured his wife. But it was; nurses were trying to turn her over. Sulwen took matters into her own hands. She told the medical centre bluntly that she was taking her daughter to a hospital that would treat her, swept aside concerns about how they would travel, and got her back to Cardiff. Professor Peter Gray, who had seen Grey-Thompson as a child, admitted her to the University Hospital of Wales, where an X-ray revealed the problem and an infected area. They decided to remove the rod, but the operation left her so weak that she couldn't race for six months and missed so much of her politics course that she decided to retake the second year.

In September 1989 she was back, competing in her first long distance race, the British Wheelchair Marathon, at Porthcawl in South Wales. It was an open race for men and women over more than 26 miles. She was up against her inspiration, Chris Hallam, in conditions of high winds and lashing rain. 'I had spiky hair and the gel kept running into my eyes and stinging.' Hallam went on to win. She came in joint thirteenth in a mediocre time of 3 hours 3 minutes. Yet she enjoyed it; she had proved she was fit again and she was on course for the London Marathon.

The following year she had a series of wins around the UK in the events she was making her own – 100m, 200m, 400m and 800m – and moved into long distance, both track and road. Here she came up against Rose Hill. The two never really got on, says Grey-Thompson, perhaps because they were at different stages in their lives – Hill was fifteen years older and had children. More probably it was because Grey-Thompson saw Hill as her main UK rival. Her friends among women athletes tended to be from other countries, like the Australian Louise Sauvage or the French Canadian Chantal Petitclerc, and from a different sports classification.

In Grey-Thompson's first London Marathon in the spring of 1990, she lost to Hill by eight seconds after a puncture had held her up; they came third and fourth in the women's section. In other races that year they battled it out, Grey-Thompson sometimes getting her revenge. By the end of the year they both shared the British Wheelchair Racing Association's Grand Prix and Grey-Thompson's marathon time had fallen to just over 2 hours 18 minutes, only 13 minutes behind the top ten men. The rivalry with Hill gave her a big incentive to do road racing. Besides, there was more money in it; she won £600 and a watch for winning the half-marathon, the Great North Run. It also built up stamina for track racing, her first love.

Unlike runners, wheelchair athletes can race long distance and sprint too because they are not using weight-bearing muscles. Grey-Thompson does everything at speed, including driving a car. Pushing on the road, she has reached over 24mph (39kph), and 50mph (80kph) going downhill, compared with nearly 22mph (35kph) on the track. Trying to train on the road at speed is a risky business, inviting collisions, and it has led to wheelchair athletes, as well as cyclists, being killed.

Grey-Thompson knew that if she could keep up with Hill during the race, she could summon a final, winning, sprint. The two women clashed regularly in the London Marathons of the 1990s; Hill won two, Grey-Thompson six. She dominated the London Marathon up to 2002, winning more races than any male wheelchair user did in theirs.

The desire for control lies deep inside Grey-Thompson, contributing to her will to win, to not give up, to be a pro. She claims she would be the same with or without spina bifida. Anaesthetic terrifies her because it feels like being 'put down'. When she raced abroad, she flew out early to settle in, avoided socialising, and got to the venue hours early so she could plan for any eventuality. The worry that her racing chair might be damaged or not appear in time was solved by having it boxed up for important races.

She has always put her trust in a few people she knows well, her 'team' of family, close friends, coach, training partner, physiotherapist, dietician, sports psychologist. She prefers to do things herself. She has kept a tight rein on her competitiveness by not training with female athletes or warming up with rivals. The sister who the family saw as the more disorganised one becomes very focused in a race environment. Yet setting goals, having a training programme, and getting all the detail right does not soothe her nerves. She is famous for throwing-up before a race, and Sian, who, with her father, was always at the big races, took it as a matter of course. 'So what?' she said to one agitated coach.

A great advantage for Grey-Thompson was that she could rely on her family's support, whether it was waving the flag (a Welsh flag as well as the Union flag) at important events, or writing a cheque when it mattered. After she left Loughborough with a lower second degree in politics and social administration, financial help from her father and grandmother meant she could put off job hunting and concentrate on the next Paralympics at Barcelona in 1992. By the time that came along she held the world record for 100m, 200m, 400m and 800m.

It was at Barcelona that she took part in her first 800m Olympic demonstration race. As a gesture to integration, major mainstream events like the World Championships or the Olympics include demonstration races, usually by wheelchair athletes. Essentially, they are a sideshow, the medals not counting towards the national tally, but for disabled athletes they provide a showcase and media coverage. Now that the Paralympics have won more equal recognition alongside the Olympics in Beijing and London, these demo races may disappear, and Grey-Thompson accepts that. But in Barcelona in 1992, the demo race was important to her, even though the discrimination was all too evident. She had to stay in a hotel some way from the Olympic village, sharing with an American rival, and there was no contact with British Olympic athletes. She was eventually allowed a British tracksuit but not the whole kit, and she could not take a coach, though athletes from other countries did. On top of these problems, she was competing against T4 athletes with less impairment, which allowed them to make a faster start. She produced her fastest time, but still came in last.

Three weeks later, she was back as a member of the British team, which felt a big step forward from Seoul because the athletes were together, not divided by disability group. Another advance on Seoul was having a fledgling British Paralympic Association (BPA), responsible for selecting and managing the squad and attracting corporate sponsorship; Royal Mail contributed £200,000.

All the hard work of the last seven years was about to pay off. In her first heat for the 400m, she broke the one minute barrier, setting a new world record of 59.20 seconds. Then she won three gold medals in her four track events, breaking her own world record in the 100m. Finally, although she came second in the 800m, she was awarded gold after the winner, Ann Cody from the USA, was disqualified for switching lanes too early in the race.

These successes, plus a spectacular pile-up in the men's 5000m race, some personalised promotion by the BPA, and the enthusiasm of BBC *Grandstand* presenter Helen Rollason (a good friend of Grey-Thompson's before her untimely death in 1999), brought the Paralympics into people's homes and Grey-Thompson into their lives. She reached a new level in the celebrity stakes. Among her awards were an MBE, BBC Wales Sports Personality of the Year (she has won three altogether), and *Sunday Times* Sportswoman of the Year. She made the *Guinness Book of Records* and had a giraffe at London zoo named after her. But what really made her feel she had arrived was taking part in the BBC quiz programme, *A Question of Sport*. The trouble was, she says, that with her knowledge of mainstream sport, her team got thrashed.

After Barcelona, Grey-Thompson became chair of the British Wheelchair Racing Association, which had been set up by the athletes themselves. It underlined the growing independence of disabled athletes in a world still dominated by the 'pat-them-on-the-head', 'keep-them-in-order' attitudes of sports administrators, coaches and volunteers. Disabled swimmers at Barcelona even suffered the humiliation of a 'swear box'.

Over the winter of 1993, Grey-Thompson soaked up sun, racing skills and information about how Australia ran disability sport. Funded by a Winston Churchill travelling fellowship, she trained with Jenni Banks, a high-ranking coach of mainstream and disabled athletes in New South Wales. Australia, she discovered, was well ahead of the UK in its attitudes to disabled athletes. She herself was respected and sports events were better integrated.

Banks remained her coach for several years, proving that a long-distance relationship can work once you know each other, even when there are different time zones. Banks devised a long-term training programme with weekly targets. Grey-Thompson was encouraged to analyse her own performance and fax back a log, then they talked each week on the phone. Together they worked on such things as keeping a relaxed rhythm over a long race and staying focused to get the best results. It was Banks who told her there was more to life than sport and talked about 'putting something back' by working in sports administration. Banks now says: 'She's not only in it for her own ends but also to assist other people, to make sport better and recognition of athletes with disabilities better. I think she's really achieved that.'

In 1994, Grey-Thompson was asked to team manage four male wheelchair athletes going to a demonstration race at the Commonwealth Games in Victoria, Canada. As an experienced athlete, who knew the rules, she seemed a reasonable choice. Norman Sarsfield, manager of the English team, did not think so. The gist of a phone call between him and Grey-Thompson was that a woman wheelchair user wouldn't be suitable as an official. The BPA warned her not to rock the boat. With the support of the athletes – including Dr Ian Thompson, whom she later married – she went anyway, forcing Sarsfield to admit later: 'We were wrong; everything worked absolutely perfectly.' The trip was an icebreaker for non-disabled and disabled English athletes; the cyclists, for example, were interested in wheelchair technology. Grey-Thompson has often said that her sport is closer to cycling than athletics.

The 1996 Paralympics in Atlanta were a serial debacle. The low status of the Games in the USA was brought home to everyone when parts of the Olympic village were dismantled before the Games even started, and the American media kept away – as did the spectators. 'The village was disgusting and there were no timetables, so nobody knew when they were meant to be competing,' recalled Grey-Thompson. She also criticised the management of the British team and 'well-meaning' coaches who lacked professional bite. Although Britain slipped from third to fourth place in the medals table, the Paralympians outperformed the British Olympic team by 39 golds to 1. It was a wake-up call for disabled athletes, coaches and disability groups to start talking to each other, says Grey-Thompson. But, more importantly, the disastrous Olympic results spawned a National Lottery funded World Class Performance Programme, aimed at winning medals, into which elite disabled athletes could tap. The growth of central funding brought not only new opportunities, but also bureaucratic controls; performance targets and medal-winning sports took precedence over grassroots development.

Other issues swirled about at Atlanta. People with learning difficulties were included in the Games for the first time, a decision Grey-Thompson and Ian Thompson had openly opposed, on the grounds that the classification system for learning disability was unreliable and could undermine the elite nature of the Games. Their view was confirmed at the Sydney Paralympics in 2000, when Spain's basketball team were stripped of their medals because most of them did not have a learning difficulty. The International Paralympic Committee (IPC) suspended the category. Swimmer Tara Flood remembers how Paralympians did not speak up for athletes with learning difficulties. 'There is this feeling that "I'm in a wheelchair but I'm not stupid,"' she says, but then concedes: 'I probably felt that way when I was competing.' A working party authorised by the IPC has been looking for criteria that would allow reinstatement by 2012. Grey-Thompson, now a member of the European Paralympic Committee, sees getting the classification system right as the first step and then there should be an open discussion because, if athletes with learning difficulties are included, smaller sports may be dropped. There are other questions too, she says. 'Is it possible in some events for athletes with learning difficulties to be included in mainstream? Is it because there is still significant discrimination that they don't have those opportunities?'

Disabled athletes are classified according to their degree of function so as to ensure fair competition. Despite changes, the system is still complex, medical, and a turn-off for the general public. It can also be political when a category is excluded because the athletes in it are severely impaired or there are not enough of them. Chris Hallam, now a national coach, noticed how athletes in the disabled British squad were growing closer to non-disabled people. At Seoul, 80 per cent of them could not get off the plane unassisted; at Atlanta, 80 per cent of them could. He blames media influence. 'Do you want to see someone nearly able bodied doing a sport that looks pretty much able bodied – long jump or whatever? Or do you want to see someone who is more severely disabled doing something that looks really slow and kind of uninteresting?' Sponsorship has also been blamed, from the top down. Certainly the Olympics have traditionally kept the Paralympics at arm's length; 2012 will be the first time they have a joint organising committee and the same logo.

The argument about more or less integration has been highlighted since 2006 by the ups and downs of Oscar Pistorius, the South African sprinter with prosthetic legs, as he fought to compete in the Beijing Olympics. Grey-Thompson has been equivocal about this. She was all for him competing, but she also saw the damage it could do. 'It's whether the Paralympics becomes in his category an event for the guys who are not good enough to make the Olympics. It's part of a much wider debate.'

When it comes to administration, she and Chris Hallam disagree. Hallam would like disability sport to be run by disability organisations, albeit without the charity connotation, while Grey-Thompson favours more integration inside the existing governing bodies, though she fears that merging the Games would exclude the smaller sports and people with more severe impairments.

Classification decisions can have a powerful impact on results. It happened in Grey-Thompson's events at Atlanta in 1996. She arrived reasonably confident: since Barcelona she had won races in faster times, breaking four of her own world records along the way. At Atlanta she found that a talented 13-year-old American, Leanne Shannon, had just been reclassified from T4 into the higher impairment T3, so would be competing against her. Grey-Thompson was not alone in thinking the decision should be reviewed, but there was no official support for a formal protest. She knew she couldn't match Shannon's starts. Although she set a world record in a 200m heat, she lost in the final and ended up with three silvers. Only over the longer distance, 800m, which gave her more time to catch up, did she win gold and set a world record. But gold medals were what counted in the world rankings. For the first time she faced pity. But she also felt some officials were pleased to see her taken down a peg. Someone in the media team thought she should retire. She was also blamed for a selection decision made by the British Wheelchair Racing Association before the Games. 'I came away feeling utterly desolate and disillusioned with the sport,' she said. She considered leaving the British squad.

Even so, when the national governing body for athletics, the British Athletic Federation, decided to bring disability athletics under its umbrella and appoint a development officer, Grey-Thompson accepted the job. 'You can't bitch about something if you're not prepared to try to change it,' she said. She left home, moved to Birmingham, and organised her training routine round the job. She was in charge of 17 regions. In some places, she said, 'we were trying to generate athletes out of nothing'. Then the Federation went bankrupt and David Moorcroft, ex-British runner and chief executive, had the job of rebuilding what became UK Athletics. He and Grey-Thompson retained a lasting respect for each other, even though she left in 1999, feeling that she had not achieved enough for grassroots development or elite sport.

She continued to share with him her frustrations about how UK Athletics put its resources into mainstream athletes at the expense of its world-class disabled athletes. But she did not go public with her complaints. It was not her thing to abuse people, she once told the television presenter Jonathan Ross, and she sympathised with Moorcroft who, she thought, had many battles on his hands and bitchy people to contend with. Moorcroft resigned in 2006. He said later that Grey-Thompson impressed him because 'she could make the transition from being a terrier on the track to being charming and sympathetic and caring about others'. But, yes, she could be 'bloody-minded'. 'It's not just that she's got a strong opinion. If you don't listen and act upon it, she'll say, "Why?"'

As an ex-athlete, he supported her decision to leave the development job. She had reconnected with her ambition and was aiming for the Sydney Paralympics. She had also married Ian Thompson, an industrial chemist, in May 1999. 'Tommo' had been a competitive cyclist before he broke his back in a road accident; he walks with a stick and uses a wheelchair for longer distances. Wheelchair racing brought them together over many years, and there was little to choose between them in commitment to their sport. Trying to beat Ian was what kept her training, jokes Grey-Thompson. The wedding featured in *Hello!* magazine, but their lifestyle was a million miles away. They belted round the streets of Cardiff independently on their wedding day, and chose Sempach in Switzerland for their honeymoon because they could keep up their training when not working companionably on their computers!

Grey-Thompson was back in Switzerland the following year competing for a place in the Sydney Olympics 800m demo race. She had one of her longest throwing-up sessions before the semi-final, but qualified for the final after talking tactics with Cheri Becerra, an American rival; Becerra got off to a fast start, and Grey-Thompson kept with her. At Sydney she came fourth.

Cooperating with another competitor is above-board. But wheelchair athletes, like cyclists, can resort to dirty tricks when they are racing in a pack – pushing, cutting each other up, and so on. In her early days, Grey-Thompson was involved in borderline cheating, when she used Ian Thompson's slipstream to help her along in a marathon and then won. The tactic had been suggested to her and she did not question its legitimacy. The officials decided she had not broken the rules. Nowadays, men and women are usually started at different times.

Doping, the bane of able-bodied sport, is comparatively unknown in disability sport. First discovered at the 1992 Barcelona Paralympics, it hit the headlines at Sydney, where nine disabled power lifters were expelled from the Games in 2000. Four years later, an anti-doping code was in place. For Grey-Thomson, doping might be deplorable, but at least it showed that the Paralympics were being taken seriously.

Her races at Sydney were preceded by a nasty shock. She was out training less than two weeks before her first race, when she felt a pain in her left side, checked herself, and found a lump. The team doctor examined her and found two. She burst into tears. Characteristically, she decided to deal with the matter there and then, not leave it until she got home. Since the British team has private health insurance abroad, she could have the tests and see a specialist. By next day, she knew there was a 70 per cent chance that she had benign cysts, not cancer. She tried to lock away her fears about the other 30 per cent and concentrate on the job in hand.

A smaller problem helped to take her mind off the bigger one. She has often dyed her hair, to be trendy and get away from the dark brown she dislikes. At Sydney, she decided to give herself some blonde highlights. It all went wrong, and she ended up shampooing her hair nine times to get rid of a pillar-box red look – to no avail. That's how she appeared on television and in photographs.

At least, in these Games, she was not competing against Leanne Shannon, who had outgrown her classification. But she came down with a cold and the rest of the team were getting ill too. As a morale booster, they created a giant fundraising thermometer to record the estimated cost of their various medical interventions. Luckily – though she doesn't believe in luck – the 800m race came first, and she won it. After winning her third race, she was jubilant. Three days later came the fourth race, the 400m. Now she was back to being jittery and sick. Winning that proved a big anticlimax – suddenly it was all over – but it was exciting to carry the Union flag at the closing ceremony and know that she had raced in front of 100,000 spectators.

The BBC pulled out all the stops for Sydney, sending teams for TV and radio, including Clare Balding for BBC Two and Peter White for BBC Radio. The Paralympic athletes had unprecedented coverage, Grey-Thompson among them. Back home, the awards came tumbling through the letter box – an OBE, honorary degrees (she now has 23) and membership of the Laureus World Sports Academy, where the great names of sport help with charitable sports projects for young people and hold glitzy annual sports awards. Attending her first event, Grey-Thompson found herself hailed by a fellow Welsh woman, Catherine Zeta-Jones, and then she had a conversation about shoes with Martina Navratilova. She and Ian found the whole thing over the top, but she admitted to being a bit star struck. 'I think it would be a shame to lose that.'

Given an all clear by the cancer clinic, she embarked, with her agent's help, on a hectic round of invitations, fitted between training and racing – BBC programmes like *Question Time* and *Mastermind*, mayoral lunches, corporate meetings and charity events where she was often the patron.

Her feelings about charity and disability have been ambivalent. Charity allowed the Paralympics to develop, paid for her first sports chair and still plays a key role in funding the chairs of young disabled athletes, as well as recruiting them. Yet her sense of independence as an elite athlete rebels against the ethos of 'deserving crips'. She disliked receiving the Helen

Rollason Award in 2000 'for outstanding courage and achievement in the face of adversity'. 'I don't think that applies to me,' she said. 'I keep working hard at telling people that I'm not struggling against the odds, but I can't escape it.'

Still, it is one thing to raise money for sick animals or the Royal National Lifeboat Institution (a lifeboat is named after her), and another to join sports celebrities in a round Britain relay on behalf of BBC's *Children in Need* appeal, when other disabled people are picketing Television Centre. That happened in 1992, the same year that disabled people brought ITV's Telethon to a halt. They were expressing their anger against a patronising society that saw disabled people as victims. You would think Grey-Thompson could identify with their protest, but their strategy was not hers. 'I get further by working with people rather than shouting at them,' she said a few years later. Also, immersed as she was in sport rather than national politics (she chose politics at Loughborough only because history had been scrapped), she was not involved with campaigning for the Disability Discrimination Act 1995 – though she was a relatively uninformed member of the National Disability Council that followed it. Direct action would probably not have served her purpose, she said later.

> You need to get into the centre of British sport to be able to say 'That's wrong, stop it now.' If I had just thrown stones from the outside, it would have been very easy in the time I grew up in sport for me to be excluded from it.

Certainly, being on the inside has given her influence. She has been on the board of UK Sport and on the Sports Council for Wales, both of which allocate funding.

Although she has been known to take a stand against airlines that patronise her, it is only latterly that she has become more confident about speaking out on disability rights, often through her freelance writing. By 2005, she was sufficiently politicised to refuse an honorary degree from Newcastle University unless she received it on the same floor level as everyone else, which happened.

Meanwhile, carefully planned between the Sydney and Athens Paralympics, her baby, Carys, arrived in February 2002. Medals might not compare, but Grey-Thompson thought she deserved one for every day she and Carys managed to be up and dressed before lunch. As with her training, she resolutely put up with discomfort. She had gladly accepted the doctor's recommendation of a Caesarean section, but she breastfed for five painful months, helped initially by savoy cabbage leaves. Carys did not sleep through the night for 18 months. Grey-Thompson remembers how one night, completely exhausted, she dropped a bottle in the cot and found next morning that the toddler had fed herself. Carys spent her early years in dungarees, so Grey-Thompson could catch her by the straps. She was soon being 'really stubborn, bit of a drama queen – like her mother.'

Mum and daughter: Tanni Grey-Thompson at home with
three-year-old Carys in June 2005. Photography taken by Mary Wilkinson

Amid all the disruption, racing continued. When Carys was three weeks old, they all went to Spain, where Ian Thompson was coaching the national squad. Grey-Thompson recorded her slowest time in the 1500m since she was 12, but managed to qualify for the World Championships. In April, when Carys was nine weeks old, Grey-Thompson won the London Marathon women's section, only eight minutes outside her winning time of the year before. All the same, sport had to give way; she cut down her races from 35 a year to about 20. That she could still do so many was because Ian shared the childcare.

Her successes at the Athens Paralympics induced another wave of establishment appreciation, including being made a Dame – belatedly, thought some people, given that the runner Kelly Holmes achieved the same honour after two golds at the Athens Olympics. She also applied for, and got, a place on the new sporting honours subcommittee. For the first meeting, she left home in Redcar, Cleveland, at 4am to be in London early morning, and wore a pair of purple, sparkly-edged trousers and sparkly flat shoes. 'Dame Tanni' likes being a dame, but on her terms.

Beneath the public froth, the status of elite wheelchair athletes remained much the same. Grey-Thompson's frustration was boiling over:

> We are athletes, we do athletics, we are funded by the National Lottery, we are part of their governing body, but we are not seen as such. So our inclusion within coaching is minimal; our inclusion within branded material, our provision of kits, everything is shrieking to me of discrimination, and I'm really tired of it.

Disabled athletes were not even visible on the UK Athletics website. She saw a lack of planning and organisation at every level, from bringing on talented young disabled athletes to running a truly elite squad.

Another frustration for her, as for other people in the sport, was the proliferation of national disability sports organisations. Communication between them and the sports governing bodies was poor, and they clogged up the system. 'Disability sport needs a big shake-up,' she declared.

Underlying these management difficulties were more fundamental problems. New countries were emerging. China topped the medals table at Athens by far, with Great Britain second. The pattern of disability in Britain was changing; the pool of active wheelchair users was dwindling, and elite athletes were retiring. Without a broad base of disabled athletes, there would be fewer new medal winners. As a result, developing talent is now seen as a priority and funding for Paralympic sport rose to £29 million for 2006–09 (Olympic funding was £192 million).

Midway through 2006, Grey-Thompson decided to retire. The main reason was not Carys, nor the punishing training schedule, nor her joints beginning to buckle under the strain; it was that she had lost heart. 'I had had enough of constantly fighting for integration and inclusion and, just, respect. Probably for the first time ever, I thought I'm not prepared to do it, someone else can do it.' She told no one outside the family. 'Being a control freak, I wanted to go on my own terms.' She decided her last race would be in May 2007 and she would miss Beijing.

Then, in January 2007, Ed Warner, the new chairman of UK Athletics, phoned her a few days into his job and invited her to a breakfast meeting. He wanted her views on athletics. 'Do you really want them?' she said. At the end, he asked if she would like to be a non-executive director.

Warner saw a feisty, forceful woman with red hair – 'You could come up with all sorts of clichés about Welsh dragons.' But her words rang true. 'If Britain's greatest ever Paralympian athlete had had to overcome petty bureaucratic inefficiency and institutional neglect of her genre of the sport, then we'd got a problem.' He wanted to harness her drive to help put things right.

Since then, UK Athletics has been restructured. There are still only two or three disabled staff in a workforce of about 70, and Grey-Thompson is one of two athletes at director level, but she was pleased about the push to include disabled athletes in the national squads and the regional training centres. In 2008 she led a review of anti-doping policy. Then came the Beijing Paralympics, where overall the GB team came second, but the athletic squad failed to reach a tough target of 30 medals, only achieving 17. Grey-Thompson was there for the BBC. The world of sport was moving on, she warned, and British athletes would have to decide if they were going to aim higher or leave it to others. With 2012 approaching, now was the time to review athletics from the grassroots up.

Since Beijing, the arrival of a global recession has ratcheted up the pressure on athletes and their organisations. Already less successful sports and the Paralympics managing body face funding cuts, while medal winning sports will get more money.

For Grey-Thompson the drive to improve is taking over from her will to win – whether it is contributing to the Paralympics, encouraging people to take up sport via a new website, working with a volunteering charity, pushing disability access on the Transport for London board, or helping to design trendy clothes for disabled adults and children. Sometimes she gets a bit preachy: *Aim High*, for the Welsh Quick Reads series, passes on to people with limited reading skills the secrets behind her success and the lessons she has learned.

Her swansong, when it came, was an anticlimax. She competed in just one race at the Visa Paralympic World Cup, on a cold, wet day in Manchester, and came second. People willed her to win, but the competition was strong and hungry for medals. Still, a public outpouring of affection helped to carry her into retirement.

Where that will lead, she doesn't know. A Jonathan Edwards of disability sport, perhaps, given that the BBC is increasing its coverage? 'It's one of those things that's really nice to do, but does it change stuff?' she asks. Yet she saw how the Athens Paralympics had a positive impact on Greek attitudes to disabled people, and the BBC sports presenter, Clare Balding, confirms it has happened in Britain. 'The effect of people watching on TV or watching live is profound. I know it because I get their feedback. It's had a huge effect on me too… and that is down to people like Tanni.'

Strangely enough, for all her success as an athlete, it is as a communicator that Grey-Thompson is seen to have made the greatest impact. 'She has done for disability sport what David Beckham has done for football or Jonny Wilkinson has done for Rugby Union,' says Richard Caborn, ex-Minister for Sport. 'She's made it cool to be a wheelchair user,' thinks Chris Hallam.

Ade Adepitan, a member of the British wheelchair basketball team before turning TV actor and presenter, is an ambassador in his own right. But he sees Grey-Thompson as 'a very special ambassador', on two counts. She has the clout, helped by being a Dame, to relate to big business and keep disability sport in the public eye, which together can stimulate essential sponsorship. And she can unite disabled and non-disabled youngsters. Adepitan has seen them shouting her name and asking for her autograph.

> You could see in their eyes they see her as an inspirational figure. And for me that's brilliant. When you have a disabled athlete who can be an ambassador for both able-bodied and disabled kids then that's the future for me, really.

# DIFFERENT LIVES, COMMON PURPOSE

Nine disabled people, nine pioneers. Let's cut across their stories to see what they have in common, where they differ, and what impact they have had overall.

To begin with, their impairment has often given them a sense of purpose. Rachel Hurst's eyes were opened to social oppression when she started using a wheelchair. Jack Ashley's deafness presented a barrier to his ministerial ambitions but diverted him into becoming a backbench social campaigner. Andrew Lee used direct action and self-advocacy to challenge those who called him a 'thicko'.

Some people have exploited their disability as well as fighting discrimination. Disability gave Tom Shakespeare a career path and Phil Friend a fresh start in training and consultancy, after he realised he was sitting on his 'biggest asset'. Once Mat Fraser accepted that phocomelia was part of him, he found a cause as well as a new dimension for his music, poetry and acting, one that still allowed him to challenge social conventions. Fraser, and to some extent Shakespeare, could also 'live up' their deviance; Fraser played on his 'freak' appearance to shock, make money and explore the history of performing freaks. Bert Massie, the pragmatist, found a job where he could use his skills and impairment in the cause of social justice. For Peter White and Tanni Grey-Thompson achievement was the objective. Blind or not, White wanted to be a broadcaster; Grey-Thompson claims that without spina bifida she would have been just as competitive. But both have been spurred to fight discrimination in their own fields; and, in White's case, to report widely on disability issues as well as on many others.

Another common denominator is ability. They are all able, imaginative people and excellent communicators. Most of them would have been leaders anyway. Lee calls for easy-read documents wherever he goes, uses 'supporters' to help him at high-level meetings and has worked out with them how to process information and control his behaviour. He has used his ability to bypass his limitations, and others have done the same. White's fine memory, and the brain–finger coordination that produces his phenomenal speed at reading Braille, along with an engaging interviewing technique, have allowed him to compete in mainstream broadcasting and advantaged him on disability programmes. Ashley contrived various ways of dealing with his deafness so that he could operate as an MP before he had a cochlear implant. He, Massie and Friend are skilled negotiators; Hurst too, when outrage doesn't get the better of her.

Ability would not have been much use without determination, which goes with hard work. Determination is part of their characters, beyond their impairment, but bringing strength to it. Ashley, for example, fought poverty and injustice in Widnes long before he was deaf. Hurst talked her way into teaching full-time and ran the local branch of a charity before she became a disability campaigner. Grey-Thompson and White have the will to win. Fraser has tried many routes to make his name. None of them takes no for an answer.

For all nine, the way they were treated by their family had a big impact on how they saw their disability and how confidently they grew up. Time and again, parents or siblings played a vital role in treating them like everyone else – supporting them, pushing them or just loving them. Everyone talked positively of their mothers. Shakespeare had a positive role model in his father, a successful GP with restricted growth. White was always trying to copy his older brother, who was also blind but had more sight. Grey-Thompson's parents encouraged her to do whatever she wanted, fought for her to have a good education and declined to help her put on her socks; she also had an older sister to compete with. Lee's parents ignored the low expectations of the medical and educational establishment and got on with giving their son all the opportunities they could.

Schooling varied from elite public school through mainstream Catholic, private or comprehensive schools to 'special' education, either day or boarding. It gave Shakespeare, White and Grey-Thompson a straight route into university; Ashley got to Cambridge via Ruskin College. For Ashley and Shakespeare university provided a leg-up into a career; for Grey-Thompson it meant first-rate sports facilities. Apart from these four, education seems to have been less decisive in their lives than their families and their own personalities. Even when it was narrow and harsh, Friend and Massie dredged something positive out of it. They thrived, perversely, on being separated from their families. Neither had much academic opportunity, but Massie learned to work the system, while Friend's leadership ability emerged in other ways and he could vent his anger in a safe environment.

The most obvious difference within the group is their eight impairments, which underlines the difficulty of bringing everyone together under one 'disability' flag. Fraser and Shakespeare are disabled by their appearance (though there are hidden side-effects in pain or dysfunction, and Shakespeare now has paraplegia too). Ashley and White have sensory impairments. Lee has learning difficulties. Hurst, Friend, Massie and Grey-Thompson all have mobility impairments of one kind or another that, as they grew older, have led them to use a wheelchair. Only Ashley acquired his impairment as an adult, although Hurst's was not diagnosed until she was nearly 40. People with acquired impairments are supposed to be less accepting of their condition and more impatient for change. Hurst and Ashley are certainly outspoken, but so are the others.

Although they all believe that disabled people should be treated as equal citizens, within that general agreement there are sharp differences. Take the social model. Only Hurst and Lee carry the banner aloft for this white hot 'idea' that gave so many disabled people in the 1980s and 1990s a common belief and purpose to fight social discrimination and oppression. Friend and Massie subscribe to it. Fraser now sets freedom of speech above the party line; Shakespeare has attacked the social model openly; Grey-Thompson has reservations; Ashley doesn't mention it; White says he's never met an intelligent disabled person who really believed it. There is a distinction here between opposing discrimination and accepting the social model's definition of disability. There are similar cracks in unity about issues like abortion, genetic research and assisted dying.

In the 1980s and 1990s, when battle was joined with the Tory government over anti-discrimination legislation and later civil rights, political unity was seen as essential; organisations of disabled people and traditional charities worked together. A disabled leader deemed not to be on side, like

Massie, was pilloried. Later, it happened to the academic, Shakespeare, who dared to question the social model and mingle with dangerous geneticists. Today, with many political battles won – comprehensive anti-discrimination law, an international human rights convention signed (though not yet ratified) by the UK, the connection between disability and poverty acknowledged, and a deadline set for disabled people to be treated equally – old allegiances have fallen away and positions have shifted. BCODP leaders who shouted on the streets are now members of the establishment; Jane Campbell, for example, is a Baroness in the House of Lords and Rachel Hurst has accepted a CBE. As disability commissioner in the Equality and Human Rights Commission, Campbell has dared to ditch the old identity politics. She now makes common cause with older people and carers to secure social care reform – alignments urged by Tom Shakespeare – and she seeks to work with other groups using ideas from the disability movement to further human rights. Bert Massie called for a broad approach like this when he launched a 'disability agenda' in 2007.

Within these general trends, the nine people here focus on what is important to them – disability sport, employment, independent living, social care, bioethics, human rights, poverty, the disability agenda inside the Equality Commission. The list covers most of the major disability issues being grappled with today.

Temperamentally, the nine have also differed in the way they fight discrimination – from the militancy of Hurst to the persistent diplomacy of Massie. But their differences are not hard and fast. Hurst can be charming and magnanimous, Massie stroppy, Ashley a firebrand and a clever politician. Both approaches – tough cop, soft cop – have been needed to effect change.

The overall impact of the nine can be judged in three ways – as exemplars, innovators of policy and practice, and opinion formers. The second two overlap.

It would be hard not to see all of them as exemplars for other disabled people: they have confounded low expectations, shown what can be achieved and given a sense of empowerment. White went where no blind person had gone before, presenting news on TV. Grey-Thompson is 'Britain's greatest ever Paralympian'. Fraser mixed rap, punk rock and the social model, bringing an iconoclastic message into disability arts and proving to young people that a disabled man could be strong and cool; later they saw him on mainstream TV. Tom Shakespeare is a positive or negative exemplar, depending on whether you agree with his views about such things as the social model, genetic research or assisted dying. He has spearheaded the bioethics debate both inside the disability community and in the mainstream media, and he has shown that writing and speaking about disability need not be worthy or dull.

As regards changes in policy and practice, Ashley has won government concessions for deaf and disabled people. His Parliamentary All Party Disability Group has provided a disability focus for peers and MPs, and played a crucial role in lobbying at all stages for the Disability Discrimination Acts 1995 and 2005 as well as other legislation, most recently the Disabled Persons (Independent Living) Bill 2006; it has also been a bridge between parliamentarians and disabled people. Massie, too, from RADAR through the DRC years to his transitional role on the Equality Commission today, has built bridges between disabled people, government ministers and civil servants, negotiating legislation and regulations, persuading companies to obey the DDA, winning special provision for disability in the Equality Commission. He has often worked behind the scenes, whereas Hurst has been effective both on demos and in debate, crawling up the steps of Parliament, writing resolutions, influencing policy and people in the European Commission and at the UN General Assembly.

Fraser, successful as a disabled performer, then an actor and presenter, has hit his head on the glass ceiling that prevents disabled actors being hired as just actors, especially for TV parts. To change that, particularly for people with obvious or less socially acceptable impairments, requires a different mindset among producers and casting directors and, preferably, pressure from above. It will be interesting to see if the BBC keeps its promise to consider disabled actors for all mainstream roles – and they get more jobs.

Even so, Fraser has helped shift attitudes, from seeing him as a scary 'freak' to just 'that guy from TV'. Grey-Thompson's regular presence on TV chat shows and as a presenter has made a wheelchair user familiar in people's homes. Ashley is a well-known public figure, and White is an institution at the BBC. In the marketplace, Phil Friend has brought mainstream employers to appreciate the business arguments for employing disabled people, as well as their duties under the DDA; the iron fist in a velvet glove has worked better than just the iron fist. At public meetings and, increasingly, in the media, Andrew Lee is a friendly but insistent spokesperson for people with learning difficulties, showing what can be achieved with the right support.

Between them, these nine leaders have helped disabled people towards their goal of social equality and human rights. Of course, they have not done it alone, and as several of them admit, it was a matter of the right person being in the right place at the right time. But that should not belittle their impact; they have helped to mainstream disability.

# BIBLIOGRAPHY

Ashley, J. (1994) *Acts of Defiance*. London: Penguin.

Campbell, J. and Oliver, M. (1996) *Disability Politics*. London: Routledge.

Corker, M. and Shakespeare, T. (eds) (2002) *Disability/Postmodernity: Embodying Disability Theory*. London and New York: Continuum.

Davies, C. (compiler) (1993) *Lifetimes*. Farnham: Understanding Disability Educational Trust.

Gooding, C. (1994) *Disabling Laws, Enabling Acts*. London: Pluto.

Grey-Thompson, T. (2007) *Aim High*. Bedlinog: Accent Press.

Grey-Thompson, T. with Broadbent, R. (2001) *Seize the Day*. London: Hodder & Stoughton.

Harrison, T. (1996) *Tanni*. London: CollinsWillow.

Kerr, A. and Shakespeare, T. (2002) *Genetic Politics: From Eugenics to Genome*. Cheltenham: New Clarion Press.

Kinrade, D. (2007) *Alf Morris: People's Parliamentarian*. London: National Information Forum.

People First (2007) *Taking the Power: From Oppression towards Independence. Real Life Stories of People with Learning Disabilities*. London: People First (Self Advocacy).

Shakespeare, T. (ed.) (1998) *The Disability Reader*. London: Cassell.

Shakespeare, T. (2000) *Help!* Birmingham:Venture Press.

Shakespeare, T. (2006) *Disability Rights and Wrongs*. London: Routledge.

Shakespeare, T., Gillespie-Sells, K. and Davies, D. (1996) *The Sexual Politics of Disability*. London: Cassell.

White, P. (2000) *See It My Way*. London: Warner.

# INDEX